Good Reasons

Designing and Writing Effective Arguments

Third Edition

Lester Faigley
University of Texas at Austin

Jack Selzer
The Pennsylvania State University

PEARSON
Longman

New York San Francisco Boston
London Toronto Sydney Tokyo Singapore Madrid
Mexico City Munich Paris Cape Town Hong Kong Montreal

Senior Acquisitions Editor: Lynn M. Huddon
Development Editor: Leslie Taggart
Senior Supplements Editor: Donna Campion
Media Supplements Editor: Jenna Egan
Senior Marketing Manager: Alexandra Rivas-Smith
Production Manager: Eric Jorgensen
Project Coordination, Text Design, and Electronic Page Makeup: Pre-Press Company, Inc.
Cover Designer/Manager: Wendy Ann Fredericks
Cover Photos: front cover: Digital Vision, Inc.; back cover: Cha Cha Royale/Brand X Pictures
Manufacturing Buyer: Roy Pickering
Printer and Binder: RR Donnelley & Sons Company
Cover Printer: Phoenix Color Corp.

For permission to use copyrighted material, grateful acknowledgment is made to
the copyright holders on p. 301 which are hereby made part of this copyright page.

Photos: pp. 1, 6, 14, 23, 30, 39, 61, 62, 63, 85, 86, 96, 97, 98, 105, 109, 127, 131, 136, 161,
189, 193, 197, 223, 238, 261: Lester Faigley Photos; p. 5 left: Cover from SILENT SPRING
by Rachel Carson (Boston: Houghton Mifflin, 2002); right: Erich Hartmann / Magnum
Photos Inc.; p. 87 top: Dorothea Lange; bottom: © 1996 Benetton Group SpA, Ph. O.
Toscani; p. 88: Arthur Rothstein, July 1938. Library of Congress; p. 89: Anti-drug ads often use visual metaphors. *Public Service Announcements provided courtesy of the Partnership
for Drug-Free America®*; p. 90 top: U.S. Army Staff Sgt. David Bennett; bottom: Marion
Post Wolcott. Belzoni, MS, October 1939. Library of Congress; p. 91: Arthur Rothstein,
1939. Library of Congress; p. 100: © 2003 America's Dairy Farmers and Milk Processors;
p. 113: Library of Congress; p. 145: NASA; p. 159: Department of Defense; p. 173:
Courtesy www.adbusters.org

Library of Congress Cataloging-in-Publication Data

Faigley, Lester, 1947–
   Good reasons: designing and writing effective arguments / Lester Faigley,
Jack Selzer.—3rd ed.
     p. cm.
   Includes index.
   ISBN 0-321-31681-9 (pbk.)
   1. English language—Rhetoric. 2. Persuasion (Rhetoric)
3. Report writing. I. Selzer, Jack. II. Title.

PE1431.F35 2005
808'.042—dc22

                                       2004060100

Visit us at http://www.ablongman.com

ISBN 0-321-31681-9

1 2 3 4 5 6 7 8 9 10—DOH—08 07 06 05

In memory of our teacher and friend,
James L. Kinneavy (1920–1999)

Contents

Preface

Like many other college writing teachers, we have come to believe that a course focusing on argument is an essential part of a college writing curriculum. Most students come to college with very little experience in reading and writing extended arguments. Because so much writing in college concerns arguments in the various disciplines, a basic course in writing arguments is part of the foundation of an undergraduate education. You will find that college courses frequently require you to analyze the structure of arguments, to identify competing claims, to weigh the evidence offered, to recognize assumptions, to locate contradictions, and to anticipate opposing views. The ability to write cogent arguments is also highly valued in most occupations that require college degrees. Just as important, you need to be able to read arguments critically and write arguments skillfully if you are to participate in public life after you leave college. The long-term issues that will affect your life after your college years—education, the environment, social justice, and the quality of life, to name a few—have many diverse stakeholders and long, complex histories. They cannot be reduced to slogans and sound bites. If you are to help make your views prevail in your communities, you must be able to participate in sustained give-and-take on a range of civic issues.

A Straightforward Approach to Argument

Good Reasons begins by considering why people take the time to write arguments in the first place. People write arguments because they want to change attitudes and beliefs about particular issues, and they want things done about problems they identify. We start out by asking you to examine exactly why you might want to write an argument and how what you write can lead to extended discussion and long-term results. We then provide you with practical means to find good reasons that support convincingly the positions you want to advocate.

A Rhetorical Approach to Finding Good Reasons

You won't find a lot of complicated terminology in *Good Reasons*. The only technical terms this book uses are the general classical concepts of *pathos, ethos*, and *logos*—sources of good reasons that emerge from the audience's most passionately held values, from the speaker's expertise and credibility, or from reasonable, commonsense thinking. The crux of teaching argument, in our view, is to get you to appreciate its rhetorical nature. A reason becomes a *good reason* when the audience accepts the writer or speaker as credible and accepts the assumptions and evidence on which the argument is based.

The Oral and Visual Aspects of Argument

Good Reasons is also distinctive in its attention to the delivery and presentation of arguments—to oral and visual aspects of argument in addition to the written word. We encourage you to formulate arguments in different genres and different media. Commonly used word processing programs and Web page editors now allow you to include pictures, icons, charts, and graphs—making design an important part of an argument. While the heart of an argument course should be the critical reading and critical writing of prose, we also believe that you should understand and use visual persuasion when appropriate.

The Value of Argument

The popularity of argument courses is not an accident. Even though we hear frequently that people have become cynical about politics, they are producing self-sponsored writing in quantities never before seen. It's almost as if people have rediscovered writing. While writing personal letters is perhaps becoming a lost art, participating in online discussion groups, writing Web logs (blogs), putting up Web sites, and sending email have become commonplace. Citizen participation in local and national government forums, in a multitude of issue-related online discussions, blogs, and in other forms such as online magazines is increasing daily. You already have many opportunities to speak in the electronic community. We want you to recognize and value the breadth of information available on the Internet and to evaluate, analyze, and synthesize that information. And we want to prepare you for the changing demands of the professions and public citizenship in your future.

Features New to This Edition

- Visual argument is emphasized throughout in order to respond to the need for greater visual literacy in our media-saturated culture.

  Chapter 1 introduces the new emphasis by including a new visual argument to accompany the chapter from Rachel Carson's classic *Silent Spring*.

  A new chapter in Part 1, Chapter 5, "Understanding Visual Arguments," discusses visual persuasion and how visuals are used as supports for textual arguments. Twenty-five photographs, icons, charts, graphs, and advertisements illustrate major points. A new student paper, "Got Roddick?" demonstrates rhetorical analysis of an advertisement.

  More visuals illustrate concepts throughout Parts 1 and 2. In Chapter 4, for example, two photos of a Roman statue exemplify textual and contextual analysis. All the photo openers in Part 2 serve a pedagogical function. In all, 50 new visuals, including 32 new photographs by Lester Faigley, appear in this edition.

- Three new chapters in Part 1 aid students in the process of creating and analyzing arguments.

A new chapter on invention. Chapter 2, "Finding Arguments," helps students decide what to argue about, how to think about audience, and how to craft a thesis statement for the argument. The chapter introduces invention strategies such as freewriting, brainstorming, using online subject directories, and making idea maps in addition to reading in the subject area. The thesis discussion includes both focusing the thesis and evaluating it.

A new chapter on rhetorical analysis. Chapter 4, "Understanding Written Arguments: Rhetorical Analysis," gives an overview of two main forms of rhetorical analysis: textual analysis (via classical rhetorical theory) and contextual analysis (text as a part of a larger conversation). Each type of analysis is demonstrated by analyzing a narrative argument from Part 2, Leslie Marmon Silko's "The Border Patrol State." A student uses both kinds of analysis in her paper "The NRA Blacklist: A Project Gone Mad."

A new chapter on visual analysis. Chapter 5, "Understanding Visual Arguments: Visual Analysis" discusses visuals that make explicit claims, photos and ads whose claims must be inferred or co-created by the viewer, and visual metaphor. The section on visual evidence discusses current and past evidence, how the significance of images can be debated, and how the contexts of images, producers, and viewers can create controversy around the use of visuals as evidence.

- A greater emphasis on student work throughout encourages students to understand themselves as agents and to see the range of topics their colleagues are investigating.

  Five new student essays appear in Parts 1 and 2, along with student-produced Web sites in Part 3.

- Expanded discussions of the process of research and MLA and APA documentation guidelines.

  Particular attention is given to using library databases and to documenting sources from library databases. A new sample student research paper using MLA style, "Need a Cure for Tribe Fever? How About a Dip in the Lake?" can be found in chapter 11.

- A new glossary of terms helps students remember important concepts.

Supplements

The **Companion Website** to accompany *Good Reasons*, Third Edition, (http://www.ablongman.com/faigley), revised by Laura McGrath, offers a wealth of resources for both students and instructors. Students can access detailed chapter summaries and objectives, writing exercises, chapter review quizzes, and links to additional Web resources for further study. Instructors will find sample syllabi, Web resources, and the Instructor's Manual available for download.

The **Instructor's Manual** that accompanies this text was revised by Iris Ralph and is designed to be useful for new and experienced instructors alike. The Instructor's Manual briefly discusses the ins and outs of teaching the material in each chapter. Also provided are in-class exercises, homework assignments, discussion questions for each reading selection, and model paper assignments and syllabi. This revised Instructor's Manual will make your work as a teacher a bit easier. Teaching argumentation and composition becomes a process that has genuine—and often surprising—rewards.

MyCompLab provides the best multimedia resources for writing, grammar, and research in one easy-to-use site. Students will find guided assistance through each step of the writing process; *Exchange*, Longman's new online peer-review program; newly revised "Avoiding Plagiarism" tutorials; "Exercise Zone" with diagnostic grammar tests and more than 3600 practice exercises; "ESL Exercise Zone" with more than 600 practice exercises; and *Research Navigator*^{TM}, a database with thousands of magazines and academic journals, the subject-search archive of the *New York Times*, "Link Library," library guides, and more. Tour the site at *www.mycomplab.com*.

Acknowledgments

We are much indebted to the work of many outstanding scholars of argument and to our colleagues who teach argument at Texas and at Penn State. In particular, we thank the following reviewers for sharing their expertise: Mary L. Dodson, Amarillo College; Jane Yellowlees Douglas, University of Florida; Daniel Ferguson, Amarillo College; Laura McGrath, Georgia Institute of Technology; JoAnn Pavletich, University of Houston, Downtown; Doreen Piano, Georgia Institute of Technology; Iris Ralph, University of Texas at Austin; Ellen Strenski, University of California, Irvine; Jacqueline Thomas, University of Texas at Austin; and Patti Wojahn, New Mexico State University. We are especially grateful to our students, who have given us opportunities to test these materials in class and who have taught us a great deal about the nature of argument.

Our editor, Eben Ludlow, convinced us we should write this book and gave us wise guidance throughout three editions. We are extremely fortunate to have Leslie Taggart as our development editor for this edition. Leslie not only brings great ideas but she also makes writing the book fun. Kelly Kessler worked with us in the revision and made many fine contributions. Katy Faria and Elsa van Bergen at Pre-Press Company and Eric Jorgensen at Pearson Longman did splendid work in preparing our book for publication. Finally we thank our families, who make it all possible.

LESTER FAIGLEY

JACK SELZER

PART 1

Persuading with Good Reasons

What Do We Mean by Argument?

For over thirty years, the debate over legalized abortion has raged in the United States. The following scene is a familiar one: Outside an abortion clinic, a crowd of pro-life activists has gathered to try to stop women from entering the clinic. They carry signs that read "ABORTION = MURDER" and "A BABY'S LIFE IS A HUMAN LIFE." Pro-choice supporters are also present in a counterdemonstration. Their signs read "KEEP YOUR LAWS OFF MY BODY" and "WOMEN HAVE THE RIGHT TO CONTROL THEIR BODIES." Police keep the two sides apart, but they do not stop the shouts of "Murderer!" from the pro-life side and "If you're anti-abortion, don't have one!" from the pro-choice side.

When you imagine an argument, you might think of two people engaged in a heated exchange, or two groups of people with different views, shouting back and forth at each other like the pro-choice and pro-life demonstrators. Or you might think of the arguing that occurs in the courthouse, where district attorneys and defense lawyers debate strenuously. Written arguments can resemble these oral arguments in being heated and one sided. For example, the signs that the pro-choice and pro-life demonstrators carry might be considered written arguments.

But in college courses, in public life, and in professional careers, written arguments are not thought of as slogans. Bumper stickers require no supporting evidence or reasons. Many other kinds of writing do not offer reasons either. An instruction manual, for example, does not try to persuade you. It assumes that you want to do whatever the manual tells you how to do; indeed, most people are willing to follow the advice, or else they would not be consulting the manual. Likewise, an article written by someone who is totally committed to a particular cause or belief often assumes that everyone should think the same way. These writers can count on certain phrases and words to produce predictable responses.

Effective arguments do not make the assumption that everyone should think the same way or hold the same beliefs. They attempt to change people's minds by convincing them of the validity of new ideas or that a particular course of action is the best one to take. Written arguments not only offer evidence and reasons but also often examine the assumptions on which they are based, think through opposing arguments, and anticipate objections. They explore positions thoroughly and take opposing views into account.

Extended written arguments make more demands on their readers than most other kinds of writing. Like bumper stickers, they often appeal to our emotions. But they typically do much more. They expand our knowledge with the depth of their analysis and lead us through a complex set of claims by providing networks of logical relations and appropriate evidence. They explicitly build on what has been written before by offering trails of sources, which also demonstrates that they can be trusted because the writers have done their homework. They cause us to reflect on what we read, in a process that we will shortly describe as *critical reading*.

Our culture is a competitive culture, and often the goal is to win. If you are a professional athlete, a top trial lawyer, or a candidate for president of the United States, it really is win big or lose. But most of us live in a world in which the opponents don't go away when the game is over. Even professional athletes have to play the team they beat in the championship game the next year.

In real life, most of us have to deal with people who disagree with us at times but with whom we have to continue to work and live in the same communities. The idea of winning in such situations can only be temporary. Soon enough other situations will come up in which we will need the support of those who were on the other side of the current issue. Probably you can think of times when friendly arguments ended up with everyone involved coming to a better understanding of the others' views. And probably you can think of other times when someone was so concerned with winning an argument that even though the person might have been technically right, hard feelings were created that lasted for years.

Usually, listeners and readers are more willing to consider your argument seriously if you cast yourself as a respectful partner rather than as a competitor and put forth your arguments in the spirit of mutual support and negotiation—in the interest of finding the *best* way, not "my way." How can you be the person that your reader will want to cooperate with rather than resist? Here are a few suggestions, both for your writing and for discussing controversial issues in class.

Strategies for Being a Respectful Partner in Argument

■ **Try to think of yourself as engaged not so much in winning over your audience as in courting your audience's cooperation.** Argue vigorously, but not so vigorously that opposing views are vanquished or silenced. Remember that your goal is to invite a response that creates a dialog.

■ **Show that you understand and genuinely respect your listener's or reader's position even if you think the position is ultimately wrong.** Often, that amounts to remembering to argue against opponents' positions, not against the opponents themselves. It often means representing an opponent's position in terms that he or she would accept. Look for ground that you already share with your reader, and search for even more. See yourself as a mediator. Consider that neither you nor the other person has arrived at a best solution, and carry on in the hope that dialog will lead to an even better course of action than the one you now recommend. Expect and assume the best of your listener or reader, and deliver your own best yourself.

■ **Cultivate a sense of humor and a distinctive voice.** Many textbooks on argument emphasize using a reasonable voice. But a reasonable voice doesn't have to be a dull one. Humor is a legitimate tool of argument. Although playing an issue strictly for laughs risks not having the reader take it seriously, nothing creates a sense of goodwill quite so much as good humor. You will be seen as open to new possibilities and to cooperation if you occasionally show a sense of humor. And a sense of humor can sometimes be especially welcome when the stakes are high, the sides have been chosen, and tempers are flaring.

Consider that your argument might be just one move in a larger process that might end up helping *you*. Most times we argue because we think we have something to offer. But in the process of developing and presenting your views, realize also that you might learn something in the course of your research or from an argument that answers your own. Holding onto that attitude will keep you from becoming too overbearing and dogmatic.

What to Argue About

A Book That Changed the World

In 1958, Rachel Carson received a copy of a letter that her friend Olga Huckens had sent to the *Boston Herald*. The letter described what had happened during the previous summer when Duxbury, Massachusetts, a small town just north of

Rachel Carson

Cape Cod where Huckens lived, was sprayed several times from an airplane with the chemical pesticide DDT to kill mosquitoes. The mosquitoes came back as hungry as ever, but the songbirds, bees, and other insects vanished except for a few dead birds that Huckens had to pick up out of her yard. Huckens asked Carson if she knew anyone in Washington who could help to stop the spraying.

The letter from Olga Huckens struck a nerve with Rachel Carson. Carson was a marine biologist who had worked for many years for the U.S. Fish and Wildlife Service and who had written three highly acclaimed books about the sea and wetlands. In 1944 she published an article on how bats use radarlike echoes to find insects, which was reprinted in *Reader's Digest* in 1945. The editors at *Reader's Digest* asked whether she could write something else for them, and Carson replied in a letter that she wanted to write about experiments using DDT. DDT was being hyped as the solution for controlling insect pests, but Carson knew in 1945 that fish, waterfowl, and other animals would also be poisoned by widespread spraying and that eventually people could die too. *Reader's Digest* was not interested in Carson's proposed article, so she dropped the idea and went on to write about other things.

Huckens's letter brought Carson back to the subject of chemical spraying. In the late 1940s and 1950s, pesticides—especially the chlorinated hydrocarbons

DDT, aldrin, and dieldrin—were sprayed on a massive scale throughout the United States and were hailed as a panacea for world hunger and famine. In 1957 much of the greater New York City area, including Long Island, was sprayed with DDT to kill gypsy moths. But there were noticeable side effects. Many people complained about not only birds, fish, and useful insects being killed but also their plants, shrubs, and pets. Other scientists had written about the dangers of massive spraying of pesticides, but they had not convinced the public of the hazards of pesticides and of the urgency for change.

Rachel Carson decided that she needed to write a magazine article about the facts of DDT. When she contacted *Reader's Digest* and other magazines, she found that they still would not consider publishing on the subject. Carson then concluded that she should write a short book. She knew that her job was not going to be an easy one because people in the United States still trusted science to solve all problems. Science had brought the "green revolution" that greatly increased crop yields through the use of chemical fertilizers and chemical pesticides. Carson's subject matter was also technical and difficult to communicate to the general public. At that time the public did not think much about air and water pollution, and most people were unaware that pesticides could poison humans as well as insects. And she was sure to face opposition from the pesticide industry, which had become a multimillion-dollar business. Carson knew the pesticide industry would do everything it could to stop her from publishing and to discredit her if she did.

Rachel Carson nonetheless wrote her book, *Silent Spring*. It sounded the alarm about the dangers caused by the overuse of pesticides, and the controversy it raised has still not ended. No book has had a greater impact on our thinking about the environment. *Silent Spring* was first published in installments in *The New Yorker* in the summer of 1962, and it created an immediate furor. Chemical companies threatened to sue Carson, and the trade associations that they sponsored launched full-scale attacks against the book in pamphlets and magazine articles. The chemical companies treated *Silent Spring* as a public relations problem; they hired scientists whose only job was to ridicule the book and to dismiss Carson as a "hysterical woman." Some even accused *Silent Spring* of being part of a communist plot to ruin U.S. agriculture.

Brown pelicans are again common along the coasts of the South and in California after they were nearly made extinct by the effects of DDT.

But the public controversy over *Silent Spring* had another effect. It helped to make the book a success shortly after it was published in September 1962. A half-million hardcover copies of *Silent Spring* were sold, keeping it on the best-seller list for thirty-one weeks. President John F. Kennedy read *Silent Spring* and met with Carson and other scientists to discuss the pesticide problem. Kennedy requested that the President's Scientific Advisory Committee study the effects of pesticides and make a report. This report found evidence around the world of high levels of pesticides in the environment, including the tissues of humans. The report confirmed what Carson had described in *Silent Spring*.

> That we still talk so much about the environment is testimony to the lasting power of *Silent Spring*.

In the words of a news commentator at the time, *Silent Spring* "lit a fire" under the government. Many congressional hearings were held on the effects of pesticides and other pollutants on the environment. In 1967 the Environmental Defense Fund was formed; it developed the guidelines under which DDT was eventually banned. Three years later, President Richard Nixon became convinced that only an independent agency within the executive branch could operate with enough independence to enforce environmental regulations. Nixon created the Environmental Protection Agency (EPA) in December 1970, and he named William Ruckelshaus as its first head. One of the missions of the EPA, according to Ruckelshaus, was to develop an environmental ethic.

The United States was not the only country to respond to *Silent Spring*. The book was widely translated and inspired legislation on the environment in nearly all industrialized nations. Moreover, it changed the way we think about the environment. Carson pointed out that the nerve gases that were developed for use on our enemies in World War II were being used as pesticides after the war. She criticized the view of the environment as a battlefield where people make war on those natural forces that they believe impede their progress. Instead, she advocated living in coexistence with the environment because we are part of it. She was not totally opposed to pesticides, but she wanted to make people more aware of the environment as a whole and how changing one part would affect other parts. Her message was to try to live in balance with nature. That we still talk so much about the environment is testimony to the lasting power of *Silent Spring*. In 1980, Rachel Carson was posthumously awarded the highest civilian decoration in the nation: the Presidential Medal of Freedom. The citation accompanying the award expresses the way she is remembered:

Never silent herself in the face of destructive trends, Rachel Carson fed a spring of awareness across America and beyond. A biologist with a gentle, clear voice, she welcomed her audiences to her love of the sea, while with an equally clear voice she warned Americans of the dangers human beings themselves pose for their own environment. Always concerned, always eloquent, she created a tide of environmental consciousness that has not ebbed.

Why *Silent Spring* Became a Classic

A book titled *Our Synthetic Environment*, which covered much of the same ground as *Silent Spring*, had been published six months earlier. The author, Murray Bookchin, writing under the pen name Lewis Herber, also wrote about the pollution of the natural world and the effects on people. Bookchin was as committed to warning people about the hazards of pesticides as Carson, but *Our Synthetic Environment* was read by only a small community of scientists. Why, then, did Carson succeed in reaching a larger audience?

Rachel Carson had far more impact than Murray Bookchin not simply because she was a more talented writer or because she was a scientist while Bookchin was not. She also thought a great deal about who she was writing for—her **audience**. If she was going to stop the widespread spraying of dangerous pesticides, she knew she would have to connect with the values of a wide audience, an audience that included a large segment of the public as well as other scientists.

The opening chapter in *Silent Spring* begins not by announcing Carson's thesis or giving a list of facts. Instead, the book starts out with a short fable about a small town located in the middle of prosperous farmland, where wildflowers bloomed much of the year, trout swam in the streams, and wildlife was abundant. Suddenly, a strange blight came on the town, as if an evil spell had been cast upon it. The chickens, sheep, and cattle on the farms grew sick and died. The families of the townspeople and farmers alike developed mysterious illnesses. Most of the birds disappeared, and the few that remained could neither sing nor fly. The apple trees bloomed, but there were no bees to pollinate the trees, and so they bore no fruit. The wildflowers withered as if they had been burned. Fishermen quit going to the streams because the fish had all died.

But it wasn't witchcraft that caused everything to grow sick and die. Carson writes that "the people had done it to themselves." She continues, "I know of no community that has experienced all the misfortunes I describe. Yet every one of these disasters has actually happened somewhere, and many real communities have already suffered a substantial number of them. A grim specter has crept upon us almost unnoticed, and this imagined tragedy may easily become a stark reality." Carson's fable did happen several times after the book was published. In July 1976, a chemical reaction went out of control at a plant near Seveso, Italy, and a cloud of powdery white crystals of almost pure dioxin fell on the town. The children ran out to play in the powder because it looked like snow. Within four days, plants, birds, and animals began dying, and the next week, people started getting sick. Most of the people had to go to the hospital, and everyone had to move out of the town. An even worse disaster happened in December 1984, when a storage tank in a pesticide plant exploded near Bhopal, India, showering the town. Two thousand people died quickly, and another fifty thousand became sick for the rest of their lives.

Perhaps if Rachel Carson were alive today and writing a book about the dangers of pesticides, she might begin differently. But remember that at the time she was writing, people trusted pesticides and believed that DDT was a miracle solution for all sorts of insect pests. She first had to make people aware that DDT could be harmful to them. In the second chapter of *Silent Spring* (reprinted at the end of this chapter), Carson continued appealing to the emotions of her audience. People in 1962 knew about the dangers of radiation even if they were ignorant about pesticides. They knew that the atomic bombs that had been dropped on Hiroshima and Nagasaki at the end of World War II were still killing Japanese people through the effects of radiation many years later, and they feared the fallout from nuclear bombs that were still being tested and stockpiled in the United States and Soviet Union.

Getting people's attention by exposing the threat of pesticides wasn't enough by itself. There are always people writing about various kinds of threats, and most aren't taken seriously except by those who already believe that the threats exist. Carson wanted to reach people who didn't think that pesticides were a threat but might be persuaded to take this view. To convince these people, she had to explain why pesticides are potentially dangerous, and she had to make readers believe that she could be trusted.

Rachel Carson was an expert marine biologist. To write *Silent Spring*, she had to read widely in sciences that she had not studied, including research about insects, toxic chemicals, cell physiology, biochemistry, plant and soil science, and public health. Then she had to explain complex scientific processes to people who had very little or no background in science. It was a very difficult and frustrating task. While writing *Silent Spring*, Carson confided in a letter to a friend the problems she was having: "How to reveal enough to give understanding of the most serious effects of the chemicals without being technical, how to simplify without error—these have been problems of rather monumental proportions."

TACTICS OF *SILENT SPRING*

Chapter 1 of *Silent Spring* tells a parable of a rural town where the birds, fish, flowers, and plants die and people become sick after a white powder is sprayed on the town. At the beginning of Chapter 2, Rachel Carson begins her argument against the mass aerial spraying of pesticides. Most of her readers were not aware of the dangers of pesticides, but they were well aware of the harmful effects of radiation. Let's look at her tactics:

The interrelationship of people and the environment provides the basis for Carson's argument.

The history of life on earth has been a history of interaction between living things and their surroundings. To a large extent, the physical form and the habits of earth's vegetation and its animal life have been molded by the environment. Considering the whole span of earthly time, the opposite effect, in which life actually modifies its surroundings, has been relatively slight. Only within the moment of time represented by the present century has one species—man—acquired significant power to alter the nature of his world.

During the past quarter century this power has not only increased to one of disturbing magnitude but it has changed in character. The most alarming of all man's assaults upon the environment is the contamination of air, earth, rivers, and sea with dangerous and even lethal materials. This pollution is for the most part irrecoverable; the chain of life it initiates not only in the world that must support life but in living tissues is for the most part irreversible. In this now universal contamination of the environment, chemicals are the sinister and little-recognized partners of radiation in changing the very nature of the world—the very nature of its life. Strontium 90, released through nuclear explosions into the air, comes to earth in rain or drifts down as fallout, lodges in the soil, enters into the grass or corn or wheat grown there, and in time takes its abode in the bones of a human being, there to remain until his death. Similarly, chemicals sprayed on croplands or forests or gardens lie long in soil, entering into living organisms, passing from one to another in a chain of poisoning and death. Or they pass mysteriously by underground streams until they emerge and, through the alchemy of air and sunlight, combine into new forms that kill vegetation, sicken cattle, and work unknown harm on those who drink from once-pure wells. As Albert Schweitzer has said, "Man can hardly even recognize the devils of his own creation."

Carson shifts her language to a metaphor of war against the environment rather than interaction with the natural world.

In 1963 the first treaty was signed by the United States and the Soviet Union that banned the testing of nuclear weapons above ground, under water, and in space.

The key move: Carson associates the dangers of chemical pesticides with those of radiation.

Albert Schweitzer (1875–1965) was a concert musician, philosopher, and doctor who spent most of his life as a medical missionary in Africa.

To make people understand the bad effects of pesticides required explaining what is not common sense: why very tiny amounts of pesticides can be so harmful. The reason lies in how pesticides are absorbed by the body. DDT is fat-soluble and gets stored in organs such as the adrenals, thyroid, liver, and kidneys. Carson explains how pesticides build up in the body:

> This storage of DDT begins with the smallest conceivable intake of the chemical (which is present as residues on most foodstuffs) and continues until quite high levels are reached. The fatty storage deposits act as biological magnifiers, so that an intake of as little as 1/10 of 1 part per million in the diet results in storage of about 10 to 15 parts per million, an increase of one hundredfold or more. These terms of reference, so commonplace to the chemist or the pharmacologist, are unfamiliar to most of us. One part in a million sounds like a very small amount—and so it is. But such substances are so potent that a minute quantity can bring about vast changes in the body. In animal experiments, 3 parts per million has been found to inhibit an essential enzyme in the heart muscle; only 5 parts per million has brought about necrosis or disintegration of liver cells.

Throughout the book, Carson succeeds in translating scientific facts into language that, to use her words, "most of us" can understand. Of course, Carson was a scientist and quite capable of reading scientific articles. She establishes her credibility as a scientist by using technical terms such as *necrosis*. But at the same time she identifies herself with people who are not scientists and gains our trust by taking our point of view.

To accompany these facts, Carson tells about places that have been affected by pesticides. One of the more memorable stories is about Clear Lake, California, in the mountainous country north of San Francisco. Clear Lake is popular for fishing, but it is also an ideal habitat for a species of gnat. In the late 1940s the state of California began spraying the lake with DDD, a close relative of DDT. Spraying had to be repeated because the gnats kept coming back. The western grebes that lived on the lake began to die, and when scientists examined their bodies, the grebes were loaded with extraordinary levels of DDD. Microscopic plants and animals filtered the lake water for nutrients and concentrated the pesticides at 20 times their level in the lake water. Small fish ate these tiny plants and animals and again concentrated the DDD at levels 10 to 100 times that of their microscopic food. The grebes that ate the fish suffered the effects of this huge magnification.

Although DDT is still used in parts of the developing world, the influence of *Silent Spring* led to the banning of it and most other similar pesticides in the United States and Canada. Rachel Carson's book eventually led people to stop relying only on pesticides and to look instead to other methods of controlling pests, such as planting crops that are resistant to insects and disease. When pesticides are used today, they typically are applied much more selectively and in lower amounts than was common when Carson was writing.

Rachel Carson's more lasting legacy is our awareness of our environment. She urges us to be aware that we share this planet with other creatures and that "we are dealing with life—with living populations and all their pressures and counterpressures, their surges and recessions." She warns against dismissing the balance of nature. She writes:

> The balance of nature is not the same today as in Pleistocene times, but it is still there: a complex, precise, and highly integrated system of relationships between living things which cannot safely be ignored any more than the law of gravity can be defied with impunity by a man perched on the edge of a cliff. The balance of nature is not a *status quo*; it is fluid, ever shifting, in a constant state of adjustment.

Since the publication of *Silent Spring*, we have grown much more conscious of large-scale effects on ecosystems caused by global warming, acid rain, and the depleted ozone layer in addition to the local effects of pesticides described in Carson's book. The cooperation of nations today in attempting to control air and water pollution, in encouraging more efficient use of energy and natural resources, and in promoting sustainable patterns of consumption is due in no small part to the long-term influence of *Silent Spring*.

ANALYZING ARGUMENTS: PATHOS, ETHOS, AND LOGOS

When the modern concept of democracy was developed in Greece in the fifth century BCE, the study of rhetoric also began. It's not a coincidence that the teaching of rhetoric was closely tied to the rise of democracy. In the Greek city-states, all citizens had the right to speak and vote at the popular assembly and in the committees of the assembly that functioned as the criminal courts. Citizens took turns serving as the officials of government. Because the citizens of Athens and other city-states took their responsibilities quite seriously, they highly valued the ability to speak effectively in public. Teachers of rhetoric were held in great esteem.

In the next century, the most important teacher of rhetoric in ancient Greece, Aristotle (384–323 BCE), made the study of rhetoric systematic. He defined **rhetoric** as the art of finding the best available means of persuasion in any situation. Aristotle set out three primary tactics of argument: appeals to the emotions and deepest-held values of the audience (**pathos**), appeals based on the trustworthiness of the speaker (**ethos**), and appeals to good reasons (**logos**).

ANALYZING ARGUMENTS: PATHOS, ETHOS, AND LOGOS *(continued)*

Carson makes these appeals with great skill in *Silent Spring*. Very simply, her purpose is to stop pesticide pollution. She first appeals to *pathos*, engaging her readers in her subject. She gives many specific examples of how pesticides have accumulated in the bodies of animals and people. But she also engages her readers through her skill as a writer, making us care about nature as well as concerned about our own safety. She uses the fate of robins to symbolize her crusade. Robins were the victims of spraying for Dutch elm disease. Robins feed on earthworms, which in turn process fallen elm leaves. The earthworms act as magnifiers of the pesticide, which either kills the robins outright or renders them sterile. Thus when no robins sang, it was indeed a silent spring.

Carson is also successful in creating a credible *ethos*. We believe her not just because she establishes her expertise. She convinces us also because she establishes her ethos as a person with her audience's best interests at heart. She anticipates possible objections, demonstrating that she has thought about opposing positions. She takes time to explain concepts that most people do not understand fully, and she discusses how everyone can benefit if we take a different attitude toward nature. She shows that she has done her homework on the topic. By creating a credible ethos, Carson makes an effective moral argument that humans as a species have a responsibility not to destroy the world they live in.

Finally, Carson supports her argument with good reasons, what Aristotle called *logos*. She offers "because clauses" to support her main claims. She describes webs of relationships among the earth, plants, animals, and humans, and she explains how changing one part will affect the others. Her point is not that we should never disturb these relationships but that we should be as aware as possible of the consequences.

Reading Arguments

If you have ever been coached in a sport or have been taught an art such as dancing or playing a musical instrument, you likely have viewed a game or a performance in two ways. You might enjoy the game or performance like everyone else, but at the same time, you might be especially aware of something that you know from your experience is difficult to do and therefore appreciated the skill and the practice necessary to develop it. A similar distinction can be made about two kinds of reading. For the sake of convenience, the first can be called **ordinary reading**, although we don't really think there is a single kind of ordinary reading. In ordinary reading, on the first time through, the reader forms a sense of content and gets an initial impression: whether it's interesting, whether the author has something important to say, whether you agree or disagree.

For most of what you read, one time through is enough. When you read for the second or third time, you start to use different strategies because you have some reason to do so. You are no longer reading to form a sense of the overall content. Often, you are looking for something in particular. If you reread a textbook chapter, you might want to make sure you understand how a key concept is being used. When you reread your apartment contract, you might want to know what is required to get your deposit back. This second kind of reading can be called **critical reading**. Critical reading does not mean criticizing what the writer has to say (although that's certainly possible). Critical reading begins with questions and specific goals.

T I P S

Become a Critical Reader

Before you start reading, find out when the argument was written, where it first appeared, and who wrote it.

Arguments don't appear in vacuums. They most often occur in response to something else that has been written or some event that has happened. You also have a title, which suggests what the argument might be about. This information will help you to form an initial impression about why the writer wrote this particular argument, who the writer imagined as the readers, and what purposes the writer might have had in mind. Then pick up your pencil and start reading.

Become a Critical Reader *(continued)*

Ask Questions

On the first time through, you need to understand what's in the argument. So circle the words and references that you don't know and look them up. If a statement part of the argument isn't clear, note that section in the margin. You might figure out what the writer is arguing later, or you might have to work through it slowly a second time through.

Analyze

On your second reading, you should start analyzing the structure of the argument. Here's how to do it:

- Identify the writer's main claim or claims. You should be able to paraphrase it if it doesn't appear explicitly.
- What are the reasons that support the claim? List them by number in the margins. There might be only one reason, or there could be several (and some reasons could be supported by others).
- Where is the evidence? Does it really support the reasons? Can you think of contradictory evidence?
- Does the writer refer to expert opinion or research about this subject? Do other experts see this issue differently?
- Does the writer acknowledge opposing views? Does the writer deal fairly with opposing views?

Respond

Write down your thoughts as you read. Often you will find that something you read reminds you of something else. Jot that down. It might be something to think about later, and it might give you ideas for writing. Think also about what else you should read if you want to write about this topic. Or you might want to write down whether you are persuaded by the argument and why.

Writers of arguments engage in critical reading even on the first time through. They know that they will have to acknowledge what else has been written about a particular issue. If the issue is new (and few are), then the writer will need to establish its significance by comparing it to other issues on which much has been written. Writers of arguments, therefore, begin reading with *questions*. They want to know *why* a particular argument was written. They want to know *what* the writer's basic assumptions are. They want to know *who* the writer had in mind when the argument was written. Critical readers most often read with pen or pencil in hand or with a window open on their computer. They write their questions in the margins or in the file.

Critical readers do more than just question what they read. They analyze how the argument works. Critical readers look at how an argument is laid out. They identify key terms and examine how the writer is using them. They consider how the writer appeals to our emotions, represents himself or herself, and uses good reasons. They analyze the structure of an argument—the organization—and the way in which it is written—the style.

Finally, critical readers often *respond* as they read. They don't just take in what they read in a passive way. They jot down notes to themselves in the margins or on the blank pages at the front and back of a book. They use these notes later when they start writing. Reading is often the best way to get started writing.

POSITION AND PROPOSAL ARGUMENTS

In *Silent Spring*, Rachel Carson made an effective argument against the massive use of synthetic pesticides. Arguing against the indiscriminate use of pesticides, however, did not solve the problem of what to do about harmful insects that destroy crops and spread disease. Carson also did the harder job of offering solutions. In her final chapter, "The Other Road," Carson gives alternatives to the massive use of pesticides. She describes how a pest organism's natural enemies can be used against it instead.

These two kinds of arguments can be characterized as *position* and *proposal* arguments.

Position Arguments

In a **position argument**, the writer makes a claim about a controversial issue.

- **The writer first has to define the issue**. Carson had to explain what synthetic pesticides are in chemical terms and how they work, and she had to give a history of their increasing use after World War II before she could begin arguing against pesticides.
- **The writer should take a clear position**. Carson wasted no time setting out her position by describing the threat that high levels of pesticides pose to people worldwide.

POSITION AND PROPOSAL ARGUMENTS *(continued)*

■ **The writer should make a convincing argument and acknowledge opposing views**. Carson used a variety of strategies in support of her position, including research studies, quotes from authorities, and her own analyses and observations. She took into account opposing views by acknowledging that harmful insects needed to be controlled and conceded that selective spraying is necessary and desirable.

Proposal Arguments

In a **proposal argument**, the writer proposes a course of action in response to a recognizable problem situation. The proposal says what can be done to improve the situation or change it altogether.

■ **The writer first has to define the problem**. The problem Carson had to define was complex. Not only was the overuse of pesticides killing helpful insects, plants, and animals and threatening people, but the harmful insects the pesticides were intended to eliminate were becoming increasingly resistant. More spraying and more frequent spraying produced pesticide-resistant "superbugs." Mass spraying resulted in actually helping bad bugs such as fire ants by killing off their competition.

■ **The writer has to propose a solution or solutions**. Carson did not hold out for one particular approach to controlling insects, but she did advocate biological solutions. She proposed biological alternatives to pesticides, such as sterilizing and releasing large numbers of male insects and introducing predators of pest insects. Above all, she urged that we work with nature rather than being at war with it.

■ **The solution or solutions must work, and they must be feasible**. The projected consequences should be set out, arguing that good things will happen, bad things will be avoided, or both. Carson discussed research studies that indicated her solutions would work, and she argued that they would be less expensive than massive spraying. Today, we can look at Carson's book with the benefit of hindsight. Not everything Carson proposed ended up working, but her primary solution—learn to live with nature—has been a powerful one. Mass spraying of pesticides has stopped in the United States, and species that were threatened by the excessive use of pesticides, including falcons, eagles, and brown pelicans, have made remarkable comebacks.

RACHEL CARSON

The Obligation to Endure

Rachel Carson (1907–1964) was born and grew up in Springdale, Pennsylvania, 18 miles up the Allegheny River from Pittsburgh. When Carson was in elementary school, her mother was fearful of infectious diseases that were sweeping through the nation and often kept young Rachel out of school. In her wandering on the family farm, Rachel developed the love of nature that she maintained throughout her life. At 22 she began her career as a marine biologist at Woods Hole, Massachusetts, and she later went to graduate school at Johns Hopkins University in Baltimore. She began working for the U.S. government in 1936 in the agency that later became the Fish and Wildlife Service, and she was soon recognized as a talented writer as well as a meticulous scientist. She wrote three highly praised books about the sea and wetlands: Under the Sea Wind *(1941),* The Sea Around Us *(1951), and* The Edge of the Sea *(1954).*

Carson's decision to write Silent Spring *marked a great change in her life. For the first time, she became an environmental activist rather than an inspired and enthusiastic writer about nature. She had written about the interconnectedness of life in her previous three books, but with* Silent Spring *she had to convince people that hazards lie in what had seemed familiar and harmless. Although many people think of birds when they hear Rachel Carson's name, she was the first scientist to make a comprehensive argument that links cancer to environmental causes. Earlier in this chapter, you saw how Carson associated pesticides with the dangers of radiation from nuclear weapons. Notice how else she gets her readers to think differently about pesticides in this selection, which begins Chapter 2 of* Silent Spring.

1   The history of life on earth has been a history of interaction between living things and their surroundings. To a large extent, the physical form and the habits of the earth's vegetation and its animal life have been molded by the environment. Considering the whole span of earthly time, the opposite effect, in which life actually modifies its surroundings, has been relatively slight. Only within the moment of time represented by the present century has one species—man—acquired significant power to alter the nature of his world.

2   During the past quarter century this power has not only increased to one of disturbing magnitude but it has changed in character. The most alarming of all man's assaults upon the environment is the contamination of air, earth, rivers, and sea with dangerous and even lethal materials. This pollution is for the most part irrecoverable; the chain of evil it initiates not only in the world that must support life but in living tissues is for

the most part irreversible. In this now universal contamination of the environment, chemicals are the sinister and little recognized partners of radiation in changing the very nature of the world—the very nature of its life. Strontium 90, released through nuclear explosions into the air, comes to earth in rain or drifts down as fallout, lodges in soil, enters into the grass or corn or wheat grown there, and in time takes up its abode in the bones of a human being, there to remain until his death. Similarly, chemicals sprayed on croplands or forests or gardens lie long in soil, entering into living organisms, passing from one to another in a chain of poisoning and death. Or they pass mysteriously by underground streams until they emerge and, through the alchemy of air and sunlight, combine into new forms that kill vegetation, sicken cattle, and work unknown harm on those who drink from once-pure wells. As Albert Schweitzer has said, "Man can hardly even recognize the devils of his own creation."

3   It took hundreds of millions of years to produce the life that now inhabits the earth—eons of time in which that developing and evolving and diversifying life reached a state of adjustment and balance with its surroundings. The environment, rigorously shaping and directing the life it supported, contained elements that were hostile as well as supporting. Certain rocks gave out dangerous radiation; even within the light of the sun, from which all life draws its energy, there were short-wave radiations with power to injure. Given time—time not in years but in millennia—life adjusts, and a balance has been reached. For time is the essential ingredient; but in the modern world there is no time.

4   The rapidity of change and the speed with which new situations are created follow the impetuous and heedless pace of man rather than the deliberate pace of nature. Radiation is no longer merely the background radiation of rocks, the bombardment of cosmic rays, the ultraviolet of the sun that have existed before there was any life on earth; radiation is now the unnatural creation of man's tampering with the atom. The chemicals to which life is asked to make its adjustment are no longer merely the calcium and silica and copper and all the rest of the minerals washed out of the rocks and carried in rivers to the sea; they are the synthetic creations of man's inventive mind, brewed in his laboratories, and having no counterparts in nature.

5   To adjust to these chemicals would require time on the scale that is nature's; it would require not merely the years of a man's life but the life of generations. And even this, were it by some miracle possible, would be futile, for the new chemicals come from our laboratories in an endless stream; almost five hundred annually find their way into actual use in the United States alone. The figure is staggering and its implications are not easily grasped—500 new chemicals to which the bodies of men and animals are required somehow to adapt each year, chemicals totally outside the limits of biologic experience.

6   Among them are many that are used in man's war against nature. Since the mid-1940s over 200 basic chemicals have been created for use in killing insects, weeds, rodents, and other organisms described in the modern vernacular as "pests"; and they are sold under several thousand different brand names.

7   These sprays, dusts, and aerosols are now applied almost universally to farms, gardens, forests, and homes—nonselective chemicals that have the power to kill every insect, the "good" and the "bad," to still the song of birds and the leaping of fish in the streams, to coat the leaves with a deadly film, and to linger on in soil—all this though the intended target may be only a few weeds or insects. Can anyone believe it is possible to lay down such a barrage of poisons on the surface of the earth without making it unfit for all life? They should not be called "insecticides," but "biocides."

8   The whole process of spraying seems caught up in an endless spiral. Since DDT was released for civilian use, a process of escalation has been going on in which ever more toxic materials must be found. This has happened because insects, in a triumphant vindication of Darwin's principle of the survival of the fittest, have evolved super races immune to the particular insecticide used, hence a deadlier one has always to be developed—and then a deadlier one than that. It has happened also because, for reasons to be described later, destructive insects often undergo a "flareback," or resurgence, after spraying, in numbers greater than before. Thus the chemical war is never won, and all life is caught in its violent crossfire.

9   Along with the possibility of the extinction of mankind by nuclear war, the central problem of our age has therefore become the contamination of man's total environment with such substances of incredible potential for harm—substances that accumulate in the tissues of plants and animals and even penetrate the germ cells to shatter or alter the very material of heredity upon which the shape of the future depends.

10   Some would-be architects of our future look toward a time when it will be possible to alter the human germ plasm by design. But we may easily be doing so now by inadvertence, for many chemicals, like radiation, bring about gene mutations. It is ironic to think that man might determine his own future by something so seemingly trivial as the choice of an insect spray.

11   All this has been risked—for what? Future historians may well be amazed by our distorted sense of proportion. How could intelligent beings seek to control a few unwanted species by a method that contaminated the entire environment and brought the threat of disease and death even to their own kind? Yet this is precisely what we have done. We have done it, moreover, for reasons that collapse the moment we examine them. We are told that the enormous and expanding use of

pesticides is necessary to maintain farm production. Yet is our real problem not one of *overproduction?* Our farms, despite measures to remove acreages from production and to pay farmers *not* to produce, have yielded such a staggering excess of crops that the American taxpayer in 1962 is paying out more than one billion dollars a year as the total carrying cost of the surplus-food storage program. And is the situation helped when one branch of the Agriculture Department tries to reduce production while another states, as it did in 1958, "It is believed generally that reduction of crop acreages under provisions of the Soil Bank will stimulate interest in use of chemicals to obtain maximum production on the land retained in crops."

12   All this is not to say there is no insect problem and no need of control. I am saying, rather, that control must be geared to realities, not to mythical situations, and that the methods employed must be such that they do not destroy us along with the insects. ■

UNION OF CONCERNED SCIENTISTS

The Impact of Global Warming in North America

In 1969 faculty members and students at the Massachusetts Institute of Technology founded the Union of Concerned Scientists dedicated to building a cleaner, healthier environment and a safer world. The UCS offers the insights of scientific analysis to both government policy makers and the general public.

One topic the UCS has addressed is global warming. Ten of the warmest years on record have occurred since 1987, and the mean surface temperature of the earth has increased 0.5°F over the past forty years. In January 2003, Dr. Sharon Locke of the University of Southern Maine and Dr. Susanne Moser of the Union of Concerned Scientists updated a world map to show the effects of global warming based on the latest scientific findings < www.climatehotmap.org/namerica.html >.

The map of North America reproduced here is one part of the world map. The map indicates "fingerprints," the documented effects of a widespread and long-term trend toward higher temperatures, with the darker shade. "Harbingers," events that foreshadow impacts that are likely to become more frequent and widespread, are indicated with the lighter shade. Direct links for the harbingers to global warming cannot be confirmed or eliminated at this time.

The world map on global warming makes an argument by accumulation of details. It attempts to convince you by supplying a mass of evidence. If you don't believe one particular piece of evidence is connected to global warming, there are still many others. This method of argument is particularly well suited to the Web because a visitor to the Web site can click on the many links the site provides.

Global warming fingerprint

Ocean warming, sea-level rise and coastal flooding

Chesapeake Bay

Marsh and island loss. The current rate of a sea level rise is three times the historical rate and appears to be accelerating. Since 1938, about one-third of the marsh at Blackwater National Wildlife Refuge has been submerged.

Global warming harbinger

Earlier spring arrival

Southeast Arizona

Mexican jays are laying eggs 10 days earlier than in 1971. The earlier breeding coincides with a nearly 5°F (2.8°C) increase in average nighttime temperatures from 1971 to 1998.

CHAPTER 2

Finding Arguments

What Exactly Is an Argument?

Many people think of the term *argument* as a synonym for *debate*. College courses and professional careers, however, require a different kind of argument—one that, most of the time, is cooler in emotion and more elaborate in detail than oral debate. At first glance an **argument** in writing doesn't seem have much in common with debate. But the basic elements and ways of reasoning used in written arguments are similar to those we use in everyday conversations. Let's look at an example of an informal debate.

When the pain in his abdomen didn't go away, Jeff knew he had torn something while lifting his friend's heavy speakers up a flight of stairs. He went to the student health center, and called his friend Maria when he returned home.

> An argument must have a claim and one or more reasons to support that claim.

JEFF: I have good news and bad news. The pain is a minor hernia that can be repaired with day surgery. The bad news is that the fee we pay for the health center doesn't cover hospital visits. We should have health coverage.

MARIA: Jeff, you didn't buy the extra insurance. Why should you get it for nothing?

JEFF: Because health coverage is a right.

MARIA: No it's not. Everyone doesn't have health insurance.

JEFF: Well, because in some other countries like Canada, Germany, and Britain, they do.

MARIA: Yes, and people who live in those countries pay a bundle in taxes for the government-provided insurance.

JEFF: It's not fair in this country because some people have health insurance and others don't.

MARIA: Jeff, face the facts. You could have bought the extra insurance. Instead you chose to buy a new car.

JEFF: It would be better if the university provided health insurance because students could graduate in four years. I'm going to have to get a second job and drop out for a semester to pay for the surgery.

MARIA: Neat idea, but who's going to pay for it?

JEFF: OK, all students should be required to pay for health insurance as part of their general fee. Most students are healthy, and it wouldn't cost that much more.

In this discussion, Jeff starts out by making a **claim** that students should have health coverage. Maria immediately asks him why students should not have to pay for health insurance. She wants a reason to accept his claim. Scholars who study argument maintain that *an argument must have a claim and one or more reasons to support that claim.* Something less might be persuasive, but it isn't an argument.

A bumper sticker that says "NO TOLL ROADS" is a claim, but it is not an argument because the statement lacks a reason. Many reasons are possible for arguing against building toll roads:

- We don't need new roads but should build light-rail instead.
- We should raise the gas tax to pay for new roads.
- We should use gas tax revenue only for roads—rather than using it for other purposes.

When a claim has a reason attached, then it becomes an argument.

The Basics of Arguments

A reason is typically offered in a **because clause**, a statement that begins with the word *because* and that provides a supporting reason for the claim. Jeff's first attempt is to argue that students should have health insurance *because* health insurance is a right.

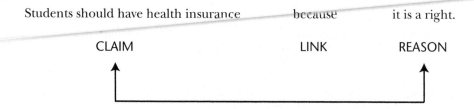

Students should have health insurance   because   it is a right.

CLAIM   LINK   REASON

The word *because* signals a **link** between the reason and the claim. Every argument that is more than a shouting match or a simple assertion has to have one or more reasons. Just having a reason for a claim, however, doesn't mean that the audience will be convinced. When Jeff tells Maria that students have a right to health insurance, Maria replies that students don't have that right. Maria will accept Jeff's claim only if she accepts that his reason supports his claim. Maria challenges Jeff's links and keeps asking "So what?" For her, Jeff's reasons are not good reasons.

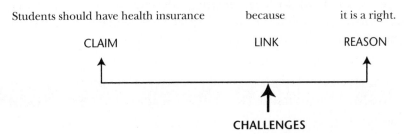

Students should have health insurance · because · it is a right.

CLAIM · LINK · REASON

CHALLENGES

(Other people in the United States do not have free health insurance. Why should students get free insurance?)

By the end of this short discussion, Jeff has begun to build an argument. He has had to come up with another claim to support his main claim: All students should be required to pay for health insurance as part of their general fee. If he is to convince Maria, he will probably have to provide a *series of claims* that she will accept as linked to his primary claim. He will also need to find evidence to support these claims.

Benjamin Franklin observed, "So convenient a thing it is to be a rational creature, since it enables us to find or make a reason for every thing one has a mind to do." It is not hard to think of reasons. What *is* difficult is to convince your audience that your reasons are **good reasons**. In a conversation, you get immediate feedback that tells you whether your listener agrees or disagrees. When you are writing, you usually don't have someone reading who can question you immediately. Consequently, you have to (1) be more specific about what you are claiming, (2) connect with the values you hold in common with your readers, and (3) anticipate what questions and objections your readers might have, if you are going to convince someone who doesn't agree with you or know what you know already.

When you write an argument, imagine a reader like Maria who is going to listen carefully to what you have to say but who is not going to agree with you automatically. Readers like Maria will expect to see:

1. A *claim* that is interesting and makes them want to find out more about what you have to say
2. At least one *good reason* that makes your claim worth taking seriously
3. Some *evidence* that the good reason or reasons are valid
4. Some acknowledgment of the *opposing views and limitations* of the claim

The remainder of this chapter will guide you through the process of finding a topic and making a claim. Chapter 3 will help you find good reasons and evidence and anticipate objections to your claim.

WHAT IS NOT ARGUABLE

Statements of *facts* are usually not considered arguable. Most facts can be verified by doing research. But even simple facts can sometimes be argued. For example, Mount Everest is usually acknowledged to be the highest mountain in the world at 29,028 feet above sea level. But if the total height of a mountain from base to summit is the measure, then the volcano Mauna Loa in Hawaii is the highest mountain in the world. Although the top of Mauna Loa is 13,667 feet above sea level, the summit is 31,784 above the ocean floor. Thus the "fact" that Mount Everest is the highest mountain on the earth depends on a definition of *highest* being the point farthest above sea level. You could argue for this definition.

Another category of claims that are not arguable are those of *personal taste*. Your favorite food and your favorite color are examples of personal taste. If you hate fresh tomatoes, no one can convince you that you actually like them. But many claims of personal taste turn out to be value judgments using arguable criteria. For example, if you think that *Alien* is the best science fiction movie ever made, you can argue that claim using evaluative criteria that other people can consider as good reasons (see Chapter 8). Indeed, you might not even like science fiction and still argue that *Alien* is the best science fiction movie ever.

Finally, many claims rest on *beliefs* or *faith*. If someone accepts a claim as a matter of religious belief, then for that person, the claim is true and cannot be refuted. Of course, people still make arguments about the existence of God and which religion reflects the will of God. Whenever an audience will not consider an idea, it's possible but very difficult to construct an argument. Many people claim to have evidence that UFOs exist, but most people refuse to acknowledge that evidence as even being possibly factual.

Find a Topic

When your instructor gives you a writing assignment, look closely at what you are asked to do. Assignments typically contain a great deal of information, and you have to *sort* that information. First, circle all the instructions about the length, the due date, the format, the grading criteria, and anything else about the production and conventions of the assignment. This information is important to you, but it doesn't tell you what the paper is supposed to be about.

Read Your Assignment Carefully

Often your assignment will contain key words such as *analyze, define, evaluate*, or *propose* that will assist you in determining what direction to take. *Analyze* can mean several things. Your instructor might want you to analyze a piece of writing (see Chapter 4), an image (see Chapter 5), or the causes of something (see Chapter 7). *Define* usually means a **definition argument**, where you argue for a definition based on the criteria you set out (see Chapter 6). *Evaluate* indicates an **evaluation argument**, where you argue that something is good, bad, best, or worst in its class according to criteria that you set out (see Chapter 8). *Write about an issue using your personal experience* indicates a **narrative argument** (see Chapter 9). *Take a position in regard to a reading* might lead you to write a **rebuttal argument** (see Chapter 10). *Propose* means that you should identify a particular problem and explain why your solution is the best one (see Chapter 11).

If you remain unclear about the purpose of the assignment after reading it carefully, talk with your instructor.

Think about What Interests You

Your assignment may specify the topic you are to write about. If your assignment gives you a wide range of options and you don't know what to write about, look first at the materials for your course: the readings, your lecture notes, and discussion boards. Think about what subjects came up in class discussion.

If you need to look outside class for a topic, think about what interests you. Subjects we argue about often find us. There are enough of them in daily life. We're late for work or class because the traffic is bad or the bus doesn't run on time. We can't find a place to park when we get to school or work. We have to negotiate through various bureaucracies for almost anything we do—making an appointment to see a doctor, getting a course added or dropped, or correcting a mistake on a bill. Most of the time we grumble and let it go at that. But sometimes we stick with a subject. Neighborhood groups in cities and towns have been especially effective in getting something done by writing about it—for example, stopping a new road from being built, getting better police and fire protection, and having a vacant lot turned into a park.

List and Analyze Issues

A good way to get started is to list possible issues to write about. Make a list of questions that can be answered "YES, because . . ." or "NO, because. . . ." (Following are some lists to get you started.) You'll find out that often before you can make a claim, you first have to analyze exactly what is meant by a phrase like *censorship of the Internet*. Does it mean censorship of the World Wide Web or of everything that goes over the Internet, including private email? To be convincing, you'll have to argue that one thing causes another, for good or bad.

Think about issues that affect your campus, your community, the nation, and the world. Which ones interest you? In which could you make a contribution to the larger discussion?

Campus

- Should students be required to pay fees for access to computers on campus?
- Should smoking be banned on campus?
- Should varsity athletes get paid for playing sports that bring in revenue?
- Should admissions decisions be based exclusively on academic achievement?
- Should knowledge of a foreign language be required for all degree plans?
- Should your college or university have a computer literacy requirement?
- Should fraternities be banned from campuses if they are caught encouraging alcohol abuse?

Community

- Should people who ride bicycles and motorcycles be required to wear helmets?
- Should high schools be allowed to search students for drugs at any time?
- Should high schools distribute condoms?
- Should bilingual education programs be eliminated?
- Should the public schools be privatized?
- Should bike lanes be built throughout your community to encourage more people to ride bicycles?
- Should more tax dollars be shifted from building highways to funding public transportation?

Nation/World

- Should advertising be banned on television shows aimed at preschool children?
- Should capital punishment be abolished?
- Should the Internet be censored?
- Should the government be allowed to monitor all phone calls and all email to combat terrorism?
- Should handguns be outlawed?
- Should beef and poultry be free of growth hormones?
- Should a law be passed requiring that the parents of teenagers who have abortions be informed?
- Should people who are terminally ill be allowed to end their lives?
- Should the United States punish nations with poor human rights records?

After You Make a List

1. Put a check beside the issues that look most interesting to write about or the ones that mean the most to you.
2. Put a question mark beside the issues that you don't know very much about. If you choose one of these issues, you will probably have to do in-depth research—by talking to people, by using the Internet, or by going to the library.

3. Select the two or three issues that look most promising. For each issue, make another list:

- Who is most interested in this issue?
- Whom or what does this issue affect?
- What are the pros and cons of this issue? Make two columns. At the top of the left one, write "YES, because." At the top of the right one, write "NO, because."
- What has been written about this issue? How can you find out what has been written?

You can get help with finding a topic, drafting a thesis, and organizing and revising your paper at your writing center.

Explore Your Topic

Once you have identified a general topic, the next step is to explore that topic. You don't have to decide exactly what to write about at this stage. Your goal is to find out how much you already know and what you need to learn more about. Experienced writers use several strategies for exploring a topic.

Freewrite

The goal of **freewriting** is to write as quickly as you can without stopping for a set time—usually five or ten minutes. Set a timer and then write as fast as you can, even if you wander off the topic. Don't stop to correct mistakes. Write the same sentence again if you get stuck momentarily. The constant flow of words will generate ideas—some useful and some not. After you've finished, read what you have written and single out any key ideas.

Freewrite on privacy

I get so much junk email and junk mail. How did so many people get my email and mail addresses? How is it collected? How does it get passed around? How do I find this out? Friend told me about a question in an interview—they had done a Google search on him. A lot of people have the same names. Easy to mix up people. Scary. How could you fix it? Amazon account tracks what I buy. Do they sell that information? What are the laws? Read that Florida made it illegal to keep track of who owns guns but they have a government list of prescription drug users. Why are prescription drug users more dangerous than gun owners?

Ideas to Use

1. *The sharing of personal information.*
2. *The misuse of personal information by corporations.*
3. *Government collected personal information.*

You may want to take one of the ideas you have identified to start another freewrite. After two or three rounds of freewriting, you should begin to identify how you might develop your topic.

Brainstorm

Another method of discovery is to brainstorm. The end result of **brainstorming** is usually a list—sometimes of questions, sometimes of statements. These questions and statements give you ways to develop your topic. Below is a list of questions on the issue of secondhand smoke.

- How much of a risk is secondhand smoke?
- What are the effects of secondhand smoke on children?

■ How do the risks of secondhand smoke compare to other kinds of pollution?

■ Which states ban all exposure to secondhand smoke? exposure in restaurants? exposure in the workplace?

■ Who opposes banning exposure to secondhand smoke?

Use an Online Subject Directory

Online subject directories can help you identify the subtopics of a large, general topic. Try the subject index of your library's online catalog. You'll likely find subtopics listed under large topics.

Yahoo! Issues and Causes directory
(dir.yahoo.com/Society_and_Culture/Issues_and_Causes/)

One of the best Web subject directories for finding arguments is Yahoo's Issues and Causes directory. This directory provides subtopics for major issues and provides links to the Web sites of organizations interested in particular issues.

Read about Your Topic

Read about your topic extensively before writing about it. Most of the writing you will do in college will be in response to what others have written about that topic. Reading will often give you ideas about where to begin in writing about your topic and will help you think of ways of developing it. Chapter 15 gives you ways of finding material to read about your topic.

Write notes as you read—in the margins, in a notebook, or on a computer. Identify the main ideas and write questions and comments. Good reading notes are like a gift when you start to write. "Talking" to a text by writing questions and comments will help you to become familiar with it. Imagine the author sitting across the table from you. What would you say to her or him? Writing responses can bring that text to life, and it can also help you realize that the author is, like you, a person with a point of view.

Make an Idea Map

When you have a number of facts and ideas about a topic, you need to begin making connections. One method of assembling ideas is an **idea map**, which describes visually how the many aspects of a particular issue relate to each other. Idea maps are useful because you can see everything at once and make connections among the different aspects of an issue—definitions, causes, proposed solutions, and opposing points of view.

A good way to get started is to write down ideas on sticky notes. Then you can move the sticky notes around until you figure out which ideas fit together. The accompanying illustration shows what an idea map on childhood obesity might look.

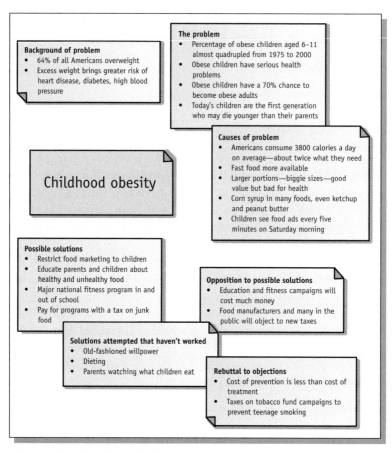

Idea map on childhood obesity

Think about Your Audience

Thinking about your audience doesn't mean telling them what they might want to hear. Instead, imagine yourself in a dialog with your audience. What questions will they likely have? How might you address any potential objections?

What Does Your Audience Know—and Not Know?

Critical to your argument is your audience's knowledge of your subject. If they are not familiar with the background information, they probably won't understand your argument fully. If you know that your readers will be unfamiliar with your subject, you will have to supply background information before attempting to convince them of your position. A good tactic is to tie your new information to what your readers already know. Comparisons and analogies can be very helpful in linking old and new information.

Another critical factor is your audience's level of expertise. How much technical language can you use? For example, if you are writing a proposal to put high-speed Internet connections into all dormitory rooms, will your readers know the difference between a T1 line and a T3 line? The director of the computation center should know the difference, but the vice president for student affairs might not. If you are unsure of your readers' knowledge level, it's better to include background information and explain technical terms. Few readers will be insulted, and they can skip over this information quickly if they are familiar with your subject.

What Is Your Audience's Attitude Toward You?

Does your audience know you at all, either by reputation or from previous work? Are you considered your reader's equal, superior, or subordinate? How your audience regards you will affect the tone and presentation of your message. Does your audience respect you and trust you? What can you include in your presentation to build trust? In many cases, your audience will know little about you. Especially in those circumstances, you can build trust in your reader by following the advice on building credibility, discussed in Chapter 3.

What Is Your Audience's Attitude Toward Your Subject?

People have prior attitudes about controversial issues that you must take into consideration as you write or speak. Imagine, for instance, that you are preparing an argument for a guest editorial in your college newspaper advocating that your state government provide parents with choices between public and private schools. You plan to argue that the tax dollars that now automatically go to public schools should go to private schools if the parents so choose. You have evidence that the sophomore-to-senior dropout rate in private schools is less than half the rate of public schools. Furthermore, students from private schools attend college at nearly twice the rate of public school graduates. You intend to argue that one of the reasons private schools are more successful is that they spend more money on instruction and less on administration. And you believe that school choice speaks to the American desire for personal freedom.

Not everyone on your campus will agree with your stand. How might the faculty at your college or university feel about this issue? the administrators? the staff? other students? interested people in the community who read the student newspaper? What attitudes toward public funding of private schools will they have before they start reading what you have to say? How are you going to deal with the objection that because many students in private schools come from more affluent families, it is not surprising that they do better?

Even when you write about a much less controversial subject, you must think carefully about your audience's attitudes toward what you have to say or write. Sometimes, your audience may share your attitudes; other times, your audience may be neutral; at still other times, your audience will have attitudes that differ sharply from your own. Anticipate these various attitudes and act accordingly. Show awareness of the attitudes of your audience, and if those attitudes are very different from yours, you will have to work hard to counter them without insulting your audience.

Write a Thesis

Once you have identified a topic and have a good sense of how to develop it, the next critical step is to write a **working thesis**. Your **thesis** states your main idea. Much writing that you will do in college and later in your career will have an explicit thesis, usually stated near the beginning. The thesis announces your topic and indicates what points you want to make about that topic.

Focus Your Thesis

The thesis can make or break your paper. If the thesis is too broad, you cannot do justice to the argument. Who wouldn't wish for fewer traffic accidents, better medical care, more effective schools, or a cleaner environment? Simple solutions for these complex problems are unlikely.

Stating something that is obvious to everyone isn't an arguable thesis. Don't settle for easy answers. It's easy to make broad generalization or make predictable statements when your topic is too broad. Narrow your focus and concentrate on the areas where you have the most questions. Those places are likely the ones where your readers will have the most questions too.

The opposite problem is less common: a too-narrow thesis. If your thesis is only a statement of a commonly known fact, then it is too narrow. For example, the growth rate of the population in the United States has doubled since 1970 because of immigration. The Census Bureau provides reasonably accurate statistical information, so this claim is not arguable. But the policies that allow increased immigration and the effects of a larger population on more crowding, congestion, and the costs of housing, education, and transportation are arguable.

> NOT ARGUABLE: The population of the United States grew faster in the 1990s than in any previous decade because Congress increased the level of legal immigration and the government stopped enforcing most laws against illegal immigration in the interior of the country.
>
> ARGUABLE: Allowing a high rate of immigration helps the United States deal with the problems of an increasingly aging society and helps provide funding for millions of Social Security recipients.
>
> ARGUABLE: The increase in the number of visas to foreign workers in technology industries is the major cause of unemployment in those industries.

Evaluate Your Thesis

Once you have a working thesis, ask these questions:

1. Is it arguable?
2. Is it specific?
3. Is it manageable in the length and time you have?
4. Is it interesting to your intended readers?

Example 1

Sample thesis:
We should take action to resolve the serious traffic problem in our city.

Arguable? The thesis is arguable, but it lacks a focus.

Specific? The thesis is too broad.

Manageable? Transportation is a complex issue. New highways and rail systems are expensive and take many years to build. Furthermore, citizens don't want new roads running through their neighborhoods.

Interesting? The topic has the potential to be interesting if the writer can propose a specific solution to a problem everyone in the city recognizes.

When a thesis is too broad, it needs to be revised to address a specific aspect of an issue. Make the big topic smaller.

Revised thesis:
The existing freight railway that runs through the center of the city should be converted to a passenger railway because it is the cheapest and quickest way to decrease traffic congestion downtown.

Example 2

Sample thesis:
Over 60% of Americans play video games on a regular basis.

Arguable? The thesis states a commonly acknowledged fact.

Specific? The thesis is too narrow.

Manageable? A known fact is stated in the thesis, so there is little to research. Several surveys report this finding.

Interesting? Video games are interesting as a cultural trend, but nearly everyone is aware of the trend. The popularity of video games is well established.

There's nothing original or interesting about stating that Americans love video games. Think about what is controversial. One debatable topic is the effects of video games on children.

Revised thesis:
Video games are valuable because they improve children's visual attention skills, their literacy skills, and their computer literacy skills.

Finding and Supporting Good Reasons

The Basics of Reasoning

You decide to pick up a new pair of prescription sunglasses at the mall on your way to class. The company promises that it can make your glasses in an hour, but what you hadn't counted on was how long it would take you to park and how long you would have to wait in line at the counter. You jog into the mall, drop off your prescription, and go out of the store to wait. There's a booth nearby where volunteers are checking blood pressure. You don't have anything better to do, so you have your blood pressure checked.

After the volunteer takes the blood pressure cuff off your arm, he asks how old you are. He asks you whether you smoke, and you say no. He tells you that your reading is 150 over 100. He says that's high for a person your age and that you ought to have it checked again. "This is all I need," you think. "I have a test coming up tomorrow, a term paper due Friday, and if I don't make it to class, I won't get my homework turned in on time. And now something bad is wrong with me."

When you get your blood pressure checked again at the student health center after your test the next day, it turns out to be 120/80, which the nurse says is normal. When you think about it, you realize that you probably had a high reading because of stress and jogging into the mall.

Your blood pressure is one of the most important indicators of your health. When the volunteer checking your blood pressure tells you that you might have a serious health problem because your blood pressure is too high, he is relying on his knowledge of how the human body works. If your blood pressure is too high, it

> A good reason works because it includes a link to your claim that your readers will find valid.

39

eventually damages your arteries and puts a strain on your entire body. But he used the word *might* because your blood pressure is not the same all the time. It can go up when you are under stress or even when you eat too much salt. And blood pressure varies from person to person and even in different parts of your body. For example, your blood pressure is higher in your legs than in your arms.

Doctors use blood pressure and other information to make diagnoses. Diagnoses are claims based on evidence. But as the blood pressure example shows, often the link is not clear, at least from a single reading. A doctor will collect several blood pressure readings over many weeks or even years before concluding that a patient has a condition of high blood pressure called *hypertension*. These readings will be compared to readings from thousands of other patients in making a diagnosis. Doctors are trained to rely on **generalizations** from thousands of past observations in medical science and to make diagnoses based on probability. In everyday life, you learn to make similar generalizations from which you make decisions based on probability. If you are in a hurry in the grocery store, you likely will go to the line that looks the shortest. You pick the shortest line because you think it will probably be the fastest.

Sometimes we don't have past experience to rely on, and we have to reason in other ways. When we claim that one thing is like something else, we make a link by **analogy**. When a United States court ruled against Microsoft in an antitrust case, Microsoft's lawyers argued by analogy against the decision. They maintained that requiring Microsoft to bundle the rival browser Netscape Navigator with their own browser, Internet Explorer, was as irrational as expecting Coca-Cola to put three cans of Pepsi in every six-pack of Coke. The analogy drew on the fierce rivalry between Coca-Cola and Pepsi, where no one would expect either to help the other to sell its product.

Another way we reason is by using **cultural assumptions**, which we often think of as common sense. For example, you walk down the street and see a 280Z speed around a car that is double-parked, cross the double line, and sideswipe a truck coming the other way. A police officer arrives shortly, and you tell her that the 280Z is at fault. Maybe you've seen many accidents before, but the reason you think the 280Z is at fault is because in the United States, drivers are supposed to stay on the right side of two-way roads. It is a part of our culture that you take for granted—that is, until you try to drive in Japan, Great Britain, or India, where people drive on the left. Driving on the left will seem unnatural to you, but it's natural for the people in those countries.

Particular cultural assumptions can be hard to challenge because you often have to take on an entire system of belief. It is much easier to use the metric system to calculate distances than it is to employ the English system of miles, feet, and inches. Nonetheless, people in the United States have strongly resisted efforts to convert to metric measures. When cultural assumptions become common sense, people accept them as true even though they often can be questioned. It seems like common sense to say that salad is good for you, but in reality it depends on what's in the salad. A salad consisting of lettuce and a mayonnaise-based dressing has little nutritional value and too much fat.

Find Good Reasons

A **good reason** works because it includes a link to your claim that your readers will find valid. Your readers are almost like a jury that passes judgment on your good reasons. If they accept them and cannot think of other, more compelling good reasons that oppose your position, you will convince them.

Most good reasons derive from mulling things over "reasonably," or, to use the technical term, from logos. *Logos* refers to the logic of what you communicate; in fact, logos is the root of our modern word *logic*. Good reasons are thus commonly associated with logical appeals. Over the years, rhetoricians have devised questions to help speakers and writers find good reasons to support their arguments. These questions will equip you to communicate more effectively when you are speaking before a group as well as writing an argument. But do not expect every question to be productive in every case. Sometimes, a certain question won't get you very far; and often, the questions will develop so many good reasons and strategies that you will not be able to use them all. You will ultimately have to select from among the best of your good reasons to find the ones that are most likely to work in a given case.

If a certain question does not seem to work for you at first, do not give up on it the next time. Get in the habit of asking these questions in the course of developing your arguments. If you ask them systematically, you will probably have more good reasons than you need for your arguments.

Can You Argue by Definition?

Probably the most powerful kind of good reason is an **argument from definition**. You can think of a definition as a simple statement: _____ *is a* _____.

You use these statements all the time. When you need a course to fulfill your social science requirement, you look at the list of courses that are defined as social science courses. You find out that the anthropology class you want to take is one of them. It's just as important when _____ *is not a* _____. Suppose you are taking College Algebra this semester, which is a math course taught by the math department, yet it doesn't count for the math requirement. The reason it doesn't count is because College Algebra is not defined as a college-level math class. So you have to enroll next semester in Calculus I.

Many definitions are not nearly as clear cut as the math requirement. If you want to argue that figure skaters are athletes, you will need to define what an athlete is. You start thinking. An athlete competes in an activity, but that definition alone is too broad, since many competitions do not require physical activity. Thus, an athlete must participate in a competitive physical activity and must train for it. But that definition is still not quite narrow enough, since soldiers train for competitive physical activity. You decide to add that the activity must be a sport and that it must require special competence and precision. Your *because clause* turns out as follows: *Figure skaters are athletes because true athletes train for and compete in physical sporting competitions that require special competence and precision.*

If you can get your audience to accept your definitions of things, you've gone a long way toward convincing them of the validity of your claim. That is why the most controversial issues in our culture—abortion, affirmative action, gay rights, pornography, women's rights, gun control, the death penalty—are argued from definition. Is abortion a crime or a medical procedure? Is pornography protected by the First Amendment, or is it a violation of women's rights? Is the death penalty just or cruel and inhuman? You can see from these examples that definitions often rely on cultural assumptions for their links.

Because cultural assumptions about controversial issues are strongly held, people usually don't care about the practical consequences. Arguing that it is much cheaper to execute prisoners who have been convicted of first-degree murder than to keep them in prison for life does not convince those who believe that it is morally wrong to kill. (See Chapter 6.)

Can You Argue from Value?

A special kind of argument from definition, one that often implies consequences, is the **argument from value**. You can support your claim with a because clause (or several of them) that includes a sense of evaluation. Arguments from value follow from claims like _____ *is a good* _____, or _____ *is not a good* _____.

You make arguments from value every day. Your old TV set breaks, so you go to your local discount store to buy a new one. When you get there, you find too many choices. You have to decide which one to buy. You have only $200 to spend, but there are still a lot of choices. Which is the best TV for $200 or less? The more you look, the more confusing it gets. There are several 20-inch TVs in your price range. All have remote control. Some have features such as front surround sound, multilingual on-screen display, and A/V inputs. But you realize that there is one test that will determine the best TV for you: the picture quality. You buy the one with the best picture.

Evaluative arguments usually proceed from the presentation of certain criteria. These criteria come from the definitions of good and bad, of poor and not so poor, that prevail in a given case. A really good 20-inch TV fulfills certain criteria; so does an outstanding movie, an excellent class, or, if you work in an office, an effective telephone system. Sometimes the criteria are straightforward, as in the TV example. The TV that you select has to be under a certain cost, equipped with a remote, and ready to hook up to your cable. After those criteria are met, the big ones are picture and sound quality. But if your boss asks you to recommend a new telephone system, then it's not quite so straightforward. You are presented with many options, and you have to decide which of them are worth paying for. You have to decide how the phone system is going to be used, examine which features will be important for your office, and then rate the systems according to the criteria you have set out. The key to evaluation arguments is identifying and arguing for the right criteria. If you can convince your readers that you have the right criteria and that your assessments are correct, then you will be convincing. (See Chapter 8).

Can You Compare or Contrast?

Evaluative arguments can generate comparisons often enough. But even if they don't generate comparisons, your argument might profit if you get in the habit of thinking in comparative terms—in terms of what things are like or unlike the topic you are discussing. **Claims of comparisons** take the form _____ *is like* _____ or _____ *is not like* _____. If you are having trouble coming up with good reasons, think of comparisons that help your readers agree with you. If you want to argue that figure skaters are athletes, you might think about how their training and competitions resemble those of other athletes. Making comparisons is an effective way of building common ground.

A particular kind of comparison is an analogy. An analogy is an extended comparison—one that is developed over several sentences or paragraphs for explanatory or persuasive purposes. Analogies take different forms. A historical analogy compares something that is going on now with a similar case in the past. One of the most frequently used historical analogies is a comparison of a current situation in which one country attacks or threatens another with Germany's seizing of Czechoslovakia in 1938 and then invading Poland in 1939, which started World War II. The difficulty with this analogy is that circumstances today are not the same as those in 1939, and it is easy to point out how the analogy fails.

Other analogies make literal comparisons. A literal analogy is a comparison between current situations, in which you argue that what is true or works in one situation should be true or should work in another. Most advanced nations provide basic health care to all their citizens either free or at minimal charge. All citizens of Canada are covered by the same comprehensive health care system, which is free for both rich and poor. Canadians go to the doctor more frequently than citizens of the United States do, and they receive what is generally regarded as better care than their southern neighbors, who pay the most expensive health care bills on the planet.

The Canadian analogy has failed to convince members of the U.S. Congress to vote for a similar system in the United States. Opponents of adopting the Canadian system argue that health care costs are also high in Canada, but Canadians pay the costs in different ways. They pay high taxes, and the Canadian national debt has increased since the universal health system was approved. These opponents of adopting the Canadian system for the United States believe that the best care can be obtained for the lowest cost if health care is treated like any other service and consumers decide what they are willing to pay. Comparisons can always work both ways.

Analogies are especially valuable when you are trying to explain a concept to a willing listener or reader, but analogies are far from foolproof if the reader does not agree with you from the outset. Using an analogy can be risky if the entire argument depends on the reader's accepting it.

Can You Argue from Consequence?

Another powerful source of good reasons comes from considering the possible consequences of your position: Can you sketch out the good things that will follow from your position? Can you establish that certain bad things will be avoided if your position is adopted? If so, you will have other good reasons to use.

Arguments from consequence take the basic form of _____ *causes* _____ (or _____ *does not cause* _____). Very often, arguments from consequence are more complicated, taking the form _____ *causes* _____ *which, in turn, causes* _____ and so on. In Chapter 1 we describe how *Silent Spring* makes powerful arguments from consequence. Rachel Carson's primary claim is that *DDT should not be sprayed on a massive scale because it will poison animals and people.* The key to her argument is the causal chain that explains how animals and people are poisoned. Carson describes how nothing exists alone in nature. When a potato field is sprayed with chemical poison such as DDT, some of that poison is absorbed by the skin of the potatoes and some washes into the groundwater, where it contaminates drinking water. Other poisonous residue is absorbed into streams, where it is ingested by insect larvae, which in turn are eaten by fish. Fish are eaten by other fish, which are then eaten by waterfowl and people. At each stage, the poisons become more concentrated. Carson shows why people are in danger from drinking contaminated water and eating contaminated vegetables and fish. Even today, over thirty years after DDT stopped being used in the United States, dangerous levels exist in the sediment at the bottom of many lakes and bays. (See Chapter 7.)

Proposal arguments are future-oriented arguments from consequence. In a proposal argument, you cannot stop with naming good reasons; you also have to show that these consequences would follow from the idea or course of action that you are arguing. As an example, let's say you want to argue that all high school graduates in your state should be computer literate. You want a computer requirement more substantial than the one computer literacy course you had in the eighth grade. You want all high school graduates to be familiar with basic computer concepts and terminology, to be able to use a word processing application and at least two other applications, and to understand issues of ethics and privacy raised by new electronic technologies.

Your strongest good reason is that high school graduates should be competent in the use of computers, the tool that they will most certainly use for most writing tasks and many other activities during their lifetime. Even if your readers accept that good reason, you still have to prove that the requirement will actually give students the competency they require. Many students pass language requirements without being able to speak, read, or write the language they have studied.

Furthermore, you have to consider the feasibility of any proposal that you make. A good idea has to be a practical one. If you want to impose a computer literacy requirement, you have to argue for increased funding for expensive technology. High school students in poor communities cannot become computer literate unless they have access to computers. More teachers might also need to be hired. And you will need to figure out how to fit the computer requirement into an already crowded curriculum. Sometimes, feasibility is not a major issue (for example, if you're proposing that the starting time for basketball games be changed by thirty minutes), but if it is, you must address it. (See Chapter 11.)

Can You Counter Objections to Your Position?

Another good way to find convincing good reasons is to think about possible objections to your position. If you can imagine how your audience might counter or respond to your argument, you will probably include in your argument precisely the points that will address your readers' particular needs and objections. If you are successful, your readers will be convinced that you are right. You've no doubt had the experience yourself of mentally saying to a writer in the course of your reading, "Yeah, but what about this other idea?"—only to have the writer address precisely this objection.

You can impress your readers that you've thought about why anyone would oppose your position and exactly how that opposition would be expressed. If you are writing a proposal argument for a computer literacy requirement for all high school graduates, you might think about why anyone would object, since computers are becoming increasingly important to our jobs and lives. What will the practical objections be? What philosophical ones? Why hasn't such a requirement been put in place already? By asking such questions in your own arguments, you are likely to develop robust because clauses that may be the ones that most affect your readers.

Sometimes, writers pose rhetorical questions such as "You might say, 'But won't paying for computers for all students make my taxes go up?'" Stating objections explicitly can be effective if you make the objections as those of a reasonable person with an alternative point of view. But if the objections you state are ridiculous ones, then you risk being accused of setting up a *straw man*—that is, making the position opposing your own so simplistic that no one would likely identify with it. (See Chapter 10.)

QUESTIONS FOR FINDING GOOD REASONS

1. Can you argue by definition—from "the nature of the thing"?

- Can you argue that while many (most) people think X is a Y, X is better thought of as a Z?
  Example: Most people do not think of humans as an endangered species, but small farmers have been successful in comparing their way of life to an endangered species and thus have extended the definition of an endangered species to include themselves.

- Can you argue that while X is a Y, X differs from other Ys and might be thought of as a Z?
  Example: Colleges and universities are similar to public schools in having education as their primary mission, but unlike public schools, colleges and universities receive only part of their operating costs from tax revenues and therefore, like a business, must generate much of their own revenue.

2. Can you argue from value?

- Can you grade a few examples of the kind of thing you are evaluating as good, better, and best (or bad and worse)?
  Example: There have been lots of great actors in detective films, but none compare to Humphrey Bogart.

- Can you list the features you use to determine whether something is good or bad and then show why one is most important?
  Example: Coach Powers taught me a great deal about the skills and strategy of playing tennis, but most of all, she taught me that the game is fun.

3. Can you compare or contrast?

- Can you think of items, events, or situations that are similar or dissimilar to the one you are writing about?
  Example: We should require a foreign language for all students at our college because our main competitor does not have such a requirement.

(continued)

QUESTIONS FOR FINDING GOOD REASONS *(continued)*

- Can you distinguish why your subject is different from one usually thought of as similar?
  Example: While poor people are often lumped in with the unemployed and those on welfare, the majority of poor people do work in low-paying jobs.

4. Can you argue from consequence?

- Can you argue that good things will happen if a certain course of action is followed or that bad things will be avoided?
  Example: Eliminating all income tax deductions would save every taxpayer many hours and would create a system of taxation that does not reward people for cheating.

- Can you argue that while there were obvious causes of Y, Y would not have occurred had it not been for X?
  Example: A 17-year-old driver is killed when her car skids across the grass median of an interstate highway and collides with a pickup truck going the other direction. Even though a slick road and excessive speed were the immediate causes, the driver would be alive today if the median had had a concrete barrier.

- Can you argue for an alternative cause rather than the one many people assume?
  Example: Politicians take credit for reducing the violent crime rate because of "get-tough" police policies, but in fact, the rate of violent crime is decreasing because more people are working.

5. Can you counter objections to your position?

- Can you think of the most likely objections to your claim and turn them into your own good reasons?
  Example: High school administrators might object to requiring computer literacy because of cost, but schools can now lease computers and put them on a statewide system at a cost less than they now pay for textbooks.

- Can the *reverse* or opposite of an opposing claim be argued?
  Example: A proposed expressway through a city is claimed to help traffic, but it also could make traffic worse by encouraging more people to drive to the city.

Find Evidence to Support Good Reasons

Good reasons are essential ingredients of good arguments, but they don't do the job alone. You must support or verify good reasons with evidence. **Evidence** consists of hard data or examples or narratives or episodes or tabulations of episodes (known as *statistics*) that are seen as relevant to the good reasons that you are putting forward. To put it another way, a writer of arguments puts forward not only claims and good reasons but also evidence that those good reasons are true. And that evidence consists of examples, personal experiences, comparisons, statistics, calculations, quotations, and other kinds of data that a reader will find relevant and compelling.

How much supporting evidence should you supply? How much evidence is enough? That is difficult to generalize about; as is usual in the case of rhetoric, the best answer is to say, "It depends." If a reader is likely to find one of your good reasons hard to believe, then you should be aggressive in offering support. You should present detailed evidence in a patient and painstaking way. As one presenting an argument, you have a responsibility not just to *state* a case but to *make* a case with evidence. Arguments that are unsuccessful tend to fail not because of a shortage of good reasons; more often, they fail because the reader doesn't agree that there is enough evidence to support the good reason that is being presented.

If your good reason isn't especially controversial, you probably should not belabor it. Think of your own experiences as a reader. How often do you recall saying to yourself, as you read a passage or listened to a speaker, "OK! OK! I get the point! Don't keep piling up all of this evidence for me because I don't want it or need it." However, such a reaction is rare, isn't it? By contrast, how often do you recall muttering under your breath, "How can you say that? What evidence do you have to back it up?" When in doubt, err on the side of offering too much evidence. It's an error that is seldom made and not often criticized.

When a writer doesn't provide satisfactory evidence for a because clause, readers might feel that there has been a failure in the reasoning process. In fact, in your previous courses in writing and speaking, you may have learned about various **fallacies** associated with faulty arguments (which are listed on page 51–52).

Strictly speaking, there is nothing false about these so-called logical fallacies. The fallacies most often refer to failures in providing evidence; when you don't provide enough good evidence to convince your audience, you might be accused of committing a fallacy in reasoning. You will usually avoid such accusations if the evidence that you cite is both *relevant* and *sufficient*.

Relevance refers to the appropriateness of the evidence to the case at hand. Some kinds of evidence are seen as more relevant than others for particular audiences. For example, in science and industry, personal testimony is seen as having limited relevance, while experimental procedures and controlled observations have far more credibility. Compare someone who defends the use of a particular piece of computer software because "it worked for me" with someone who defends it because "according to a journal article published last month, 84 percent of the users of the software were satisfied or very satisfied with it." On the other hand, in writing to the general public on controversial issues such as gun control, personal experience is often considered more relevant than other kinds of data. The so-called Brady Bill, which requires a mandatory waiting period for the purchase of handguns, was named for President Ronald Reagan's press secretary, James Brady, who was permanently disabled when John W. Hinckley, Jr., made an assassination attempt on the president in 1981. James Brady's wife, Sarah, effectively told the story of her husband's suffering in lobbying for the bill.

Sufficiency refers to the amount of evidence cited. Sometimes a single piece of evidence or a single instance will carry the day if it is especially compelling in some way—if it represents the situation well or makes a point that isn't particularly controversial. More often, people expect more than one piece of evidence if they are to be convinced of something. Convincing readers that they should approve a statewide computer literacy requirement for all high school graduates will require much more evidence than the story of a single graduate who succeeded with her computer skills. You will likely need statistical evidence for such a broad proposal.

If you anticipate that your audience might not accept your evidence, face the situation squarely. First, think carefully about the argument you are presenting. If you cannot cite adequate evidence for your assertions, perhaps those assertions must be modified or qualified in some way. If you remain convinced of your assertions, then think about doing more research to come up with additional evidence. If you anticipate that your audience might suspect you have overlooked or minimized important information, reassure them that you have not and deal explicitly with conflicting arguments. Another strategy is to acknowledge explicitly the limitations of your evidence. Acknowledging limitations doesn't shrink the limitations, but it does build your credibility and convinces your audience that alternatives have indeed been explored fully and responsibly. If you are thinking of your reader as a partner rather than as an adversary, it is usually easy to acknowledge limitations because you are looking not for victory and the end of debate but for a mutually satisfactory situation that might emerge as a result of the communication process that you are part of.

CHAPTER 3 *Finding and Supporting Good Reasons* **51**

FALLACIES IN ARGUMENTS

Reasoning in arguments depends less on *proving* a claim than it does on finding evidence for the claim that readers will accept as valid. Logical fallacies in argument reflect a failure to provide adequate evidence for the claim that is being made. Among the most common fallacies are the following.

- **Bandwagon appeals.** *It doesn't matter if I cheat on a test because everyone else does.* This argument suggests that everyone is doing it, so why shouldn't you? Close examination may reveal that in fact everyone really isn't doing it—and in any case, it may not be the right thing to do.

- **Begging the question.** *People should be able to use land any way they want to because using land is an individual right.* The fallacy of begging the question occurs when the claim is restated and passed off as evidence.

- **Either-or.** *Either we build a new freeway crossing downtown or else there will be perpetual gridlock.* The either-or fallacy suggests that there are only two choices in a complex situation. This is rarely, if ever, the case. (In this example, the writer ignores other transportation options besides freeways.)

- **False analogies.** *The Serbian seizure of Bosnian territory was like Hitler's takeover of Czechoslovakia in 1938, and having learned the hard way what happens when they give in to dictators, Western nations stood up to Serbian aggression.* Analogies always depend on the degree of resemblance of one situation to another. In this case, the analogy fails to recognize that Serbia in 1993 was hardly like Nazi Germany in 1938.

- **Hasty generalization.** *We had three days this summer when the temperature reached an all-time high; that's a sure sign of global warming.* A hasty generalization is a broad claim made on the basis of a few occurrences. The debate over global warming takes into account climate data for centuries. Individual climate events such as record hot days do not confirm trends.

- **Name calling.** Name calling is as frequent in political argument as on the playground. Candidates are "accused" of being tax-and-spend liberals, ultraconservatives, radical feminists, and so on. Rarely are these terms defined; hence they are meaningless.

- **Non sequitur.** *A university that can afford to build a new football stadium should not have to raise tuition.* A non sequitur (a Latin term meaning "it does not follow") ties together two unrelated ideas. In this case, the argument fails to recognize that the money for new stadiums is often donated for that purpose and is not part of a university's general revenue.

FALLACIES IN ARGUMENTS *(continued)*

- **Oversimplification.** *No one would run stop signs if we had a mandatory death penalty for doing it.* This claim may be true, but the argument would be unacceptable to most citizens. More complex, if less definitive, solutions are called for.

- **Polarization.** *Feminists are all man haters.* Polarization, like name calling, exaggerates positions and groups by representing them as extreme and divisive.

- **Post hoc fallacy.** *I ate a hamburger last night and got deathly sick—must have been food poisoning.* The post hoc fallacy (from the Latin *post hoc ergo hoc,* "after this, therefore this") assumes that things that follow in time have a causal relationship. In this example, you may have simply started coming down with the flu—as would be obvious two days later.

- **Rationalization.** *I could have done better on the test if I thought the course mattered to my major.* People frequently come up with excuses and weak explanations for their own and others' behavior that avoid actual causes.

- **Slippery slope.** *We shouldn't grant amnesty to illegal immigrants now living in the United States because it will mean opening our borders to a flood of people from around the world who want to move here.* The slippery slope fallacy assumes that if the first step is taken, other steps necessarily follow.

- **Straw man.** *Environmentalists won't be satisfied until not a single human being is allowed to enter a national park.* A straw man argument is a diversionary tactic that sets up another's position in a way that can be easily rejected. In fact, only a small percentage of environmentalists would make an argument even close to this one.

Organize Good Reasons

Asking a series of questions can generate a list of because clauses, but even if you have plenty, you still have to decide which ones to use and in what order to present them. How can you decide which points are likely to be most persuasive? In choosing which good reasons to use in your arguments, consider your readers' attitudes and values and the values that are especially sanctioned by your community.

When people communicate, they tend to present their own thinking—to rely on the lines of thought that have led them to believe as they do. That's natural enough, since it is reasonable to present to others the reasons that make us believe what we are advocating in writing or speech. People have much in common, and it is natural to think that the evidence and patterns of thought that have guided your thinking to a certain point will also guide others to the same conclusions.

But people are also different, and what convinces you might not always convince others. When you are deciding what because clauses to present to others, try not so much to recapitulate your own thinking process as to influence the thinking of others. Ask yourself not just why you think as you do but also what you need to convince others to see things your way. Don't pick the because clauses that seem compelling to you; pick those that will seem compelling to your audience.

Create Credibility

You have probably noticed that many times in the course of reading, you get a very real sense of the kind of person who is doing the writing. Even if you have never read this person's writing before, even if you really know nothing about the actual person behind the message, you still often get a sense of the character and personality of the writer just by reading. How you respond to the message to some extent depends on how you respond to the person who delivers it.

In March 1997, scientists at the Oregon Regional Primate Research Center held a press conference to announce that they had successfully cloned two rhesus monkeys from early-stage embryos. They had taken a set of chromosomes from cells in a primitive monkey embryo and inserted them into egg cells from which the original DNA had been removed. These embryos were then implanted in the wombs of host mothers using in vitro fertilization techniques. The monkeys were born normally and were expected to live as long as twenty years. Donald Wolf, a senior scientist at the center, called the cloning a major breakthrough, since it would remove some of the uncertainties in animal research that might have been attributed to genetic differences among animals.

Other people were greatly alarmed by the cloning of the monkeys that followed closely the announcement of the successful cloning of sheep. The U.S. Congress organized hearings that began in March 1997 to examine the implications of cloning research. Following are two examples of letters sent to the House Science Subcommittee on Technology following the hearings. What persona did the writer of each of the following letters create? Both letters contain the same major points, and both are passionate in demanding legislation to end cloning of animals. Both assert that cloning monkeys for research purposes is wrong because it lacks scientific and ethical justification. But they stand apart in the ethos of the writer.

The writer of the first letter, Helen Barnes, attempts to establish common ground by noting that nearly everybody is opposed to the cloning of humans. Barnes makes a bridge to her issue by noting that the terms used for human cloning—*repulsive, repugnant, offensive*—should also be used for the cloning of animals. She urges Representative Morella to look at monkeys as beings rather than genetic material for the use of researchers. She points out the absence of any voices opposed to the use of monkeys for experiments at the hearings on cloning. She takes a strong stand at the end, but she uses "we," inviting Representative Morella to join her.

Rep. Connie Morella, Chairperson
House Science Subcommittee on Technology
2319 Rayburn House Office Building
Washington, DC 20515

Dear Representative Morella:

I am pleased to see among members of Congress great concern that humans should not be cloned. What perplexes me is the lack of protest against cloning animals. "Repulsive," "repugnant," "offensive"—scientists and politicians alike have used these words to describe human cloning experiments, but these adjectives should also be invoked to describe cloning experiments on animals.

There are both ethical and scientific reasons to oppose the cloning of animals. Animals are simply not commodities with whose genetic material we can tamper in pursuit of human ends. M. Susan Smith, director of the Oregon Primate Research Center, where Rhesus monkeys were cloned from embryo cells, says that we should be glad that scientists will now need to use "only" 3 or 4 animals instead of 20 or 30. But Smith and other proponents of animal experimentation really just don't get it. What about the 3 or 4 beings who will suffer and die in experiments? We don't bargain with lives—3 or 40—it's their use in experiments that's wrong.

Smith and other scientists justify their work by stating that genetically identical monkeys will help research into AIDS, alcoholism, depression and other illnesses. Scientists can clone a million monkeys, but they still won't be good models for human disease. It is not genetic variability that limits the effectiveness of animal experimentation—it's that the physiology of animal species differs. Animals are not "little humans," and there's no way that researchers can clone themselves around that reality.

At the recent Congressional hearings on the ethics of cloning, testimony was heard from the following: the director of National Institutes of Health, the largest funding agency of animal experimentation in the country; the head of Genzyme Transgenics Corporation, a company that seeks to profit from genetically manipulated animals; a representative from the U.S. Department of Agriculture, which is interested in the potential of cloning animals for food; Smith of Oregon Primate Research Center; and an ethicist who declared (and numerous exposés of animal experiments refute) that we do not permit research that is cruel to animals in our society.

There was a voice missing from this panel biased in favor of animal cloning: someone to represent the animals, whose lives and interests are so readily dismissed. We all need to speak up for them now and demand legislation to ban all cloning experiments.

Sincerely,
Helen Barnes

The writer of the second letter, by contrast, is confrontational from the outset. Ed Younger accuses Representative Morella of stacking the deck by inviting only proponents of cloning to the hearing. He insinuates that she is stupid if she doesn't realize the cloned monkeys will be killed and that the use of animals for testing has not produced cures for diseases such as cancer and AIDS. He suggests that she is a dupe of high-tech companies by taking their side. He ends with a threat to vote her out of office. His persona is clearly that of angry citizen.

Rep. Connie Morella, Chairperson
House Science Subcommittee on Technology
2319 Rayburn House Office Building
Washington, DC 20515

Dear Representative Morella:

I cannot believe you actually pretended to have a hearing on animal cloning and only invited people in favor of cloning. Why didn't you invite someone to speak for the animals? What a waste of our tax dollars! You should be passing laws against cloning instead of trying to justify it.

Don't you understand that the monkeys are being cloned to be killed? Thousands of monkeys have died in research on cancer and AIDS, and we're still no closer to finding cures. Don't you see that such research is useless? It's not that difficult to figure out. Monkeys are not people. It doesn't matter if they have identical genes or not.

We see what's happening. This is another example of government protecting big business over the interests of the people. The only people who will benefit from cloning animals are the big executives of the high-tech companies and a few scientists who will make big profits.

Haven't you read the polls and noticed that the great majority of Americans are opposed to cloning? You'll find out how we feel when you have to run for reelection!

Sincerely,
Ed Younger

Representatives often receive more than a thousand letters, faxes, and emails each day, and they have to deal with letters from angry people all the time. Usually, staff members answer the mail and simply tally up who is for and against a particular issue. Often, the reply is a form letter thanking the writer for his or her concern and stating the representative's position. But sometimes, representatives personally write detailed answers to letters from their constituents. Imagine that you are Representative Morella and you have to answer these two letters. Ed Younger's persona makes it difficult to say more than "I appreciate hearing your opinion on this issue." Helen Barnes's persona leaves open the possibility of an exchange of ideas.

People make judgments about you that are based on how you represent yourself when you write. Sometimes the angry voice is the one to present if you believe that your readers need a wake-up call. However, most people don't like to be yelled at. Just as you can change your voice orally when the situation calls for it—just as you can speak in a friendly way, in an excited way, or in a stern way in different circumstances—so too you should be able to modulate your voice in writing, depending on what is called for. Some important factors are the following:

- **Your relationship with your audience** (Your voice can be less formal when you know someone well or when you are communicating with people in the same circumstances than when you are communicating with a relative stranger or with someone above or below you in an organization.)
- **Your audience's personality** (Different people respond sympathetically to different voices.)
- **Your argument** (Some arguments are more difficult to make than others.)

ARGUE RESPONSIBLY

In Washington, D.C., cars with diplomatic license plates often park illegally. Their drivers know they will not be towed or have to pay a ticket. For people who abuse the diplomatic privilege, the license plate says in effect, "I'm not playing by the rules."

In a similar way, you announce you are not playing by the rules when you begin an argument by saying "in my opinion." First, a reader assumes that if you make a claim in writing, you believe that claim. More important, it is rarely *only* your opinion. Most beliefs and assumptions are shared by many people. If it is only your opinion, it can be easily dismissed. But if your position is likely to be held by at least a few other members of your community, then a responsible reader must consider your position seriously.

- **Your purpose** (You may take a more urgent tone if you want your readers to act immediately.)
- **Your genre** (Arguments in formal proposals usually have a different voice from arguments in newspaper sports and opinion columns.)

Choose an Appropriate Voice

Arguments that are totally predictable quickly lose their effectiveness. Being aware of your options in creating a **voice** when you write is one of the secrets of arguing successfully. Before those options are described for a specific argument, a little background for the case in point will be useful. In June 1989, the Supreme Court ruled in *Texas v. Johnson* to uphold the First Amendment right to burn the U.S. flag as symbolic political speech. An outraged Congress approved the Flag Protection Act of 1989, but the Senate voted down an amendment to the Constitution. After the Flag Protection Act became law, there were many protests against it. Some protesters were arrested, but the courts ruled that the Flag Protection Act was unconstitutional. Pressure built to get a flag protection amendment into the Constitution, and legislation has been introduced for such an amendment in every session of Congress since 1995. Imagine that you have decided to argue that flag burning should be protected as free speech. You think that people could find better ways to protest than by burning the flag, but nonetheless, they still should have that right. When you start researching the issue and look at the text of laws that have been passed against flag burning, you discover that the laws are vague about defining what a flag is. You realize that people could be arrested and put in prison for cutting a cake with an image of the flag in the icing at a Fourth of July picnic. You decide that examining definitions of the U.S. flag is a great way to begin your paper because if the flag cannot be defined, then you have a good argument that attempts to ban burning of the flag are doomed to failure. Congress cannot pass an amendment against something that it cannot accurately define. You look up the U.S. Code about the flag that was federal law from 1968 to 1989, when it was overturned in the Supreme Court case of *Texas v. Johnson*. It reads:

> Whoever knowingly casts contempt upon any flag of the United States by publicly mutilating, defacing, defiling, burning, or trampling upon it shall be fined not more than $1,000 or imprisoned for not more than one year, or both.
>
> The term "flag of the United States" as used in this section, shall include any flag, standard colors, ensign, or any picture or representation of either, or of any part or parts of either, made of any substance or represented on any substance, of any size evidently purporting to be either of said flag, standard, color, or ensign of the United States of America, or a picture or a representation of either, upon which shall be shown the colors, the stars and the stripes, in any number of either thereof, or of any part or parts of either, by which the average person seeing the same without deliberation may believe the same to represent the flag, standards, colors, or ensign of the United States of America.

You think the definition in the second paragraph is ridiculous. It could apply to red-and-white striped pants or almost anything that has stars and is red, white, and blue. But the question is how to make the point effectively in your analysis. Here are three versions of an analysis paragraph that would come after you quote the above law:

Version 1 (Distant, balanced)
The language of the 1968 law, passed in the midst of the protest over the Vietnam War, demonstrates the futility of passing laws against flag burning. Congress realized that protesters could burn objects that resembled the American flag and evade prosecution, so they extended the law to apply to anything "the average person" believed to represent the flag. The great irony was that the major violators of this law were the most patriotic people in America, who put flags on their cars and bought things with images of flags. When they threw away their flag napkins, they desecrated the flag and violated the law.

Version 2 (Involved, angry)
The 1968 law against flag burning is yet another example of why the Washington bureaucrats who love big government always get it wrong.

They see on TV something they don't like—protesters burning a flag. So they say, "Let's pass a law against it." But for the law to have teeth, they realize that it has to be far reaching, including every imagined possibility. So they make the law as broad as possible so the police can bust the heads of anyone they want to. The attempt to ban flag burning shows how people with good intentions take away your liberties.

Version 3 (Comedic)
"Wait a second!" you're probably saying to yourself. "Any number of stars? Any part or parts of either? On any substance? Or a picture or representation?" You bet. Burning a photo of a drawing of a three-starred red, white, and blue four-striped flag would land you in jail for a year. I'm not making this up. Do you still trust them to define what a flag is? I don't.

You can hear the differences in voices of these paragraphs. The first is the modulated voice of a radio or television commentator, appearing to give a distanced and balanced perspective. The second is the voice of an angry libertarian, asserting that the government that governs best is the one that governs least. The third is the voice of Comedy Central or the alternative press, laughing at what government tries to do. Once again, the point is not which one is most effective, because each could be effective for different audiences. The point is to be aware that you can take on different voices when you write and to learn how to control these voices.

CHAPTER 4

Understanding Written Arguments: Rhetorical Analysis

What Is Rhetorical Analysis?

To many people, the term *rhetoric* means speech or writing that is highly ornamental or deceptive or manipulative. You might hear someone say, "That politician is just using a bunch of rhetoric" or "the rhetoric of that advertisement is very deceptive." But as you have already learned, the term **rhetoric** is also used in a positive sense.

It is commonly used as a neutral synonym for all kinds of writing or speech, for instance ("*Silent Spring* is one of the most influential pieces of environmental rhetoric ever written"), and it is sometimes used as the name of a college course ("English 101: Rhetoric and Composition") or even a college major. As a subject of study, rhetoric is usually associated with how to produce effective pieces of communication, following Aristotle's classic definition of rhetoric as "the art of finding in any given case the available means of persuasion." But in recent years rhetoric has also taken on an interpretive or analytical function. It has come to be used not just as a means of *producing* effective communications but also as a way of *understanding* communication. The two aspects mutually support one another: Becoming a better writer makes you a better interpreter, and becoming a better interpreter makes you a better writer. This chapter is designed to give you a good understanding of the key concepts involved in rhetorical analysis and to make you comfortable conducting rhetorical analyses on your own.

The Goals of Rhetorical Analysis

Aristotle's emphasis on persuasion has been influential in the history of rhetoric. It is now common to understand rhetoric as fundamentally involved in the study of persuasion. **Rhetorical analysis**, therefore, can be defined as an effort to understand how people in specific social situations attempt to influence others through language. But not *just* through language: Rhetoricians today attempt to understand better every kind of important symbolic action—speeches and articles, yes, but also architecture (isn't it clear that the U.S. Capitol in Washington makes an argument as a building?), movies and television shows (doesn't *The Bachelor* have designs on viewers' values and attitudes?), memorials (don't the AIDS quilt and the Vietnam Veterans Memorial make arguments about AIDS and about our national understanding of the Vietnam war?), as well as visual art, Web sites, advertisements, photos and other images, dance, and popular songs.

Through rhetorical analysis, people strive to understand better how particular rhetorical acts are persuasive. They get a better sense of the values and beliefs and attitudes that are conveyed in specific rhetorical moments. It might be helpful to think of rhetorical analysis as a kind of critical reading: Whereas "ordinary" reading involves experiencing firsthand a speech or text or TV show or advertisement and then reacting (or not reacting) to it, **critical reading**—rhetorical analysis, that is—involves studying carefully some kind of symbolic action in order to understand it better and appreciate its tactics. The result is a heightened awareness of the message and an appreciation for the ways people manipulate language and other symbols for persuasive purposes.

Rhetorical analysis examines how an idea is shaped and presented to an audience in a particular form for a specific purpose. There are many approaches to rhetorical analysis and no one "correct" way to

The statue of Castor stands at the entrance of the Piazza del Campidoglio in Rome. A textual analysis focuses on the statue itself. The size and realism of the statue makes it a masterpiece of classical Roman sculpture.

do it. But generally approaches to rhetorical analysis can be placed between two broad extremes—not mutually exclusive categories but extremes along a continuum. At the one end of the continuum are analyses that concentrate more on texts than contexts. They typically use rhetorical concepts to analyze the features of texts. Let's call this approach **textual analysis**. At the other extreme are approaches that emphasize **context** over text. These emphasize reconstructing the cultural environment or context that existed when a particular rhetorical event took place, and then to depend on that re-creation to produce clues about the persuasive tactics and appeals. Those who undertake **contextual analysis**—as we'll call this second approach—regard particular rhetorical acts as parts of larger communicative chains, or "conversations."

> Rhetorical analysis examines how an idea is shaped and presented to an audience in a particular form for a specific purpose.

Now let's discuss those two approaches in detail.

A contextual analysis focuses on the surroundings and the history of the statue. Legend has Castor and his twin brother Pollux, the mythical sons of Leda, assisting Romans in an early battle. Romans built a large temple in the Forum to honor them. The statues of Castor and Pollux were uncovered in sixteenth-century excavations and brought in 1583 to stand at the top of the Cordonata, a staircase designed by Michelangelo as part of a renovation of the Piazza del Campidoglio commissioned by Pope Paul III Farnese in 1536.

Textual Analysis: Using Rhetorical Concepts as an Analytical Screen

Just as expert teachers in every field of endeavor—from baseball to biology—devise vocabularies to facilitate specialized study, rhetoricians too have developed a set of key concepts to permit them to describe rhetorical activities. A fundamental concept in rhetoric, of course, is *audience*. But there are many others. Classical rhetoricians in the tradition of Aristotle, Quintilian, and Cicero developed a range of terms around what they called the "canons" of rhetoric in order to describe some of the actions of communicators: *inventio* (invention—the finding or creation of information for persuasive acts, and the planning of strategies), *dispostio* (or arrangement), *elocutio* (or style), *memoria* (the recollection of rhetorical resources that one might call upon, as well as the memorization of what has been invented and arranged), and *pronuntiatio* (or delivery). These five canons generally describe the actions of any persuader, from preliminary planning to final delivery.

Over the years, and as written discourse gained in prestige against oral discourse, four canons (excepting *memoria*) especially encouraged the development of concepts and terms useful for rhetorical analysis. Terms like *ethos, pathos*, and *logos*, all associated with invention, account for features of texts related to the trustworthiness and credibility of the writer or speaker (ethos), for the persuasive good reasons in an argument that derive from a community's mostly deeply and emotionally held values (pathos), and for the good reasons that emerge from intellectual reasoning (logos). Arrangement has required terms like *exordium* (introduction), *narratio* (generally equivalent to what we refer to today as "forecasting"), *confirmatio* (proof), *refutatio* (answering the objections of others), and *peroration* (conclusion) to describe the organization of speeches and essays. Delivery has given rise to a discussion of things like voice, gesture, and expression (in oral discourse) and to voice and visual impact (in written). And a whole series of technical terms developed over the years to describe effective maneuvers of style (*elocutio*)—many of them still in common use, such as antithesis, irony, hyperbole, and metaphor. Fundamental to the classical approach to rhetoric is the concept of *decorum*, or "appropriateness": Everything within a persuasive act can be understood as in keeping with a central rhetorical goal that any communicator consistently keeps in mind and that governs consistent choices according to occasion and audience. The concept of decorum lies behind rhetorical analysis in that decisions by a communicator are understood as rational and consistent and thus, available for systematic analysis.

Perhaps an example will make textual rhetorical analysis clearer. If you have not done so already, take a few minutes to read "The Border Patrol State" by Leslie Marmon Silko (pp. 164–169). We use the concepts of classical rhetoric to understand it better.

Silko's Purpose and Argument

What is the purpose of Silko's essay? Silko wrote the essay well over a decade ago, but you probably find it to be interesting and readable still, in part at least because it concerns the perennial American issue of civil rights. In this case, Silko is taking issue with practices associated with the Border Patrol of the Immigration and Naturalization Service (INS): They are reenacting, she feels, the long subjugation of native peoples by the Anglo majority. Silko proposes that the power of the Border Patrol be sharply reduced so that the exploitation of her people might be curtailed, and she supports that thesis with an essay that describes and condemns the Border Patrol tactics. Essentially the argument comes down to this: The Border Patrol must be reformed for two good reasons: because "the Immigration and Naturalization Service and Border Patrol have implemented policies that interfere with the rights of U.S. citizens to travel freely within our borders" (para. 8), and because efforts to restrict immigration are ineffective, doomed to fail ("It is no use; borders haven't worked, and they won't work" in para. 16). Her essay amounts to an evaluation of the Border Patrol's activities, an evaluation that finds those activities wanting on ethical and practical grounds.

Silko's Use of Logos, Pathos, and Ethos

All that is easy enough to see. But note that the because-clauses used by Silko that we have just named derive from logos and pathos. When she condemns the unethical actions of the border police early in the essay, she does so in a way that is full of evidence and other appeals to readers' minds— including appeals to our sense of what is legal, constitutional, fair, and honorable. When she explains the futility of trying to stop immigration, she appeals again to her readers' reasonableness: Constructing walls across the border with Mexico is foolish because "border entrepreneurs have already used blowtorches to cut passageways through the fence" (para. 15), because "a mass migration is already under way" (para. 16), and because "The Americas are Indian country, and the 'Indian problem' is not about to go away" (para. 17). The bulk of "The Border Patrol State" amounts to an argument by example wherein the single case—Silko's personal experience, as a native American, with the border police—stands for many such cases. This case study persuades as other case studies and narratives do—by being presented as representative. Silko creates through her narrative a representative example that stands for the treatment of many native Americans. The particular details provided in the essay are not mere "concrete description" but hard, logical evidence summoned to support Silko's thesis.

Those logical appeals are reinforced by Silko's more emotional good reasons:

- The border patrol is constructing an "Iron Curtain" that is as destructive of human rights as the Iron Curtain that the Soviet Union constructed around Eastern Europe after World War II (para. 15).
- "Proud" and "patriotic" Native American citizens are being harassed, such as "old Bill Pratt [who] used to ride his horse 300 miles overland . . . every summer to work as a fire lookout" (para. 1).
- American citizens can be terrified by border police in a way that is chillingly reminiscent of "the report of Argentine police and military officers who became addicted to interrogation, torture, and murder" (paras. 3–5).

The most emotional moment of all in the essay may be when Silko describes how the border patrol dog, trained to find illegal drugs and other contraband, including human contraband, seems to sympathize with her and those she is championing: "I saw immediately from the expression in her eyes that the dog hated them" (para. 6); "the dog refused to accuse us: She had an innate dignity that did not permit her to serve the murderous impulses of those men" (para. 7). Clearly the good reasons in "The Border Patrol State" appeal in a mutually supportive way to the reason and emotions of Silko's audience. She appeals to the whole person.

Why do we take Silko's word about the stories she tells? It is because she establishes her ethos, her trustworthiness, early in the article. Of course any item in print gains a certain credibility from being printed, and Silko can also count on being widely recognized for her accomplishments as a writer. But just to be sure that she comes off as credible, Silko reminds her readers that she is a respected, published author who has been on a book tour to publicize her novel *Almanac of the Dead* (para. 3). She quotes widely, if unobtrusively, from books and reports to establish that she has studied the issues thoroughly; note how much she displays her knowledge of INS policies in paragraph 9, for instance. She cites the stories not only of her own encounters with the border police (experiences that are a source of great credibility), but also of others whom she lists, name after careful name, in order that we might trust her account. She knows history and geography. She also ties herself to traditional American values such as freedom (para. 1), ethnic pride, tolerance, and even the love of dogs. While her political biases and values might be known from other sources and while even this essay, because of its anti-authoritarian strain, might seem to display politically progressive attitudes at times, in general Silko comes off as hard-working, honest, educated, even patriotic. And definitely credible.

Silko's Arrangement

Silko arranges her essay appropriately as well. In general the essay follows a traditional pattern. She begins with a long concrete introductory story that "hooks" the reader and leads to her thesis in paragraph 8. Next, in the body of her essay, she supports her thesis by evaluating the unethical nature of INS policies: She cites their violation of constitutional protections, their similarity to tactics used in nations that are notorious for violating the rights of citizens, and their fundamental immorality; and she emphasizes how those policies are racist in nature (e.g., paras. 11–13). After completing her moral evaluation of INS policy, she turns beginning with paragraph 14 to the practical difficulties of halting immigration: NAFTA permits the free flow of goods, and even drugs are impossible to stop, so how can people be stopped from crossing borders; efforts to seal borders are "pathetic" in their ineffectuality (para. 15). This all lays the groundwork for the surprising and stirring conclusion: "The great human migration within the Americas cannot be stopped; human beings are natural forces of the earth, just as rivers and winds are natural forces" (para. 16); "the Americas are Indian country, and the 'Indian problem' is not about to go away" (para. 17); the mythic "return of the Aztlan" is on display in the box cars that go by as the essay closes. In short, this essay unfolds in a conventional way: It has a standard beginning, middle, and end.

Silko's Style

What about Silko's style? How is it appropriate to her purposes? Take a look at paragraphs 3 and 4: you will notice that nearly all of the fourteen sentences in those paragraphs are simple in structure. There are only five sentences that use any form of *subordination* (clauses that begin with *when*, *that*, or *if*). Many of the sentences either consist of one clause or of two clauses joined by simple *coordination* (such as *and* or *but* or a semicolon).

Several of the sentences and clauses are unusually short. Furthermore, Silko never in these paragraphs uses metaphors or other sorts of poetic language, and her **diction**—the words she uses—is as simple as her sentences. It all reminds you of the daily newspaper, doesn't it? Silko chooses a style similar to one used in newspaper reporting—simple, straightforward, unadorned—because she wants her readers to accept her narrative as credible and trustworthy. Her tone and voice reinforce her ethos.

There is more to say about the rhetorical choices that Silko made in crafting "The Border Patrol State." But this analysis is enough to illustrate our main point. Textual rhetorical analysis employs rhetorical terminology—in this case, terms borrowed from classical rhetoric such as ethos, pathos, logos, arrangement, style, and tone—as a way of helping us to understand a piece of writing better, as a way of understanding how a writer makes choices to achieve certain effects. And it cooperates with contextual analysis.

METAPHORS IN ADS

Advertisers have long understood the critical role that words play in persuading people. The writers of advertising copy are well aware that the average American is exposed to over three thousand ads a day and that such oversaturation has made people cynical about ads. Advertisers have to be clever to get our attention, so ads often use the tactics of poets and comedians. Words in ads often use puns and metaphors to draw our attention to the products they promote. A watch ad runs with the banner "Every second counts." An ad for a coffeemaker asks, "Who better to handle his ugly mug in the morning?" A plastic wrap ad shows two chicken legs under the headline "Stop our legs from drying out." A used-car ad appears under the words "Born again."

But it is not just clever plays on words that do the work in the language of advertising. We often find words in ads that do not make much sense at first reading. For example, a Nikon camera ad displays in big bold letters, "It's a stealth bomber with fuzzy dice." Calling a camera a "stealth bomber with fuzzy dice" is an example of metaphor. **Metaphor** is a Greek term that means "carry over," which describes what happens when you encounter a metaphor. You carry over the meaning from one word to another. Metaphor is but one kind of **figurative language**. Also common in advertising are **synecdoche**, in which the part is used to represent the whole (a hood ornament represents a car), and **metonymy**, in which something stands for something else with which it is closely associated (using flowers to represent a product's fresh scent).

METAPHORS IN ADS *(continued)*

There are other kinds of figurative language, but all involve the transfer of meaning from one word or phrase to another. How this transfer works is complicated. If we encounter an unfamiliar metaphor such as the stealth bomber example, we do our best to make sense of what the writer means. What meanings, then, is the reader supposed to carry over from "stealth bomber with fuzzy dice" to a Nikon camera? Cameras don't have wings, wheels, jet engines, or bomb bays, nor are they covered with fake fur. The advertisers didn't want the reader to work too hard, so they put in fine print at the bottom their interpretation of the metaphor: "The technology of a serious camera. The spontaneity of a point-and-shoot. Now you don't have to choose between the two."

Contextual Analysis: Communication as Conversation

Notice that in the previous discussion the fact that Leslie Marmon Silko's "The Border Patrol State" was originally published in the magazine *The Nation* did not matter too much. Nor did it matter when the essay was published (October 17, 1994) or who exactly read it or what their reaction was or what other people at the time were saying. Textual analysis, strictly speaking, need not attend to such matters; it can proceed as if the item under consideration "speaks for all time" somehow, as if it is a sort of museum piece unaffected by time and space just as surely as, say, an ancient altarpiece once housed in a church might be placed on a pedestal in a museum. There's nothing wrong with museums, of course; they certainly permit people to observe and appreciate objects in an important way. But just as certainly museums often fail to retain a vital sense of an artwork's original context and cultural meaning; in that sense museums can diminish understanding as much as they contribute to it. Contextual rhetorical analysis, however, as an attempt to understand communications through the lens of their environments, does examine the setting or scene out of which any communication emerges.

And, as in the case of textual analysis, contextual analysis may be conducted in any number of ways. But *contextual rhetorical analysis always proceeds from a description of the rhetorical situation* that motivated the item in question. It demands an appreciation of the social circumstances that call rhetorical events into being and that orchestrate the course of those events. It regards communications as anything but self-contained:

- Each communication is considered as a response to other communications (and to other social practices).

- Communications (and social practices more generally) are considered to reflect the attitudes and values of the communities that sustain them.

- Evidence is sought about how those other communications (and social practices) are reflected in texts.

Rhetorical analysis from a contextualist perspective understands individual pieces as parts of ongoing conversations.

The challenge is to reconstruct the conversation surrounding a specific piece of writing or speaking. Sometimes it is fairly easy to do so. You may have good background information on the topic and a feel for what is behind what people are writing or saying about it. People who have strong feelings about the environment or stem cell research (or about same-sex marriage, the lack of competitive balance in major league baseball, or any number of other current issues) are well informed about the arguments that are converging around those topics.

But other times it takes some research to reconstruct the conversations and social practices related to a particular issue. You need to see how the debate is conducted in current magazines, newspapers, talk shows, movies and TV shows, Web sites, and so forth (if the issue concerns current events), or do archival research into historical collections of newspapers, magazines, books, letters, and other documentary sources (if the item being analyzed was from an earlier time period). That research usually involves libraries, special research collections, or film and television archives where it is possible to learn quite a bit about context.

Again, an example will clarify how contextual analysis works to "open up" an argument to analysis: let's return again to a discussion of Silko's "The Border Patrol State." It will take a bit of research to reconstruct some of the "conversations" that Silko is participating in, but the result will be an enhanced understanding of the essay as well as an appreciation for how you might do a contextual rhetorical analysis.

Silko's Life and Works

You can begin by learning more about Silko herself. The essay itself gives some facts about her (e.g., that she is a native American writer of note who has lived in the Southwest); the headnote on page 164 gives additional information (that her writing usually develops out of native American traditions and tales); and you can learn still more about her from the Internet. Thus Silko's credibility, her ethos, is established not just by her textual moves but by her prior reputation, especially for readers of *The Nation* who would recognize and appreciate her accomplishments. Perhaps the most relevant information on the Web is about *Almanac of the Dead*, the novel Silko refers to in paragraph 3. That novel, set mainly in Tucson, revolves around a native American woman psychic who is in the process of transcribing the lost histories of her dead ancestors into "an almanac of the dead"—into a history of her people. That history is from the point of view of the conquered, not the conqueror; "The Border Patrol State," it seems, is an essayistic version of *Almanac of the Dead* in that like the novel it protests what has been lost—and what is still being lost—in the clash between Anglo and native cultures. It is a protest against the tactics of the border police. Or is it?

The Context of Publication

Through a consideration of the conversations swirling around it, contextual analysis actually suggests that "The Border Patrol State" is just as much about immigration policy as it is about the civil rights of native Americans. The article first appeared in *The Nation*, a respected, politically progressive magazine that has been appearing weekly for decades. Published in New York City, it is a magazine of public opinion that covers the theater, film, music, fiction, and other arts; politics and public affairs; and contemporary culture. If you want to know what left-leaning people are thinking about an issue, *The Nation* is a good magazine to consult. You can imagine that Silko's essay therefore reached an audience of sympathetic readers—people who would be receptive to her message. They would be inclined to sympathize with Silko's complaints and to heed her call for a less repressive border patrol.

But what is interesting is that Silko's essay appeared on October 17, 1994 in a special issue of *The Nation* given over to "The Immigration Wars," a phrase very visible on the cover of that issue. Hers was one of several articles that appeared under that banner, an indication that Silko's argument is not just about the violation of the civil rights of native Americans but also about the larger issue of immigration policy. "The Border Patrol State" appeared after David Cole's "Five Myths about Immigration"; Elizabeth Kadetsky's "Bashing Illegals in California"; Peter Kwong's "China's Human Traffickers"; two editorials about immigration policy; and short columns on immigration by *Nation* regulars Katha Pollitt, Aryeh Neier, and Christopher Hitchens. Together the articles in this issue of *The Nation* mounted a sustained argument in favor of a liberal immigration policy.

The Larger Conversation

Why did *The Nation* entitle its issue "The Immigration Wars"? Immigration was a huge controversy in October 1994, just before the 1994 elections. When the 1965 Immigration Act was amended in 1990, the already strong flow of immigrants to the United States became a flood. While many immigrants previously came to the United States from Europe, most recent immigrants have come from Asia, Latin America, and the Caribbean islands, and Africa. While those earlier immigrants typically passed through Ellis Island and past the Statue of Liberty that welcomed them, most recent immigrants in 1994 were coming to Florida, Texas, and California. The arrival of all those new immigrants revived old fears about immigrants that have been in the air for decades (that they take away jobs from native-born Americans, that they undermine national values by resisting assimilation and clinging to their own cultures, that they reduce standards of living by stressing educational and social welfare budgets). Many people countered those claims by indicating that immigrants create jobs and wealth, enhance the vitality of American culture, become among the proudest of Americans, and contribute to the tax base of their communities. But those counterarguments were undermined when a tide of illegal immigrants—up to 300,000 per year—was arriving at the time Silko was writing.

The Immigration Wars were verbal wars. In the 1994 election, Republicans had united under the banner of a "Contract with America." Some three hundred Republican congressional candidates, drawn together by conservative leader Newt Gingrich, agreed to run on a common platform in an ultimately successful effort to gain control of the House of Representatives. The Contract offered a number of conservative initiatives, among them a reduction in the size of government, a balanced budget amendment, crime legislation, a reduction in welfare benefits and capital gains taxes, and benefits increases for seniors on social security. More to the point here, it also proposed changes in laws in order to curtail immigration, reduce illegal immigration, and deny benefits to illegal residents, including health care and education. Title IV of the proposed Personal Responsibility Act would have declared resident aliens ineligible for welfare assistance and restricted their eligibility for health, social service, and education benefits (see www.house.gov/house/Contract/CONTRACT.html). In this way, the

Contract with America offered support for California's Proposition 187, another important 1994 proposal. This so-called "Save Our State" initiative was designed to "prevent California's estimated 1.7 million undocumented immigrants from partaking of every form of public welfare including non-emergency medical care, pre-natal clinics and public schools," as Kadetsky explained her essay in *The Nation*. In the words of the proposition itself, "The People of California find and declare as follows: That they have suffered and are suffering economic hardship caused by the presence of illegal aliens in this state. That they have suffered and are suffering personal injury and damage caused by the criminal conduct of illegal aliens. That they have a right to the protection of their government from any person or persons entering this country illegally." The Republican Contract for America and California's proposed Proposition 187 together constituted the nation's leading domestic issue in October 1994. A war of words about them was evident in the magazines, books, newspapers, talk shows, barber shops, and hair salons of America.

Silko's Political Goals

In this context, it is easy to see that Silko's essay is against more than the border patrol. It is an argument in favor of relatively unrestricted immigration, especially from Mexico and especially for native Americans. Moreover, it is a direct refutation of the Contract for America in general and Proposition 187 in particular. Where the proposition stated "that [the People of California] have suffered and are suffering economic hardship caused by the presence of illegal aliens in this state, that they have suffered and are suffering personal injury and damage caused by the criminal conduct of illegal aliens, [and] that they have a right to the protection of their government from any person or persons entering this country illegally," Silko turns the claim around. It is the border patrol that is behaving illegally. It is the border patrol that is creating economic hardship. It is the border police that is creating personal injury and damage through criminal conduct. Finally, it is the U.S. government that is acting illegally by ignoring the treaty of Guadalupe Hidalgo, which "recognizes the right of the Tohano O'Odom (Papago) people to move freely across the U.S.-Mexico border without documents," as Silko puts it in her footnote. Writing just before the election of 1994, then, and in the midst of a spirited national debate (and in the pages of an immigration issue of *The Nation*), Silko had specific political goals in mind. A contextual analysis of "The Border Patrol State" reveals that the essay is, at least in part, an eloquent refutation of the Contract for America and Proposition 187—two items that are not even named explicitly in the essay!

We could do more in the way of contextual analysis here. We could cite many more articles and books and reports and TV broadcasts that can be compared with "The Border Patrol State," including speeches and television interviews by Pat Buchanan, who ran for the Republican presidential nomination in 1992 and 1996 on an anti-immigration stance and who was in the process of writing an incendiary book entitled *The Death of the West: How Mass Immigration, Depopulation, and a Dying Faith Are Killing Our Culture and the Country*. A discussion of the conversation about immigration in 1994 and about Leslie Marmon Silko's specific contribution to that conversation could be extended for a long time—indefinitely, in fact. There is no need to belabor the point, however: our purpose has been simply to illustrate that contextual analysis of a piece of rhetoric can enrich our understanding.

Write a Rhetorical Analysis

Effective rhetorical analysis, as we have seen, can be generally textual or contextual in nature. But we should emphasize again that these two approaches to rhetorical analysis are not mutually exclusive. Indeed, many if not most analysts operate some place between these two extremes; they consider the details of the text, but they also attend to the particulars of context as well. Textual analysis and contextual analysis inevitably complement each other. Getting at what is at stake in "The Border Patrol State" or any other sophisticated argument takes patience and intelligence. Like Silko's essay, many arguments have designs on the attitudes and beliefs of audiences. Rhetorical analysis, as a way of understanding how people argue, is both enlightening and challenging.

Try to use elements of both kinds of analysis whenever you want to understand a rhetorical event more completely. Rhetoric is "inside" texts, but it is also "outside": specific rhetorical performances are an irreducible mixture of text and context, and so interpretation and analysis of those performances must account for both as well. Remember, however, the limitations of your analysis; realize that your analysis will always be somewhat partial and incomplete, ready to be deepened, corrected, modified, and extended by the insights of others. Rhetorical analysis can itself be part of an unending conversation—a way of learning and teaching within a community.

Sample Student Rhetorical Analysis

Erica Strausner is a sophomore at Pennsylvania State University, where she majors in psychology and minors in Spanish. She is a member of the Phi Eta Sigma honor society and the National Society of Collegiate Scholars. Strausner's professional goal is to earn a PhD in order to pursue a career as a clinical psychologist. She wrote this essay in a first-year composition course.

Strausner 1

Erica Strausner

Ms. Kale

English 15

November 11, 2003

The NRA Blacklist: A Project Gone Mad

The National Rifle Association is naming names? Recently the NRA decided to assign its staff researchers to dig up every anti-gun remark ever made, no matter how slight, and to put those who made the remark on a nineteen-page list accessible through the NRA Web site. It's called the NRA blacklist. How are people reacting to that list? Bob Herbert, an editorial columnist for The New York Times and one of those named on the list, isn't too happy at all. An examination of how Herbert writes his response to the NRA blacklist, "The NRA Is Naming Names," combined with another essay by Herbert in the same New York Times, "More Guns for Everyone!," will indicate how Herbert persuades his readers to reject the NRA.

"More Guns for Everyone!" indicates without a doubt Herbert's views on gun control. In commenting on a ruling by Attorney General John Ashcroft, he states,

Strausner 2

The NRA has seldom had a better friend in the
government than Mr. Ashcroft. That was proved
again on Monday, when the Justice Department,
in a pair of briefs, rejected the long-held
view of the court, the Justice Department
itself, and most legal scholars that the
Second Amendment protects only the right of
state-owned militias to own firearms.

This passage indicates that Herbert is anti-NRA, but
not that he is necessarily anti-gun. In fact, he even
refers to his days in the army, when he "had a .45
caliber pistol hanging low on my hip," to show that he
is not completely against guns. Rather, Herbert
believes only that not everyone has a legitimate reason
to own a gun and that there should be some restrictions
on them. It would be safer to say that Herbert is
cautious about gun distribution because he has seen
that guns in the wrong hands can be detrimental to
society. "No gun is more suited to criminal misuse than
a handgun, and that's exactly the type of weapon that
Mr. Ashcroft and his NRA pals are trying to make
available," Herbert notes in "More Guns for Everyone";
but "I'm not anti-gun."

With this background in mind, one can see that
Herbert wrote "The NRA Is Naming Names" at a crucial
time. Gun laws have always been an issue, and there will
always be proposals to restrict gun distribution as long
as people use firearms to kill other people. Particularly
in recent days, however, there have been crucial

Strausner 3

high-spirited arguments between NRA supporters and detractors. The NRA posted its list in a secluded space on its Web site on July 17, 2003, but quite possibly Herbert saw the list only much later because it was buried deep within the organization's Library of the Institute for Legislative Action. According to Andrew Arulanandum, Director of Public Affairs for the NRA, the posting of the list was a "response to many requests by our members wanting to know which organizations support the rights of law-abiding Americans to keep and bear arms" (NRA). Herbert found himself on the NRA hate list even though he supports only some restrictions on handguns—along with responsible people like football player Doug Flutie and admired organizations like Ben and Jerry's.

To defend himself, Herbert wrote his response to the NRA in the New York Times. His voice and tone express exactly how he feels and how vehemently he stands up for himself and others on the blacklist. Because readers of the New York Times can be considered informed on current affairs and generally educated, Herbert uses language that is appropriate to them. His vocabulary is not difficult or pedantic; his language is suited to the average person. Editorial opinion columns are much more opinionated in tone than objective news stories, but Herbert strengthens his argument in the fashion of a news report by using sources and interviewing critical people.

Actually, Herbert addresses several kinds of readers in his essay, all of them within the readership

Strausner 4

of the Times. Most importantly, he addresses NRA
members. He addresses the irrational assumptions made by
the NRA about others and about himself. Gun lobbyists
will also read Herbert's essay, so Herbert makes
comments about legislation currently under consideration
in Congress. Lastly and mainly, Herbert addresses those
who are sympathetic to his own views on gun legislation.
For all these readers Herbert establishes his
credibility very carefully. He has experience,
obviously, or else he would not be on the NRA list. He
responds to the list as any wronged person would, with
well-placed outrage. Since he is a regular New York
Times writer, he obviously has already established some
credibility with his readers as well, and they have come
to trust him because he produces hard facts, not just
opinions, and is knowledgeable about current events.

Herbert also appeals to his readers logically. He
burrows down into the root of the problem, the NRA, by
interviewing the Director of Public Affairs about why
the list was compiled and what significance it holds. The
interview also affects his argument positively because
he sheds light on both sides of the story. Herbert also
depends on statistics: e.g., "more than one million
Americans were killed by firearms" (NRA). He also cites
as evidence important pieces of current legislation,
such as President Clinton's 1994 bill banning the
distribution of assault weapons: he explains how gun
lobbyists will do anything to kill any piece of gun
control legislation. Herbert also supplies several

logical reasons why his being listed is unfair, most
notably the fact that "I am not anti-gun." By saying
that he believes people should have a legitimate reason
to own a gun, and that city slickers or suburbanites
seldom have any reason to have a gun, he establishes
that he is not really an enemy of guns, just an enemy of
their abuse. What he says makes sense because
suburbanites and city dwellers do not hunt for food.
Yes, they do have a right to protect their homes, and in
some areas that might be necessary; but the majority of
people have no use for guns.

    Finally, Herbert appeals to his readers' emotions.
Since the essay is an op-ed piece, a slightly sarcastic
or pejorative air hangs on some of Herbert's phrases:
e.g., "I'm sure there's a method to the NRA's madness,
but to tell you the truth, all I can see is the madness."
After that comment he drops the cynicism and turns to a
description of The Year the Dream Died: Revisiting 1968
in America by Jules Witcover. The book movingly describes
the assassinations of Robert Kennedy and Martin Luther
King, Jr. Just as he has his readers hooked on the
tragedy of these deaths, he returns to a cynical tone by
remarking, "Both were killed by freaks with guns." He
then returns to a somber tone by offering cold statistics
on deaths by firearms and details on gun legislation.
Then, just as quickly, he gives his final, clinching quip:
"Ah, free expression." It is this alternation of two
opposite emotions that strengthens his argument because
it forces readers to think about his and their feelings.

Strausner 6

By examining how Herbert writes his response to the NRA blacklist and comparing it to another essay by him that states his views on gun control, one can see that Herbert has intrigued not only his usual readers but the members of the NRA. Herbert effectively argues his point, and he provides every reason for the NRA to remove him from its blacklist. In fact, he makes it seem that the NRA cannot be considered responsible since it keeps a blacklist in the first place, and then includes people on it inaccurately. Such an organization cannot be trusted or taken seriously.

Strausner 7

Works Cited

Herbert, Bob. "More Guns for Everyone!" Editorial. New York Times 9 May 2002, late ed.: A39.

---. "The NRA Is Naming Names" Editorial. New York Times 13 Oct. 2003, late ed.: A17.

National Rifle Association. "National Organizations with Anti-Gun Policies." NRA-ILA Fact Sheets. 2003. National Rifle Association Institute for Legislative Action. 14 Oct. 2003 <http://www.nraila.org//issues/factsheets/read.aspx?id=15>.

Steps to a Rhetorical Analysis

Step 1 Select an argument to analyze

Find an argument to analyze: a speech or sermon designed to persuade, an op-ed item in a newspaper, an ad in a magazine designed for a particular audience, a commentary on a talk show.

Examples

- You can find arguments on the editorial pages of newspapers; in opinion features in magazines such as *Time, Newsweek,* and *U.S. News & World Report;* in magazines that take political positions such as *National Review, Mother Jones, New Republic, Nation,* and the online journal *Slate;* and the Web sites of activist organizations.
- Letters to the editor and online newsgroup postings probably won't work for this assignment unless they are long and detailed.

Step 2 Analyze the context

Who is the author?

Through research in the library or on the Web, learn all you can about the author of the argument.

- How does the argument you are analyzing repeat arguments previously made by the author?
- Does the author borrow arguments and concepts from previous things he or she has written?
- What motivated the author to write?

Who is the audience?

Through research, learn all you can about the place where the argument appeared and the audience.

- Who is the anticipated audience?
- How do the occasion and forum for writing affect the argument?
- How would the argument have been written differently if it had appeared elsewhere?
- What motivated the newspaper or magazine (or other venue) to publish it?

What is the larger conversation?

Through research, find out what else was being said about the subject your selection discusses. Track down any references made in the text you are examining.

■ When did the argument appear?
■ Why did it get published at that particular moment?
■ What other concurrent pieces of "cultural conversation" (e.g., TV shows, other articles, speeches, Web sites) does the item you are analyzing respond to or "answer"?

Step 3 Analyze the text

Summarize the argument

■ What is the main claim?
■ What reasons are given in support of the claim?
■ How is the argument organized? What are the component parts, and why are the parts presented in that order?

What is the medium and genre?

■ What is the medium? A newspaper? a scholarly journal? a Web site?
■ What is the genre? An editorial? an essay? a speech? an advertisment? What expectations does the audience have about this genre?

What appeals are used?

■ **Analyze the ethos**. How does the writer represent himself or herself? Does the writer have any credentials to be an authority on the topic? Do you trust the writer? Why or why not?
■ **Analyze the logos**. Where do you find facts and evidence in the argument? What kinds of facts and evidence does the writer present? Direct observation? statistics? interviews? surveys? secondhand sources such as published research? quotations from authorities?
■ **Analyze the pathos**. Are there any places where the writer attempts to invoke an emotional response? Where do you find appeals to shared values with the audience? You are a member of that audience, so what values do you hold in common with the writer? What values do you not hold in common?

How would you characterize the style?

■ Is the style formal, informal, satirical, or something else?
■ Are any metaphors used?

Step 4 Write a draft

Introduction

- Describe briefly the argument you are analyzing, including where it was published, how long it is, and who wrote it.
- If the argument is on an issue unfamiliar to your readers, you may have to supply some background.

Body

- Analyze the context, following Step 2.
- Analyze the text, following Step 3.

Conclusion

- Do more than simply summarize what you have said. You might, for example, end with an example that typifies the argument.
- You don't have to end by either agreeing or disagreeing with the writer. Your task in this assignment is to analyze the strategies the writer uses.

Step 5 Revise, edit, proofread

- For detailed instructions, see Chapter 12.
- For a checklist to use to evaluate your draft, see pages 217–222.

Understanding Visual Arguments

What Is a Visual Argument?

We live in a world where we are surrounded by images. They pull on us, compete for our attention, push us to do things. But unlike verbal arguments, we rarely think about how they do their work.

Arguments in written language are in one sense visual: We use our eyes to read the words on the page. But without words, can there be a visual argument? Certainly some visual symbols take on conventional meanings. Think about the signs in airports or other public places, designed to communicate with speakers of many languages.

Some visual symbols even make explicit claims. A one-way street sign says that drivers should travel in the same direction. But are such signs arguments? In Chapter 2 we point out that scholars of argument do not believe that everything's an argument. Most scholars define an argument as a claim supported by one or more reasons. A one-way sign has a claim: All drivers should go in the same direction. But is there a reason? Of course we all know an

> Visual arguments are often powerful because they invite viewers to co-create the claims and links.

unstated reason the sign carries: Drivers who go the wrong way violate the law and risk a substantial fine (plus they risk a head-on collision with other drivers).

Visual arguments often are powerful because they invite viewers to co-create claims and links. For example, the artists who decorated medieval cathedrals taught religious lessons. The facade of the Last Judgment on the front pillar of the Duomo in Orvieto, Italy, depicts Christ as judge damning sinners to hell. The facade makes a powerful visual argument about the consequences that await the unfaithful.

Facade of Last Judgment, Orvieto, Italy. ca. 1310–1330.

Other visual arguments cannot be explained this easily, even ones that purport to make claims. Beginning in 1935, the Farm Security Administration, a U.S. government agency, hired photographers to document the effects of the Great Depression and the drought years on Americans. One of the photographers, Dorothea Lange, shot a series of photographs of homeless and destitute migrant workers in California that have become some of the most familiar images of America in the 1930s. Lange had an immediate goal—getting the government to build a resettlement camp for the homeless workers. She wrote to her boss in Washington that her images were "loaded with ammunition."

Lange titled one of her images *Eighteen-year-old mother from Oklahoma, now a California migrant.* The young woman and child in the photograph are obviously quite poor if we assume the tent is where they live. Yet the image doesn't seem one of suffering. Dorothea Lange was a portrait

Eighteen-year-old mother from Oklahoma, now a California migrant. Photo by Dorothea Lange. March 1937.

photographer before becoming a documentary photographer, and her experience shows. She takes advantage of the highlighting of the woman's hair from the sun behind her contrasted with the dark interior of the tent to draw our eyes to the woman's face. She doesn't appear to be distressed—just bored. Only later do we notice the dirty face of the child and other details. With another caption—perhaps "Young mother on a camping trip left behind while the father went for a hike"—we might read the photograph to say something else. And even if we take the image as evidence of poverty, the claim is not evident, just as images of homeless people today do not necessarily make arguments.

Visual Persuasion

The Italian clothing retailer Benetton for many years has run ad campaigns intended to raise social awareness on issues including AIDS, hunger, pollution, and racism. The campaign against racism featured images of black and white children playing together, black and white hands overlapping, black and white arms handcuffed together, and similar contrasting themes. One ad shows three human hearts with the labels "BLACK," "WHITE," and "YELLOW," with a small label "United Colors of Benetton" on

one side. The image of the three hearts makes a straightforward visual argument. The claim and reason might be phrased in words: "Prejudice based on skin color is wrong because we're all alike inside."

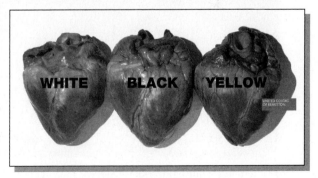

Hearts. Benetton Ad Campaign. 1996.

The particular genre—an advertisement—suggests there may be more arguments in the ad than the one that is most apparent. Benetton advertises for the same reason other companies advertise—to get consumers to buy their products. They do place their name on all their ads. The question then becomes how the controversial ads influence consumers to purchase Benetton clothing. Perhaps consumers identify with the messages in Benetton's ads and consequently identify with their clothing. Benetton says on its Web site that its ad campaigns "have succeeded in attracting the attention of the public and in standing out amid the current clutter of images." At the very least the ads give Benetton name-recognition. You may have other ideas about why the Benetton ads have been successful, but here's the point we're making: Explicit claims and reasons are often hard to extract from images.

Indeed, most ads lack explicit reasons and claims beyond "Buy this product." Throughout most of the 1900s, print ads and broadcast ads associated something desirable with purchase of a product. Romantic fulfillment was one common theme, financial success another. Unglamorous products were often placed in glamorous settings. Arthur Rothstein, a colleague of Dorothea Lange in documenting the Great Depression, photographed steelworkers' children in a homemade swimming pool in front of a billboard depicting beer as a family beverage for the wealthy.

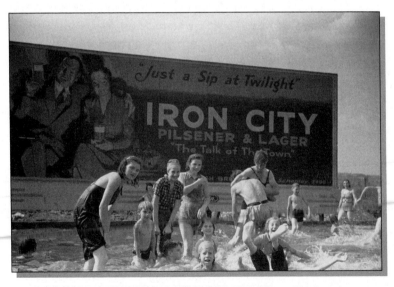

Homemade swimming pool for steelworkers' children, Pittsburgh, Pennsylvania. Photo by Arthur Rothstein. July 1938.

By the 1980s advertisers realized that the old tactics would not work for an audience saturated with advertising. Advertisers began to create ads that were entertaining, often recirculating images from the media and the larger culture. Many ads today base their images on something else—familiar images (for example, the *Mona Lisa* has been used many times in ads), old television shows, movies, even other ads.

One attention-getting tactic is **visual metaphor**—the use of an image that represents an abstract concept to make a visual analogy. The viewer is invited to make the connection between the image and the concept. Antidrug ads have used visual metaphors extensively, especially to portray the effects of drugs on the brain. The image of the brain as a scrambled egg is one example. Other metaphors represent drugs as self-destructive weapons.

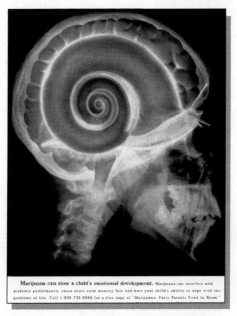

Marijuana can slow a child's emotional development. Marijuana can interfere with academic performance, cause short-term memory loss and hurt your child's ability to cope with the problems of life. Call 1-800-729-6686 for a free copy of "Marijuana: Facts Parents Need to Know."

Antidrug ads often use visual metaphors.

Visual Evidence

Photographs

Images and graphics seldom make arguments on their own, but they are frequently used to support arguments. Photographs are commonly used as factual evidence. When United States soldiers captured Saddam Hussein on

Saddam Hussein shortly after he was captured on December 13, 2003. Photo by Staff Sgt. David Bennett.

December 13, 2003, the military immediately released photographs of the former leader of Iraq, whom they declared a prisoner of war, even though releasing images of a POW is technically a violation of Geneva Convention rules. But even nations critical of the United States didn't raise this issue. The demand for proof of Saddam's capture was overwhelming.

Photographs also provide evidence of the past. They provide a cultural memory of earlier times. The segregation of white and African Americans in the South before the 1960s would now be hard to imagine without images from the time that depict separate water fountains and separate entrances to public buildings.

Just as for other kinds of evidence, the significance of images can be contested. In 1936, 21-year-old Arthur Rothstein worked as a photographer for the Resettlement Administration, a federal agency created to help people living in rural poverty. Rothstein sent a photograph of a bleached cow's

"Colored" entrance to a movie theater, Belzoni, Mississippi, October 1939. Photo by Marion Post Wolcott.

skull lying on cracked dirt to Roy Stryker, his boss in Washington. Stryker saw the image as representing the plight of Midwestern plains states in the midst of a severe drought.

But not all people living in plains states found the image and others like it representative. A newspaper in Fargo, North Dakota, published one of Rothstein's photographs on the front page under the headline, "It's a fake." The newspaper accused journalists in general of making the situation on the plains appear worse than it was and accused Rothstein in particular of using a movable prop to make a cheap point. Furthermore, the newspaper contended that the cracked earth was typical of the badlands at all times but didn't represent the soil condition in most of the state. Close examination of the set of photographs of the skull revealed the skull had been moved about 10 feet, which Rothstein admitted. But he protested that the drought was real enough and there were plenty of cow bones on the ground. Rothstein followed a long practice among photographers in altering a scene for the purpose of getting a better photograph.

Photographs were often manipulated in the darkroom, but realistic results required a high skill level. Digital photography and the image editing software have made it relatively easy to alter photographs. Thousands of altered images are circulated daily that put heads on different bodies and put people in different places, often within historical images. The ease of cropping digital photographs reveals an important truth about photography. A high-resolution picture of a crowd can be divided into many smaller images that each say something different about the event. The act of pointing the camera in one direction and not in another shapes how photographic evidence will be interpreted.

The bleached skull of a steer on the dry, sun-baked earth of the South Dakota Badlands, 1939. Photo by Arthur Rothstein.

Tables

Statistical information is frequently used as evidence in arguments. For example, gun control advocates point to comparisons between the United States and other advanced nations of the world, all of which have much stricter gun laws than the United States and much lower rates of deaths by firearms. The rate of firearm deaths in the United States is three times higher than Canada's, four times higher than Australia's, nine times higher than Germany's, twenty-four times higher than the United Kingdom's (even including Northern Ireland), and almost two hundred times higher than Japan's.

The problem with giving many statistics in words is that readers shortly lose track of the numbers. Readers require formats where they can take in a mass of numerical data at once. Tables are useful for presenting an array of numerical data. Below is a comparison of the death rates due to firearms in the United States and other advanced nations.

	Deaths Due to Firearms (rates are per 100,000 people)							
	Total Firearm Deaths		**Firearm Homicides**		**Firearm Suicides**		**Fatal Firearm Accidents**	
	Rate	Number	Rate	Number	Rate	Number	Rate	Number
United States (1995)	13.7	35,957	6	15,835	7	18,503	0.5	1,225
Australia (1994)	3.05	536	0.56	96	2.38	420	0.11	20
Canada (1994)	4.08	1,189	0.6	176	3.35	975	0.13	38
Germany (1995)	1.47	1,197	0.21	168	1.23	1,004	0.03	25
Japan (1995)	0.07	93	0.03	34	0.04	49	0.01	10
Sweden (1992)	2.31	200	0.31	27	1.95	169	0.05	4
Spain (1994)	1.01	396	0.19	76	0.55	219	0.26	101
United Kingdom (1994)	0.57	277	0.13	72	0.33	193	0.02	12

Source: United Nations. *United Nations International Study on Firearms Regulation*. Vienna, Austria: United Nations Crime Prevention and Criminal Justice Division, 1997. 109.

Charts and Graphs

While tables can present an array of numbers at once, they too lack the dramatic impact of charts. Charts visually represent the magnitude and proportion of data. The differences in death rates due to firearms is striking when presented as a chart.

Column and Bar Charts

One of the easiest charts to make is a simple column or bar chart (column charts are vertical; bar charts are horizontal).

The options in creating charts involve rhetorical decisions. The lengths of the axes on a column or bar chart either exaggerate or minimize differences. The unit of measurement also determines the appearance of a chart.

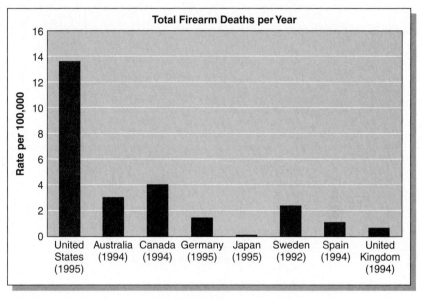

Figure 5.1   Column chart of firearm deaths by country.

Line Graphs

People have difficulty visualizing trends if they are given a long list of numbers, but they can recognize a visual pattern at a glance, which is why line graphs are commonly used to represent statistical trends across time. In Figure 5.2, it's easy to see that the number of handgun homicides rose in the early 1990s but then declined in the late 1990s.

Pie Charts

Pie charts are especially useful for representing percentages, but they work only if the percentages of the parts add up to one hundred percent. Gun control advocates frequently cite a study done in Seattle that identified all gunshot

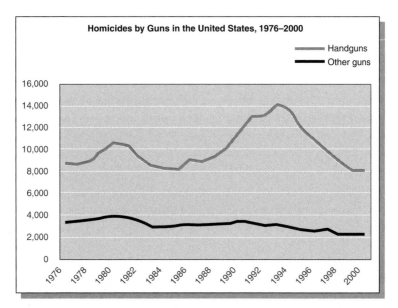

Figure 5.2   Line graph of homicides by guns in the United States, 1976–2000 Source: United States. Department of Justice. *Homicide Trends in the U.S.* 21 Nov. 2002. 2 Dec. 2003 <http://www.ojp.usdoj.gov/bjs/homicide/weapons.htm>.

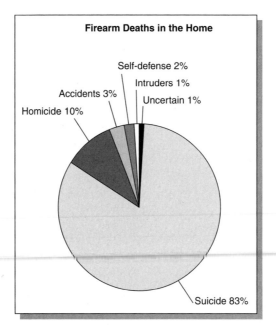

Figure 5.3   Pie chart of causes of firearm deaths in the home.

deaths over a six-year period (A. L. Kellermann and D. L. Reay. "Protection or Peril: An Analysis of Firearm-Related Deaths in the Home." *New England Journal of Medicine* 314 (1986): 1557–60). Of the 733 deaths by firearms, a majority of 398 occurred in the home in which the firearm involved was kept. Of that 398,333 (83.6%) were suicides, 41 (10.3%) were criminal homicides, 12 (3.0%) were accidental, 7 (1.7%) were justifiable self-defense, and only 2 (0.5%) involved an intruder shot during an attempted entry.

Gun control advocates use this study to question the advisability of keeping firearms in the home for protection. Gun rights advocates, however, fault the study because there is no evidence for how many attempts to enter the home might be prevented because intruders fear that the owner is armed.

EVALUATING CHARTS AND GRAPHS

Computer software makes it simple to create charts and graphs. This ease, however, does not tell you which kind of chart or graph is best to use and the purpose of including a chart or graph. Ask these questions when you are analyzing charts and graphs.

1. Is the type of chart appropriate for the information presented? For example, a pie chart is inappropriate if the parts do not add up to 100 percent of the whole.

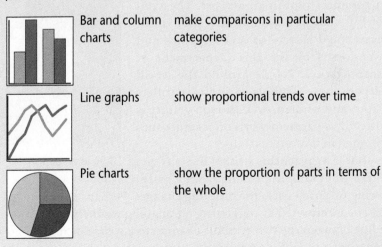

	Bar and column charts	make comparisons in particular categories
	Line graphs	show proportional trends over time
	Pie charts	show the proportion of parts in terms of the whole

(Continued)

EVALUATING CHARTS AND GRAPHS *(continued)*

2. Does the chart have a clear purpose?
3. Does the title indicate the purpose?
4. What do the units represent (dollars, people, voters, percentages, and so on)?
5. What is the source of the data?
6. Is there any distortion of information? A bar chart can exaggerate small differences if intervals are manipulated (for example, 42 can look twice as large as 41 on a bar chart if the numbering begins at 40).

Write a Visual Analysis

Few images and graphics by themselves convey definite meanings. But words often don't have definite meanings either. Consider this sentence: "Sheila will give you a ring tomorrow." Is Sheila going to call you or give you a piece of jewelry to wear on your finger? Usually we never think of the alternative meaning because the context makes clear which meaning of *ring* is intended.

Many signs are highly abstract, but we seldom confuse their meaning. Look again at a common sign in an airport. The symbols for man and woman are part of an international system of hieroglyphics and are endorsed by the U.S. Department of Transportation. People around the world interpret these symbols to indicate toilets for men and women, even though gender is marked by a garment worn only sometimes by women in Western nations.

Sign in an airport.

But if we place this symbol in a different context—for example, placing it over a graffiti drawing of closed fists—the meaning changes. Perhaps the composite image could be interpreted as suggesting an ongoing war between the sexes. If so, the line between the two symbols changes to a wall. The immediate context often gives a way of interpreting an image, and if the image is placed in a strange context, the meaning often isn't as clear.

A conventional symbol placed in a new context.

We use more than the immediate context to interpret images. We use our knowledge of images to classify them into types or genres. We recognize the image of the three individuals shown here as a snapshot, a kind of image that has been enormously popular since the appearance of the inexpensive Brownie camera in 1888. We know from how cameras are typically used in our culture that the woman in the center is probably a tourist who asked the two police officers to pose with her.

A tourist in New York City.

Another detail gives an important clue to how to read the photograph. The woman is wearing an NYPD cap, which were seldom worn by people other than police officers before September 11, 2001. The cap tells us that the location is probably New York City and the date of the photo was sometime after September 11. In addition to the immediate context, we use our knowledge of the broader historical and cultural contexts to interpret an image.

The great majority of visual arguments we see each day are advertisements, but there are other important kinds of visual arguments. One is public art and sculpture, which often celebrates the importance of people and events. On one of the bridge houses of the Michigan Avenue Bridge cross-

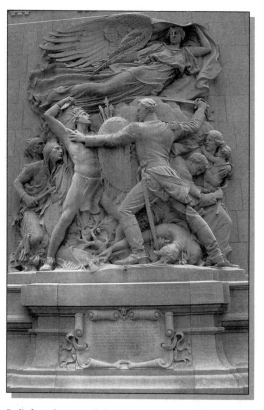

Relief sculpture of the Fort Dearborn Massacre on the Michigan Avenue Bridge, Chicago.

ing the Chicago River in downtown Chicago is a large relief sculpture depicting the massacre of settlers fleeing Fort Dearborn in 1812. The size of the sculpture and its placement on the busiest and most famous street in Chicago attests to its significance at the time it was commissioned.

Two central figures—an American soldier and a Potawatomi Indian—battle as an angel hovers above. On the left another Indian is stealthily approaching, crouched with a tomahawk in hand. On the right a man shields a woman and a child from the threat. The sculpture uses a familiar stereotype of American Indians to make a visual argument: the Indians are attacking because they are bloodthirsty and sneaky; the innocent white people bravely resist. The sculpture does not speak to the circumstances of the massacre. The Potawatomis allied with the British during the War of 1812 to resist settlers who were taking their land. The settlers waited too long to evacuate Fort Dearborn in the face of growing numbers of Indians surrounding the fort.

It's not surprising that the sculpture represents the settlers as heroic. The bridge and monument were part of a grand plan to enhance Chicago's waterfront, begun in 1909. Thus the monument plays its part in obscuring the actual history of the area. Viewers who are unaware of the facts may feel a sense of patriotic pride in the actions of the soldier and the woman. Viewers who are familiar with the whole story may take a more cynical view of the intended message.

Sample Student Visual Analysis

Angela Yamashita wrote the following essay while a first-year student at Pennsylvania State University. Yamashita is majoring in bioengineering and is an avid lacrosse player.

Yamashita 1

Angela Yamashita

Dr. Sanchez

English 15

12 December 2003

Got Roddick?

Andy Roddick is one of the hottest up-and-coming athletes of today. In 2003 he became the youngest American to finish ranked number one in the ATP rankings, and he's known not only for his excellent playing skills but also for his good looks and easygoing attitude. Boyfriend to popular singer Mandy Moore, Roddick has been thrown into the spotlight and is now a teenage crush. It was his picture that stopped me while leafing through Seventeen and made me take a longer look. Roddick stands staring at the viewer, racquet over his shoulder, leaning against the net on the court. More prominent than his

white pants, white tennis shirt, and white towel draped
around his neck is the white milk mustache above his
upper lip. The ad reads: "Now serving. I'm into power. So
I drink milk. It packs 9 essential nutrients into every
glass. Which comes in handy whether you're an athlete or
an energetic fan." At the bottom of the page is the ad
slogan (also in white) "Got Milk?"

The "Got Milk?" campaign has been going on since
1993 and has published numerous ads that try to convince
adults to drink more milk. Everyone from rock groups to
actors to athletes have participated in this campaign.
In today's caffeine-obsessed society of coffee and soda
drinkers, America's Dairy Farmers and Milk Processors
(the association that sponsors the "Got Milk?" campaign)
felt the need to reverse the decline in milk consumption
by advertising milk in a new way. The catchy "Got Milk?"
proved to be highly successful, and the campaign has
been mimicked by many others including "Got cookies?"

CHAPTER 5 *Understanding Visual Arguments* **101**

"Got fish?" "Got sports?" and even "Got Jesus?"

(Philpot). The Andy Roddick ad is typical of the "Got

Milk?" series, urging people young and old to drink milk

to remain healthy and strong. The Roddick ad primarily

uses the appeals ethos and pathos to persuade its

audience. (The one gesture toward logos in the ad is the

mention that milk has nine nutrients.)

America's Dairy Farmers and Milk Processors use

celebrity endorsements to establish the ethos of their

ads. The "Got Milk?" campaign has enlisted a range of

celebrities popular with young audiences from Amy Grant

to Austin Powers, Britney Spears to Brett Farve, T-Mac

(Tracy McGrady) to Bernie Mac. Choosing Andy Roddick,

the dominant young male player in American tennis, fits

squarely in this lineup. Admired by a strong following

of young adults (girls for his looks, boys for his

athletic ability), Roddick is an ideal spokesman for

establishing that milk is a healthy drink. Implicit in

the ad is that milk will help you become a better

athlete and better looking too.

Pathos in the ad is conveyed not simply through

Roddick's good looks. His pose is casual, almost

slouching, yet his face is serious, one that suggests

that he not only means business about playing tennis but

also about his drink of choice. The words "I'm into

power" don't mess around. They imply that you too can be

more powerful by drinking milk. "Now serving" is also in

your face, making a play on the word "serving" both as a

tennis and a drink term.

Yamashita 4

The effectiveness of the "Got Milk?" campaign is demonstrated in gallons of milk sold. The campaign began in California in 1993 at a time when milk sales were rapidly eroding. A San Francisco ad agency developed the milk mustache idea, which is credited for stopping the downward trend in milk consumption in California. In 1995 the campaign went national. By 2000 national sales of milk remained consistent in contrast to annual declines in the early 1990s (Stamler). "Got Milk?" gave milk a brand identity that it had previously lacked, allowing it to compete with the well-established identities of Pepsi and Coca-Cola. Milk now has new challengers with more and more people going out to Starbuck's and other breakfast bars. Nonetheless, the original formula of using celebrities like Andy Roddick who appeal to younger audiences continues to work. Milk isn't likely to go away soon as a popular beverage.

Yamashita 5

Works Cited

"Andy Roddick." Got Milk? 2003. Milk Processor Education
    Program. 18 Nov. 2003 <http://www.whymilk.com/
    celebrity_archive.htm>.
Philpot, Robert. "Copycats Mimic 'Got Milk' Ads."
    Milwaukee Journal Sentinel 12 May 2002, final ed.: D3.
Stamler, Bernard. "Got Sticking Power?" New York Times
    30 July 2001, late ed.: C11.

Steps to a Visual Analysis

Step 1 Select an example of visual persuasion to analyze

Many visual objects and images intend to persuade. Of course, all forms of advertising fall into the category of persuasion.

Examples

- Analyze a map. What is represented on a map? What is most prominent? What is left out? Maps most often do not make explicit claims, but they are persuasive nonetheless.
- Analyze a popular consumer product. Why did iPods became the hottest-selling MP3 player? What made the iPod stand out?
- Analyze a public building in your city or town. What messages does it convey?
- Analyze images on an online real estate site. Why are particular pictures of a house displayed? What arguments do those images make?

Step 2 Analyze the context

What is the context?
- Why was this image made or object created?
- What was the purpose?
- Where did it come from?

Who is the audience?
- What can you infer about the intended audience?
- What did the designer(s) assume the audience knew or believed?

Who is the designer?
- Do you know the identity of the author?
- What else has the designer done?

Step 3 Analyze the text

What is the subject?
- Can you describe the content?
- How is the image or object arranged?

What is the medium and genre?

■ What is the medium? A printed photograph? an oil painting? an outdoor sign? a building?
■ What is the genre? An advertisement? a monument? a portrait? a cartoon? What expectations does the audience have about this genre?

Are words connected to the image or object?

■ Is there a caption attached to the image or words in the image?
■ Are there words on the building or object?

What appeals are used?

■ Are there appeals to ethos—the character of what is represented?
■ Are there appeals to logos—the documentation of facts?
■ Are there appeals to pathos—the values of the audience? Are there elements that can be considered as symbolic?

How would you characterize the style?

■ Is the style formal, informal, comic, or something else?
■ Are any visual metaphors used?

Step 4 Write a draft

■ Introduce the image or object and give the background.
■ Make a claim about the image or object you are analyzing. For example, *the "Got Milk?" ad featuring Andy Roddick relies on the appeals of ethos and pathos.*
■ Support your claim with close analysis of the image or object. Describe key features.

Step 5 Revise, edit, proofread

■ For detailed instructions, see Chapter 12.
■ For a checklist to use to evaluate your draft, see pages 217–222.

PART 2

Putting Good Reasons into Action

Options for Arguments

Imagine that you bought a new car in June and you are taking some of your friends to your favorite lake over the Fourth of July weekend. You have a great time until, as you are heading home, a drunk driver—a repeat offender—swerves into your lane and totals your new car. You and your friends are lucky not to be hurt, but you're outraged because you believe that repeat offenders should be prevented from driving, even if that means putting them in jail. You also remember going to another state that had sobriety checkpoints on holiday weekends. If such a checkpoint had been at the lake, you might still be driving your new car. You live in a town that encourages citizens to contribute to the local newspaper, and you think you could get a guest editorial published. The question is: How do you want to write the editorial?

- You could tell your story about how a repeat drunk driver endangered the lives of you and your friends.
- You could define driving while intoxicated (DWI) as a more legally culpable crime.
- You could compare the treatment of drunk drivers in your state with the treatment of drunk drivers in another state.

- You could cite statistics that drunk drivers killed 17,013 people in 2003, a figure that was down from previous years but still represented too many needless deaths.
- You could evaluate the present drunk driving laws as insufficiently just or less than totally successful.
- You could propose taking vehicles away from repeat drunk drivers and forcing them to serve mandatory sentences.
- You could argue that your community should have sobriety checkpoints at times when drunk drivers are likely to be on the road.
- You could do several of the above.

You're not going to have much space in the newspaper, so you decide to argue for sobriety checkpoints. You know that they are controversial. One of your friends in the car with you said that they are unconstitutional because they involve search without cause. However, after doing some research to find out whether checkpoints are defined as legal or illegal, you learn that on June 14, 1990, the U.S. Supreme Court upheld the constitutionality of using checkpoints as a deterrent and enforcement tool against drunk drivers. But you still want to know whether most people would agree with your friend that sobriety checkpoints are an invasion of privacy. You find opinion polls and surveys going back to the 1980s that show that 70 to 80 percent of those polled support sobriety checkpoints. You also realize that you can argue by analogy that security checkpoints for alcohol are similar in many ways to airport security checkpoints that protect the passengers. You decide you will finish by making an argument from consequence. If people who go to the lake with plans to drink a lot know in advance that there will be checkpoints, they will find a designated driver or some other means of safe transportation, and everyone else will also be a little safer.

The point of this example is that people very rarely set out to define something in an argument for the sake of definition, compare for the sake of comparison, or adopt any of the other ways of structuring an argument. Instead, they have a purpose in mind, and they use the kinds of arguments that are discussed in Part 2—most often in combination—as means to an end. Most arguments use multiple approaches and multiple sources of good reasons. Proposal arguments in particular often analyze a present situation with definition, causal, and evaluative arguments before advancing a course of future action to address that situation. The advantage of thinking explicitly about the structure of arguments is that you often find other ways to argue. Sometimes you just need a way to get started writing about complex issues.

Using Different Approaches to Construct an Argument

An even greater advantage of thinking explicitly about specific kinds of arguments is that they can often give you a *sequence* for constructing arguments. Take affirmative action policies for granting admission to college as an example. No issue has been more controversial on college campuses during the last ten years.

Definition

What exactly does *affirmative action* mean? You know that it is a policy that attempts to address the reality of contemporary inequality based on past injustice. But injustice to whom and by whom? Do all members of minorities, all women, and all people with disabilities have equal claims for redress of past injustices? If not, how do you distinguish among them? And what exactly does affirmative action entail? Do all students who are admitted by affirmative action criteria automatically receive scholarships? Clearly, you need to define affirmative action first before proposing any changes in the policy.

Cause and Effect

Since affirmative action policies have been around for a few years, you might next investigate how well they have worked. If you view affirmative action as a cause, then what have been its effects? You might find, for example, that the percentage of African Americans graduating from college dropped from 1991 through 2001 in many states. Furthermore, affirmative action policies have created a backlash attitude among many whites who believe, rightly or wrongly, that they are victims of reverse racism. But you might find that enrollment of minorities at your university has increased substantially since affirmative action policies were instituted. And you might come across a book by the then-presidents of Princeton and Harvard, William G. Bowen and Derek Bok, entitled *The Shape of the River: Long-Term Consequences of Considering Race in College and University Admissions*, which examines the effects of affirmative action policies at twenty-eight of the nation's most select universities. They found that African American graduates of elite schools were more likely than their white counterparts to earn graduate degrees and to take on civic responsibilities after graduation.

Evaluation

With a definition established and evidence collected, you can move to evaluation. Is affirmative action fair? Is affirmative action just? Is the goal of achieving diversity through affirmative action admissions policies a worthy one because white people enjoyed preferential treatment until the last few decades? Or are affirmative action admissions policies bad because they continue the historically bad practice of giving preference to people of certain races and because they cast into the role of victims the people they are trying to help?

Proposal

When you have a definition with evidence and have made an evaluation, you have the groundwork for making a recommendation in the form of a proposal. A proposal argues what should be done in the future or what should not be done and what good or bad consequences will follow.

Your Goals for Argument

Even though types of argument are distinguished in Part 2, they are closely linked parts of a whole. Each type of argument can stand alone but always involves multiple aspects. If you are clear in your purpose for your argument and have a good sense of the knowledge and attitudes of the people your argument is aimed toward, then the most effective types of arguments will be evident to you. You might find yourself using several different approaches at once.

CHAPTER 6

Definition Arguments

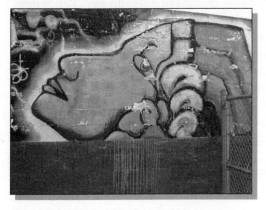

> What a quintessential marriage of cool and style to write your name in giant separate living letters, large as animals, lithe as snakes, mysterious as Arabic and Chinese curls of alphabet.
>
> NORMAN MAILER,
> THE *FAITH OF GRAFFITI*, 1973

> "It's expression, you know," one 15-year-old tagger, who would give his name only as Chris, said. "Most taggers aren't in gangs," he added. "They're not shooting people. It's not that big a problem, if you stop and think. It's really art."
>
> No, Chris, it's not art—it's vandalism when you deface the property of another without permission.
>
> EDITORIAL, *DENVER POST*,
> JUNE 10, 2003

From cave paintings made over thirty thousand years ago to artwork spanning from Egyptian and Roman times to the present, people have been writing and painting on walls. The present trend in graffiti grew up along with hip-hop in New York City in the 1970s and has evolved from simple "tagging" of names to large, sophisticated murals.

But what is graffiti—art or vandalism? Some graffiti artists have been hired to paint murals in public spaces and some even have been honored with exhibits in major art museums. Yet graffiti is also defined as a crime, either a misdemeanor or a felony. For some, graffiti is a means of self-expression and a vibrant form of urban diversity. For others, graffiti is visual pollution, even a kind of domestic terrorism that says no one is safe and that blights neighborhoods and destroys small businesses.

The continuing controversy about graffiti illustrates why definitions often matter more that we might think at first. People argue about definitions because of the consequences of something being defined in a certain way. The controversy over graffiti also illustrates three very important principles that operate when definitions are used in arguments.

> Definition arguments are the most powerful arguments.

First, people make definitions that benefit their interests. You learned very early in life the importance of defining actions as "accidents." Windows can be broken through carelessness, especially when you are tossing a ball against the side of the house, but if it's an accident, well, accidents just happen (and don't require punishment).

Second, most of the time when you are arguing a definition, your audience will either have a different definition in mind or be unsure of the definition. Your mother or father probably didn't think breaking the window was an accident, so you had to convince Mom or Dad that you were really being careful, but the ball just slipped out of your hand. It's your job to get them to accept your definition.

Third, if you can get your audience to accept your definition, then usually you succeed. For this reason, definition arguments are the most powerful arguments.

Kinds of Definitions

Rarely do you get far into an argument without having to define something. Imagine that you are writing an argument about the United States' decades-old and largely ineffective "war on drugs." We all know that the war on drugs is being waged against drugs that are illegal, like cocaine and marijuana, and not against the legal drugs produced by the multibillion-dollar drug industry. Our society classifies drugs into two categories: "good" drugs, which are legal, and "bad" drugs, which are illegal.

How exactly does our society arrive at these definitions? Drugs would be relatively easy to define as good or bad if the difference could be defined at the molecular level. Bad drugs would contain certain molecules that define them as bad. The history of drug use in the United States, however, tells us that it is not so simple. In the last century alcohol was on the list of illegal drugs for over a decade, while opium was considered a good drug and distributed in many patent medicines by pharmaceutical companies. Similarly, LSD and MDMA (ecstasy) were developed by the pharmaceutical industry but later placed in the illegal category. In a few states marijuana is now crossing over to the legal category for medicinal use.

If drugs cannot be classified as good or bad by their molecular structure, then perhaps society classifies them by effects. It might be reasonable to assume that drugs that are addictive are illegal, but that's not the case. Nicotine is highly addictive and is a legal drug; so too are many prescription medicines. Neither are drugs taken for the purpose of offering pleasure necessarily illegal (think of alcohol and Viagra), nor are drugs that alter consciousness or change personality (Prozac).

How a drug is defined as legal or illegal apparently is determined by *example*. The nationwide effort in the United States to stop people from drinking alcohol during the first decades of the twentieth century led to the passage of the Eighteenth Amendment and the ban on sales of alcohol from 1920 to 1933, known as Prohibition. Those who argued for Prohibition used examples of drunkenness, especially among the poor, to show how alcohol broke up families and left mothers and children penniless in the street. Those who opposed Prohibition initially pointed to the consumption of beer and wine in many ethnic traditions. Later they raised examples of the bad effects of Prohibition—the rise of organized crime, the increase in alcohol abuse, and the general disregard for laws.

When you make a definitional argument, it's important to think about what kind of definition you will use. Descriptions of three types follow.

Formal Definitions

Formal definitions typically categorize an item into the next higher classification and give distinguishing criteria from other items within that classification. Most dictionary definitions are formal definitions. For example, fish are cold-blooded aquatic vertebrates that have jaws, fins, and scales and are distinguished from other cold-blooded aquatic vertebrates (such as sea snakes) by the presence of gills. If you can construct a formal definition with specific criteria that your audience will accept, then likely you will have a strong argument. The key is to get your audience to agree to your criteria.

Operational Definitions

Many concepts cannot be easily defined by formal definitions. Researchers in the natural and social sciences must construct operational definitions that they use for their research. For example, researchers who study binge drinking among college students define a binge as five or more drinks in one sitting for a man, and four or more drinks for a woman. Some people think this standard is too low and should be raised to six to eight drinks to distinguish true problem drinkers from the general college population. No matter what the number, researchers must argue that the particular definition is one that suits the concept.

Definitions from Example

Many human qualities such as honesty, courage, creativity, deceit, and love must be defined by examples that the audience accepts as representative of the concept. Few would not call the firemen who entered the World Trade Center on September 11, 2001, courageous. Most people would describe someone with a diagnosis of terminal cancer who refuses to feel self-pity as courageous. But what about a student who declines to go to a concert with her friends so she can study for an exam? Her behavior might be admirable, but most people would hesitate to call it courageous. The key to arguing a definition from examples is that the examples must strike the audience as in some way typical of the concept, even if the situation is unusual.

Building a Definitional Argument

Because definition arguments are the most powerful arguments, they are often at the center of the most important debates in American history. The major arguments of the civil rights movement were definition arguments, none more

Martin Luther King, Jr.

eloquent than Martin Luther King, Jr.'s "Letter from Birmingham Jail." From 1957 until his assassination in April 1968, King served as president of the Southern Christian Leadership Conference, an organization of primarily African American clergymen dedicated to bringing about social change. King, who was a Baptist minister, tried to put into practice Mahatma Gandhi's principles of nonviolence in demonstrations, sit-ins, and marches throughout the South. During Holy Week in 1963, King led demonstrations and a boycott of downtown merchants in Birmingham, Alabama, to end racial segregation at lunch counters and discriminatory hiring practices.

On Wednesday, April 10, the city obtained an injunction directing the demonstrations to cease until their legality could be argued in court. But after meditation, King decided, against the advice of his associates, to defy the court order and proceed with the march planned for Good Friday morning. On Friday morning, April 12, King and fifty followers were arrested. King was held in solitary confinement until the end of the weekend, allowed neither to see his attorneys nor to call his wife. On the day of his arrest, King read in the newspaper a statement objecting to the demonstrations signed by eight white Birmingham clergymen of Protestant, Catholic, and Jewish faiths, urging that the protests stop and that grievances be settled in the courts.

On Saturday morning, King started writing an eloquent response that addresses the criticisms of the white clergymen, who are one primary audience of his response. But King intended his response to the ministers for widespread publication, and he clearly had in mind a larger readership. The clergymen gave him the occasion to address moderate white leaders in the South as well as religious and educated people across the nation and supporters of the civil rights movement. King begins "Letter from Birmingham Jail" by addressing the ministers as "My Dear Fellow Clergymen," adopting a conciliatory and tactful tone from the outset but at the same time offering strong arguments for the necessity of acting now rather than waiting for change. A critical part of King's argument is justifying disobedience of certain laws. The eight white clergymen asked that laws be obeyed until they are changed. Here's how King responds:

> You express a great deal of anxiety over our willingness to break laws. This is certainly a legitimate concern. Since we so diligently urge people to obey the Supreme Court's decision of 1954 outlawing segregation in the public schools, at first glance it may seem rather paradoxical for us consciously to break laws. One may well ask: "How can you advocate breaking some laws and obeying others?" The answer lies in the fact that there are two types of laws: just and unjust. I would be the first to advocate obeying just laws. One has not only a legal but a moral responsibility to obey just laws. Conversely, one has a moral responsibility to disobey unjust laws. I would agree with St. Augustine that "an unjust law is no law at all."
>
> Now, what is the difference between the two? How does one determine whether a law is just or unjust? A just law is a man-made code that squares with the moral law or the law of God. An unjust law is a code that is out of harmony with the moral law. To put it in the terms of St. Thomas Aquinas: An unjust law is a human law that is not rooted in eternal law and natural law. Any law that uplifts human personality is just. Any law that degrades human personality is unjust. All segregation statutes are unjust because segregation distorts the soul and damages the personality. It gives the segregator a false sense of superiority and the segregated a false sense of inferiority. Segregation, to use the terminology of the Jewish philosopher Martin Buber, substitutes an "I-it" relationship and ends up relegating persons to the status of things. Hence segregation is not only politically, economically and sociologically unsound, it is morally wrong and sinful. Paul Tillich has said that sin is separation. Is not segregation an existential expression of man's tragic separation, his awful estrangement, his terrible sinfulness? Thus it is that I can urge men to obey the 1954 decision of the Supreme Court, for it is morally right; and I can urge them to disobey segregation ordinances, for they are morally wrong.

Martin Luther King's analysis of just and unjust laws is a classic definitional argument. Definitional arguments take this form:

> SOMETHING is a _____ if it possesses certain criteria that differentiate it from other similar things in its general class.

According to King, a *just law* possesses the criteria of being consistent with moral law and uplifting human personality. Just as important, King sets out the criteria of an *unjust law*, when something is not a _____. Unjust laws have the criteria of being out of harmony with moral law and damaging human personality. The criteria are set out in because-clauses: SOMETHING *is a* _____ *because it has these criteria.* The criteria provide the link shown in Figure 6.1. The negative can be argued in the same way, as shown in Figure 6.2.

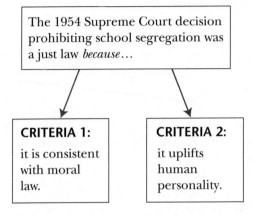

Figure 6.1

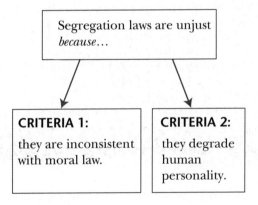

Figure 6.2

An extended definition like King's is a two-step process. First you have to determine the criteria. Then you have to argue that what you are defining possesses these criteria. If you want to argue that housing prisoners in unheated and non-air-conditioned tents is cruel and unusual punishment, then you have to make exposing prisoners to hot and cold extremes one of the criteria of cruel and unusual punishment. The keys to a definitional argument are getting your audience to accept your criteria and getting your audience to accept that the case in point meets those criteria. King's primary audience was the eight white clergymen; therefore, he used religious criteria and cited Protestant, Catholic, and Jewish theologians as his authority. His second criterion about just laws uplifting the human personality was a less familiar concept than the idea of moral law. King therefore offered a more detailed explanation drawing on the work of Martin Buber.

But King was smart enough to know that not all of his potential readers would put quite so much stock in religious authorities. Therefore, he follows the religious criteria with two other criteria that appeal to definitions of democracy:

> Let us consider a more concrete example of just and unjust laws. An unjust law is a code that a numerical or power majority group compels a minority group to obey but does not make binding on itself. This is *difference* made legal. By the same token, a just law is a code that a majority compels a minority to follow and that it is willing to follow itself. This is *sameness* made legal.
>
> Let me give another explanation. A law is unjust if it is inflicted on the minority that, as a result of being denied the right to vote, has no part in enacting or devising the law. Who can say that the legislature of Alabama which set up that state's segregation laws was democratically elected? Throughout Alabama all sorts of devious methods are used to prevent Negroes from becoming registered voters, and there are some counties in which, even though Negroes constitute a majority of the population, not a single Negro is registered. Can any law enacted under such circumstances be considered democratically structured?

King expands his criteria for just and unjust laws to include four major criteria, and he defines both by classifying and by giving examples. (See Figure 6.3.)

King's "Letter from Birmingham Jail" draws much of its rhetorical power from its reliance on a variety of arguments that are suited for different readers. An atheist could reject the notion of laws made by God but could still be convinced by the criteria that segregation laws are undemocratic and therefore unjust.

To make definitional arguments work, often you must put much effort into identifying and explaining your criteria. You must convince your readers that your criteria are the best ones for what you are defining and that they apply to the case you are arguing. King backs up his assertion—that Alabama's segregation laws in 1963 were unjust because the Alabama legislature was not democratically elected—by pointing to counties that had African American majorities but no African American voters.

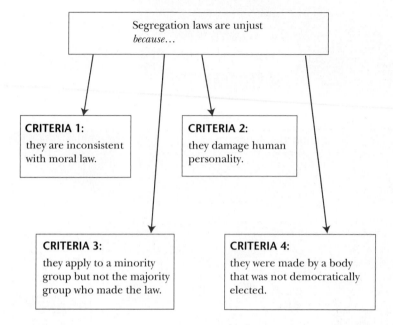

Figure 6.3

SCOTT MCCLOUD

Setting the Record Straight

Scott McCloud is the pseudonym of Scott Willard McLeod, who was born in Boston in 1960 and graduated from Syracuse University in 1982. After a short stint in the production department at DC Comics, he quickly became a highly regarded writer and illustrator of comics. His works include the ten-issue series Zot! *(1984–1985)* Destroy!! *(1986), and the nonfiction* Understanding Comics: The Invisible Art *(Northampton, MA: Tundra, 1993), from which this selection is taken.*

Understanding Comics is a brilliant explanation of how comics combine words and pictures to achieve effects that neither words nor pictures can do alone. At the beginning of the book, McCloud finds it necessary to define what comics are and are not before he can begin to analyze the magic of comics. Notice how he has to refine his criteria several times before he has an adequate definition.

Understanding Comics *Copyright © 1993, 1994 by Scott McCloud. Published by Kitchen Sink Press. Reprinted by permission of HarperCollins Publishers Inc.*

*EISNER'S OWN *COMICS AND SEQUENTIAL ART* BEING A HAPPY EXCEPTION.

*JUXTAPOSED= ADJACENT, SIDE-BY-SIDE. GREAT ART SCHOOL WORD.

Steps to a Definition Argument

Step 1 Make a claim

Make a definitional claim on a controversial issue that focuses on a key term.

Formula

- SOMETHING is (or is not) a _____ because it has (or does not have) features A, B, and C (or more).

Examples

- Hate speech (or pornography, literature, films, and so on) is (or is not) free speech protected by the First Amendment because it has (does not have) these features.
- Hunting (or using animals for cosmetics testing, keeping animals in zoos, wearing furs, and so on) is (or is not) cruelty to animals because it has (or does not have) these features.
- Doctors should be (should not be) allowed to assist patients to die if they are terminally ill and suffering.
- Displaying pinup calendars (or jokes, innuendo, rap lyrics, and so on) is (is not) an example of sexual harassment.

Step 2 Think about what's at stake

- Would nearly everyone agree with you? Then your claim probably isn't interesting or important. If you can think of people who would disagree, then something is at stake.
- Who argues the opposite of your claim?
- Why or how do they benefit from a different definition?

Step 3 List the criteria

- Which criteria are necessary for SOMETHING to be a _____?
- Which are not necessary?
- Which are the most important?
- Does your case in point meet all the criteria?

Step **4** Analyze your potential readers

- Who are your readers?
- How does the definitional claim you are making affect them?
- How familiar will they be with the issue, concept, or controversy that you're writing about?
- What are they likely to know and not know?
- Which criteria are they most likely to accept with little explanation, and which will they disagree with?
- Which criteria will you have to argue for?

Step **5** Write a draft

Introduction

- Set out the issue, concept, or controversy.
- Explain why the definition is important.
- Give the background that your intended readers will need.

Body

- Set out your criteria and argue for the appropriateness of the criteria.
- Determine whether the criteria apply to the case in point.
- Anticipate where readers might question either your criteria or how they apply to your subject.
- Address opposing viewpoints by acknowledging how their definitions might differ and by showing why your definition is better.

Conclusion

- Do more than simply summarize. You can, for example, go into more detail about what is at stake or the implications of your definition.

Step **6** Revise, edit, proofread

- For detailed instructions, see Chapter 12.
- For a checklist to use to evaluate your draft, see pages 217–222.

CHAPTER 7

Causal Arguments

In a 5–4 decision, the U.S. Supreme Court has ruled that the U.S. Corps of Army Engineers cannot regulate isolated wetlands merely because passing birds might land on such property. . . . The decision, says the National Association of Home Builders (NAHB), is "a major legal victory for home builders and other private property owners."

REALTY TIMES, JANUARY 10, 2001

According to the U.S. Fish and Wildlife Service, more than 120,000 acres of wetlands are destroyed annually. And with the leveling of these wetlands go entire delicate ecosystems—and the plants, insects, and animals they support.

NATIONAL PARKS CONSERVATION
ASSOCIATION, 2004
http://www.npca.org/marine%5Fand
%5Fcoastal/wetlands/

Many biologists now believe that within one hundred years as many as half the species on earth will become extinct or else be relegated to ghost status, surviving in zoos or as DNA samples. It's not that plants and animals are going to vanish; they will still be abundant but the number of different species will be radically fewer. Why is this mass extinction occurring? And why are many animal and plant species now thriving when so many others are disappearing?

Biologists have found a complex set of factors that are changing the composition of living things on earth: rising human population, habitat destruction, habitat fragmentation, overkill, pollution, the disruption of ecosystems, and invasive species. The species that survive will be ones that can thrive in human-dominated environments. Wildlife will consist of rats, roaches, squirrels, house sparrows, crows, starlings, pigeons, and white-tailed deer. For example, the population of raccoons is five times greater in suburban areas than in wild areas. David Quammen compares these species to weeds, ones that reproduce quickly, spread widely, tolerate a broad range of conditions, and resist efforts at eradication. Even when land is set aside in preserves, often it is surrounded by human development and weedy species to eventually overrun the species the preserve was created to protect.

To slow the loss of biological diversity we will require far more knowledge than we possess today about the intricate connections of the causes of species decline. But even in our daily lives, we are confronted with numerous questions of causation. Why did the driver who passed you on a blind curve risk his life to get one car ahead at the next traffic light? Why is it hard to recognize people you know when you run into them unexpectedly in an unfamiliar setting? Why do nearly all kids want the same toy each Christmas, forcing their parents to stand in line for hours at—sometimes outside—the toy store? Why does your mother or father spend an extra hour plus the extra gas driving to a supermarket across town just to save a few pennies on one or two items on sale? Why do some of your friends keep going to horror films when they can hardly sit through them and have nightmares afterward?

> Effective causal arguments move beyond the obvious to get at underlying causes.

Life is full of big and little mysteries, and people spend a lot of time speculating about the causes. Most of the time, however, they don't take the time to analyze in depth what causes a controversial trend, event, or phenomenon. But before and after you graduate, you likely will have to write causal arguments that require in-depth analysis. In a professional career you will have to make many detailed causal analyses: Why did a retail business fail when it seemed to have an ideal location? What causes cost overruns in the development of a new product? What causes people in some circumstances to prefer public transportation over driving? What causes unnecessary slowdowns in a local computer network? Answering any of these questions requires making a causal argument, which takes a classic form:

SOMETHING causes (or does not cause) SOMETHING ELSE.

The causal claim is at the center of a causal argument. Therefore, to get started on a causal argument, you need to propose one or more causes.

Methods of Finding Causes

The big problem with causal arguments is that any topic worth writing about is likely to be complex. Identifying causes usually isn't easy. The philosopher John Stuart Mill recognized this problem long ago and devised four methods for finding causes:

1. *The Common Factor Method.* When the cause-and-effect relationship occurs more than once, look for something in common in the events and circumstances of each effect; any common factor could be the cause. Scientists have used this method to explain how seemingly different phenomena are associated. There were a variety of explanations of fire until, in the 1700s, Joseph Priestley in England and Antoine Lavoisier in France discovered that oxygen was a separate element and that burning was caused by oxidation.

2. *The Single Difference Method.* This method works only when there are at least two similar situations, one that leads to an effect and one that does not. Look for something that was missing in one case and present in another—the single difference. The writer assumes that if everything is substantially alike in both cases, then the single difference is the (or a) cause. At the Battle of Midway in 1942, the major naval battle of World War II in the Pacific, the Japanese Navy had a 4-to-1 advantage over the U.S. Navy. Both fleets were commanded by competent, experienced leaders. But the U.S. commander, Admiral Nimitz, had a superior advantage in intelligence, which proved to be decisive.

3. *Concomitant Variation.* This tongue twister is another favorite method of scientists. If an investigator finds that a possible cause

and a possible effect have a similar pattern of variation, then one can suspect that a relationship exists. For example, scientists noticed that peaks in the eleven-year sunspot cycle have predictable effects on high-frequency radio transmission on the earth.

4. *Process of Elimination.* Many possible causes can be proposed for most trends and events. If you are a careful investigator, you have to consider all that you can think of and eliminate the ones that cannot be causes.

For an example of how these methods might work for you, suppose you want to research the causes of the increase in legalized lotteries in the United States. You might discover that lotteries go back to colonial times. Harvard and Yale have been longtime rivals in football, but the schools' rivalry goes back much further. Both ran lotteries before the Revolutionary War! In 1747 the Connecticut legislature voted to allow Yale to conduct a lottery to raise money to build dormitories, and in 1765 the Massachusetts legislature gave Harvard permission for a lottery. Lotteries were common before and after the American Revolution, but they eventually ran into trouble because they were run by private companies that failed to pay the winners. After 1840, laws against lotteries were passed, but they came back after the Civil War in the South. The defeated states of the Confederacy needed money to rebuild the bridges, buildings, and schools that had been destroyed in the Civil War, and they turned to selling lottery tickets throughout the nation, tickets that ironically were very popular in the North. Once again, the lotteries were run by private companies, and scandals eventually led to their banning.

In 1964 the voters in New Hampshire approved a lottery as a means of funding education—in preference to an income tax or sales tax. Soon other northeastern states followed this lead, establishing lotteries with the reasoning that if people are going to gamble, the money should remain at home. During the 1980s, other states approved not only lotteries but also other forms of state-run gambling such as keno and video poker. By 1993 only Hawaii and Utah had no legalized gambling of any kind.

If you are analyzing the causes of the spread of legalized gambling, you might use the **common factor method** to investigate what current lotteries have in common with earlier lotteries. That factor is easy to identify: It's economic. The early colonies and later the states have turned again and again to lotteries as a way of raising money that avoids unpopular tax increases. But why have lotteries spread so quickly and seemingly become so permanent since 1964, when before that, they were used only sporadically and were eventually banned? The **single difference method** points us to the major difference between the lotteries of today and those of previous eras:

Lotteries in the past were run by private companies, and inevitably someone took off with the money instead of paying it out. Today's lotteries are owned and operated by state agencies or else contracted under state control, and while they are not immune to scandals, they are much more closely monitored than lotteries were in the past.

The controversies over legal gambling now focus on casinos. In 1988 Congress passed the Indian Gaming Regulatory Act, which started a new era of casino gambling in the United States. The world's largest casino, Foxwoods Casino in Connecticut, owned by the Mashantucket Pequot Tribe, became a huge moneymaker—paying along with nearby Mohegan Sun Casino over $400 million into the Connecticut state treasury. Other tribes and other states were quick to cash in on casino gambling. Iowa legalized riverboat gambling in 1989, followed shortly by Louisiana, Illinois, Indiana, Mississippi, and Missouri. As with lotteries, the primary justification for approving casino gambling has been economic. States have been forced to fund various programs that the federal government used to pay for. Especially in states where lottery revenues had begun to sag, legislatures and voters turned to casinos to make up the difference.

The 350 tribal casinos in the United States produce over $16 billion in revenues each year.

Casinos, however, have been harder to sell to voters than lotteries. For many voters, casinos are a NIMBY ("not in my back yard") issue. They may believe that people should have the right to gamble, but they don't want a casino in their town. Casino proponents have tried to overcome these objections by arguing that casinos bring added tourist dollars, benefiting the community as a whole. Opponents argue the opposite: that people who go to casinos spend their money on gambling and not on tourist attractions. The cause-and-effect benefit of casinos to community businesses can be examined by **concomitant variation**. Casino supporters argue that people who come to gamble spend a lot of money elsewhere. Opponents of casinos claim that people who come for gambling don't want to spend money elsewhere. Furthermore, they point out that gambling represents another entertainment option for people within easy driving distance and can hurt area businesses such as restaurants, amusement parks, and bowling alleys. So far, the record has been mixed, some businesses being helped and others being hurt when casinos are built nearby.

Many trends don't have causes as obvious as the spread of legalized gambling. One such trend is the redistribution of wealth in the United States since 1970. During the 1950s and 1960s, businesses in the United States grew by 90 percent, and the resulting wealth benefited all income classes. Since 1970, however, almost all the growth in wealth has gone to people at the top of the economic ladder. Analysis of census data by the Congressional Budget Office found that the richest 1 percent of American households received $515,600 in after-tax income adjusted for inflation in 1999 compared with $234,700 in 1977. The incomes of the bottom 20 percent of households fell from $10,000 in 1977 to $8,800 in 1999. The higher on the economic ladder, the more extreme the gains. Those on the very highest rung in the 99.9 percentile—13,400 households out of 134 million taxpaying households—received 5% of the total income of the country, almost $24 million per household. In 1970, this top group received 1% of the total national income with $3.6 million per household.

The increasing divide between the rich and the rest of the people in the United States is well documented, but economists don't agree about the reasons why the richest Americans have become astonishingly more wealthy and why those who are in the bottom 90 percent have lost ground since 1970. The explanations that have been given include the tax cuts of 1986, the decline of labor unions, the downsizing of corporations, the increase in corporate mergers, automation, competition from low-wage nations, and simple greed. Although each of these may be a contributing cause, there must be other causes too.

The **process of elimination method** can be a useful tool when several possible causes are involved. The shift in income to the wealthy started before the tax cuts of 1986, so the tax cuts cannot be the only cause. Low-wage nations now produce cheap exports, but the sectors of the U.S. economy that compete directly with low-wage nations make up a small slice of the total pie (about 2 percent). And it's hard to explain why people might be greedier now than in earlier decades; greed has always been a human trait.

In a book published in 1995 entitled *The Winner-Take-All Society*, Robert H. Frank and Phillip J. Cook argue that changes in attitudes help to account for the shifts in wealth since 1973. In an article summarizing their book, published in *Across the Board* (33:5 [May 1996]: 4), they describe what they mean by the winner-take-all society:

Our claim is that growing income inequality stems from the growing importance of what we call "winner-take-all markets"—markets in which small differences in performance give rise to enormous differences in economic reward. Long familiar in entertainment, sports, and the arts, these markets have increasingly permeated law, journalism, consulting, medicine, investment banking, corporate management, publishing, design, fashion, even the hallowed halls of academe.

An economist under the influence of the human-capital metaphor might ask: Why not save money by hiring two mediocre people to fill an important position instead of paying the exorbitant salary required to attract the best? Although that sort of substitution might work with physical capital, it does not necessarily work with human capital. Two average surgeons or CEOs or novelists or quarterbacks are often a poor substitute for a single gifted one.

The result is that for positions for which additional talent has great value to the employer or the marketplace, there is no reason to expect that the market will compensate individuals in proportion to their human capital. For these positions—ones that confer the greatest leverage or "amplification" of human talent—small increments of talent have great value and may be greatly rewarded as a result of the normal competitive market process. This insight lies at the core of our alternative explanation of growing inequality.

A winner-take-all market is one in which reward depends on relative, not absolute, performance. Whereas a farmer's pay depends on the absolute amount of wheat he produces and not on how that compares with the amounts produced by other farmers, a software developer's pay depends largely on her performance ranking. In the market for personal income-tax software, for instance, the market reaches quick consensus on which among the scores or even hundreds of competing programs is the most comprehensive and user-friendly. And although the best program may be only slightly better than its nearest rival, their developers' incomes may differ a thousandfold.

Frank and Cook find that technology has accelerated the trend toward heaping rewards on those who are judged best in a particular arena. In the 1800s, for example, a top tenor in a major city such as London might have commanded a salary many times above that of other singers, but the impact of the tenor was limited by the fact that only those who could hear him live could appreciate his talent. Today, every tenor in the world competes with Luciano Pavarotti because opera fans everywhere can buy Pavarotti's CDs. This worldwide fan base translates into big money. It's no surprise that Michael Jordan received more money for promoting Nike shoes than the combined annual payrolls for all six factories in Indonesia that made the shoes bearing his name. What is new is how other professions have become more like sports and entertainment.

The Winner-Take-All Society is a model of causal analysis that uses the process of elimination method. The authors

- Describe and document a trend
- Set out the causes that have been previously offered and show why together they are inadequate to explain the trend, and then
- Present a new cause, explaining how the new cause works in concert with those that have been identified

But it's not enough just to identify causes. They must be connected to effects. For trends in progress, such as the growing divide between the rich and the rest in the United States, the effects must be carefully explored to learn about what might lie ahead. Frank and Cook believe that the winner-take-all attitude is detrimental for the nation's future because, like high school basketball players who expect to become the next Kobe Bryant, many people entering college or graduate school grossly overestimate their prospects for huge success and select their future careers accordingly:

> The lure of the top prizes in winner-take-all markets has also steered many of our most able graduates toward career choices that make little sense for them as individuals and still less sense for the nation as a whole. In increasing numbers, our best and brightest graduates pursue top positions in law, finance, consulting, and other overcrowded arenas, in the process forsaking careers in engineering, manufacturing, civil service, teaching, and other occupations in which an infusion of additional talent would yield greater benefit to society.
>
> One study estimated, for example, that whereas a doubling of enrollments in engineering would cause the growth rate of the GDP to rise by half a percentage point, a doubling of enrollments in law would actually cause a decline of three-tenths of a point. Yet the number of new lawyers admitted to the bar each year more than doubled between 1970 and 1990, a period during which the average standardized test scores of new public-school teachers fell dramatically.
>
> One might hope that such imbalances would fade as wages are bid up in underserved markets and driven down in overcrowded ones, and indeed there have been recent indications of a decline in the number of law-school applicants. For two reasons, however, such adjustments are destined to fall short.
>
> The first is an informational problem. An intelligent decision about whether to pit one's own skills against a largely unknown field of adversaries obviously requires a well-informed estimate of the odds of winning. Yet people's assessments about these odds are notoriously inaccurate. Survey evidence shows, for example, that some 80 percent of us think we are better-than-average drivers and that more than 90 percent of workers

consider themselves more productive than their average colleague. Psychologists call this the "Lake Wobegon Effect," and its importance for present purposes is that it leads people to overestimate their odds of landing a superstar position. Indeed, overconfidence is likely to be especially strong in the realm of career choice, because the biggest winners are so conspicuous. The seven-figure NBA stars appear on television several times each week, whereas the many thousands who fail to make the league attract little notice.

The second reason for persistent overcrowding in winner-take-all markets is a structural problem that economists call "the tragedy of the commons." This same problem helps explain why we see too many prospectors for gold. In the initial stages of exploiting a newly discovered field of gold, the presence of additional prospectors may significantly increase the total amount of gold that is found. Beyond some point, however, additional prospectors contribute very little. Thus, the gold found by a newcomer to a crowded gold field is largely gold that would have been found by others.

This short example illustrates why causal arguments for any significant trend that involves people almost necessarily have to be complex. Most people don't quit their day job expecting to hit it big in the movies, the record business, or professional athletics, yet people do select fields such as law that have become in many ways like entertainment, with a few big winners and the rest just getting by. Frank and Cook point to the "Lake Wobegon Effect" (named for Garrison Keillor's fictional town where "all children are above average") to give an explanation of why people are realistic about their chances in some situations and not in others.

Building a Causal Argument

Effective causal arguments move beyond the obvious to get at underlying causes. The immediate cause of the growing income inequality in the United States is that people at the top make a lot more now than they did thirty years ago, while people in the middle make the same and people at the bottom make less. Those changes are obvious to anyone who has looked at the numbers. What isn't obvious is why those changes occurred.

Insightful causal analyses of major trends and events avoid oversimplification by not relying on only one direct cause but instead showing how that cause arises from another cause or works in combination with other causes. Indeed, Frank and Cook have been criticized for placing too much emphasis on the winner-take-all hypothesis.

The great causal mystery today is global warming. Scientists generally agree that the average surface temperature on earth has gone up by one degree Fahrenheit or 0.6 degrees Celsius over the last hundred years and that the amount of carbon dioxide has increased by 25 percent. But the causes of those facts are much disputed. Some people believe that the rise in temperature is a naturally occurring climate variation and that the increase in carbon dioxide is only minimally the cause or not related at all. Others argue that the burning of fossil fuels and the cutting of tropical forests have led to the increase in carbon dioxide, which in turn traps heat, thus increasing the temperature of the earth. The major problem for all participants in the global warming debate is that the causation is not a simple, direct one.

Scientists use powerful computer models to understand the causes and effects of climate change. These models predict that global warming will affect arctic and subarctic regions more dramatically than elsewhere. In Iceland, average summer temperatures have risen by 0.5 to 1.0 degrees Celsius since the early 1980s. All of Iceland's glaciers except a few that surge and ebb independent of weather are now in rapid retreat, a pattern observed throughout regions in the far north. Arctic sea ice shrank by 6 percent from 1978 to 1998, and Greenland's massive ice sheet has been thinning by more than three feet a year. Environmentalists today point to the melting of the glaciers and sea ice as proof that human-caused global warming is taking place.

Scientists, however, are not so certain. Their difficulty is to sort human causes from naturally recurring climate cycles. Much of the detailed data about the Great Melt in the north goes back only to the early 1990s—not long enough to rule out short-term climate cycles. If we are in a regular, short-term warming cycle, then the question becomes how does greenhouse warming interact with that cycle? Computer models suggest there is a very low probability that such rapid change could occur naturally. But the definitive answers to the causes of the Great Melt are probably still a long way off.

Another pitfall common in causal arguments using statistics is mistaking correlation for causation. For example, the FBI reported that criminal victimization rates in the United States in 1995 dropped 13 percent for personal crimes and 12.4 percent for property crimes, the

Glaciers in retreat

largest decreases ever. During that same year, the nation's prison and jail populations reached a record high of 1,085,000 and 507,000 inmates, respectively. The easy inference is that putting more people behind bars lowers the crime rate, but there are plenty of examples to the contrary. The drop in crime rates in the 1990s remains quite difficult to explain. Others have argued that the decline in SAT verbal scores during the late 1960s and 1970s reflected a decline in literacy caused by an increase in television viewing. But the fact that the number of people who took the SAT during the 1970s greatly increased suggests that there was not an actual decline in literacy, only a great expansion in the population who wanted to go to college.

Sample Student Causal Argument

Jennifer May majors in communication disorders and intends to go to graduate school to study speech pathology. She wrote this essay for a composition course at Pennsylvania State University. After the semester in which she wrote it, May studied in Sydney, Australia, where she paraglided, snorkelled, and parasailed her way through the semester.

                                                            May 1

        Jennifer May

        Professor Reynolds

        English 102

        20 April 2002

                    Why Are Teenage Girls Dying to Be Thin?

                Imagine waking up every morning, looking into the

        mirror, and thinking no one loves you because you are

        overweight. Imagine stepping onto a scale, weighing in

        at 80 pounds, and thinking that is too high. Imagine

        staring at the food on your plate, trying to eat and

        thinking about the number of calories in each bite.

        Imagine that this is your life. It is hard to picture a

May 2

life without food, self-confidence, and love. Anorexia,
which commonly affects girls, is a mental disease that
becomes physical and a physical disease that becomes
emotional. What causes a person to slowly kill herself
in an effort to be thin? Are the principal causes nature
(biological) or nurture (environmental)? While there are
many reasons that may lead a girl to become anorexic,
the causes depend on the individual and usually include
a combination of both nature and nurture.

Eating disorders, especially anorexia nervosa,
consume health and body one bite at a time. The American
Academy of Arts and Sciences stated in 1992 that "the
disorder affects 10 out of every 100 American females at
some time in their life" (qtd. in Verdon 158). Anorexia
is characterized by excessive activity or exercise along
with self-starvation, fear of gaining weight, and a
distorted body image (Verdon 160). This disorder usually
affects white adolescent females of normal weight. They
become "15% or more underweight," yet still feel fat and
thus continue to starve (Myers 371). Anorexia is the
relentless pursuit of a perfect body, a constant
struggle to stay thin, and if left untreated, a
life-threatening obsession.

Nurture, the surrounding environment, is a major
influence on anorexia. Nurture involves parents and
family upbringing, social pressures, and cultural
influences. A family can give a child support, love, and
trust; or a family can pressure, reject, and become
detached. Parents or caregivers may exhibit one or all
of these characteristics during the child's upbringing.

May 3

An anorexic person cannot accept the love that a
caregiver may offer and feels only neglect. Parents must
show support, hoping that the feeling of abandonment and
loneliness will vanish.

The pressures surrounding an adolescent each day
are immense and sometimes too difficult for someone with
an eating disorder to handle. In a culture that admires
Barbie doll figures and is infatuated with dieting, it is
difficult not to become self-conscious about your body.
Beautiful women in magazines and on television, singers
with perfect voices, dancers and athletes with gorgeous
bodies, parents who expect straight As, coaches who
believe winning is everything, and peers who say "you're
fat" are all contributors to adolescent stress.

Nature refers to the innate biological aspects of a
person. Along with genetic make-up, nature includes the
personality of an individual. Low self-confidence and
perfectionism are prominent personality traits among
anorexics, who fear failing, getting fat, and letting
people down. Roger Verdon says that many anorexics "are
perfectionists in an imperfect world" (161).
Perfectionists often are high achievers, but they are
never satisfied by their performance.

Feeling that one's life is ruled by others (parents,
media, school) leads to a need for control of something
else. Anorexics become obsessed with numbers on the
scale or if their pants are fitting a little too tight.
It is an ongoing struggle in the mind, a seclusion from
the rest of the world, a battle that is fought alone.
Here is a journal entry from a friend (I'll refer to her

May 4

as "Jessica") who is contemplating whether to tell people
about her illness.

> Everyone will be watching me, noticing,
> thinking, wondering . . . questioning why this
> is happening to me, why I let it happen to me,
> why I don't stop it. People don't realize the
> difficulty involved, the emotional pain, the
> physical risks and consequences, the deep,
> dark truth behind it. Why can't I just be
> normal? Everybody else thinks I am. I am
> living a lie, and I know it. Should I keep it
> this way? How can I impose on other people by
> telling them my problems, making them witness
> it, make them feel obligated to help.

Female athletes, especially gymnasts, are at risk
for anorexia. Training for nine hours a day, eating only
one apple, and getting little sleep leads to anorexia
because the body adapts to deprivation. Christy Hendrich,
champion of the 1989 Gymnastic World Games, was both
anorexic and bulimic. Although the causes are different
for each individual, similar feelings and emotions are
common. Before dying at the weight of sixty pounds,
Hendrich said: "My life is a horrifying nightmare; there
feels like a beast is inside of me" (qtd. in Myers 372).

The effects of anorexia range from short-term
hospitalization to death from malnutrition. Because
anorexia nervosa usually occurs during puberty, a time
when bone growth is crucial, those who suffer from
this disease may have bone fractures and osteoporosis at
a young age from lack of calcium. Reproductive organs

May 5

may not fully develop, so menstrual abnormalities may occur and lead to pregnancy problems later in life. Malnutrition can also lead to brain damage and can affect mood and behavior (Seidenfeld and Rickert 444).

Recovery from anorexia is a long process. Relapses are common, and complete recovery can take years. Jessica says: "Mentally, I'm doing worse; my physical signs are better, but underneath the outer parts, it's doing worse. My body has adjusted to a lower caloric intake, and my metabolism has dropped again regardless of running every day." As much as Jessica wants to be cured, she keeps getting pulled back into this destructive pattern. I've learned from Jessica that anorexia can happen to any young woman, and for even those as aware as she is of what is happening, the pattern is not easy to break.

May 6

Works Cited

"Jessica." Email to the author. 2 Oct. 2001.

Myers, David G. <u>Psychology</u>. New York: Worth, 1998.

Seidenfeld, Margorie, and Vaugh Rickert. "Impact of Anorexia, Bulimia, and Obesity on the Gynecologic Health of Adolescents." <u>American Family Physician</u> 64 (2000): 444-45.

Verdon, Roger. "Mirror, Mirror on the Wall, Who Is the Thinnest of Them All?" <u>Reclaiming Children and Youth</u> 9.3 (2000): 157-61.

Steps in a Causal Argument

Step 1 Make a claim

Make a causal claim on a controversial trend, event, or phenomenon.

Formula

- SOMETHING does (or does not) cause SOMETHING ELSE.
  –or–
- SOMETHING causes SOMETHING ELSE, which, in turn, causes SOMETHING ELSE.

Examples

- One-parent families (or television violence, bad diet, and so on) is (or is not) the cause of emotional and behavioral problems in children.
- Firearms control laws (or right-to-carry-handgun laws) reduce (or increase) violent crimes.
- The trend toward home schooling (or private schools) is (or is not) improving the quality of education.
- The length of U.S. presidential campaigns forces candidates to become too much influenced by big-dollar contributors (or prepares them for the constant media scrutiny that they will endure as president).
- Putting grade school children into competitive sports teaches them how to succeed in later life (or puts undue emphasis on winning and teaches many who are slower to mature to have a negative self-image).

Step 2 What's at stake in your claim?

- If the cause is obvious to everyone, then it probably isn't worth writing about.

Step 3 Think of possible causes

- Which are the immediate causes?
- Which are the background causes?
- Which are the hidden causes?
- Which are the causes that most people have not recognized?

Step **4** Analyze your potential readers

- Who are your readers?
- How familiar will they be with the trend, event, or phenomenon that you're writing about?
- What are they likely to know and not know?
- How likely are they to accept your causal explanation?
- What alternative explanation might they argue for?

Step **5** Write a draft

Introduction
- Describe the controversial trend, event, or phenomenon.
- Give the background that your intended readers will need.

Body
- For a trend, event, or phenomenon that is unfamiliar to your readers, you can explain the cause or chain of causation. Remember that providing facts is not the same thing as establishing causes, although facts can help to support your causal analysis.
- Another way of organizing the body is to set out the causes that have been offered and reject them one by one. Then you can present the cause that you think is most important.
- A third way is to treat a series of causes one by one, analyzing the importance of each.

Conclusion
- Do more than simply summarize. You might consider additional effects beyond those that have been previously noted.

Step **6** Revise, edit, proofread

- For detailed instructions, see Chapter 12.
- For a checklist to use to evaluate your draft, see pages 217–222.

CHAPTER 8

Evaluation Arguments

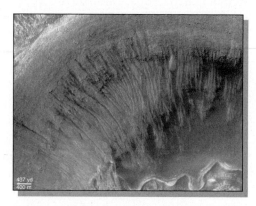

The Mars Orbiter Camera found evidence of water recently on the surface of Mars. Scientists believe that the gullies and finger-like deposits at the base of the wall were formed by flowing water and debris flows.

The solar-powered Field Integrated Design and Operations (FIDO) rover is tested in the Nevada desert to simulate driving conditions on Mars.

Robots have dug in the dirt on Mars, flown in the atmosphere of Jupiter, driven by the moons of Neptune and plopped down on an asteroid. A few are even flirting with the boundary of the solar system. Humans, on the other hand, have been relegated mostly to going in circles, barely above the surface of the planet. . . . Given the danger, the costs and the setbacks, why send humans into space at all?

RICHARD STENGER, CNN.COM, FEBRUARY 18, 2003

Returning to the moon is an important step for our space program. . . . With the experience and knowledge gained on the moon, we will then be ready to take the next steps of space exploration: human missions to Mars and to worlds beyond. . . . Probes, landers and other vehicles of this kind continue to prove their worth, sending spectacular images and vast amounts of data back to Earth. Yet the human thirst for knowledge ultimately cannot be satisfied by even the most vivid pictures or the most detailed measurements. We need to see and examine and touch for ourselves.

PRESIDENT GEORGE W. BUSH, SPEECH, JANUARY 14, 2004

The tragic loss of seven space shuttle astronauts in February 2003 revived a long-running debate over the value of sending humans into space. Humans must carry their environment with them when they venture into space. Robotic probes do not require water, air, and food and can travel for a fraction of the cost. Space shuttle missions typically cost around $500 million, while a satellite can be launched for $20 million. Even unmanned flights to Mars have cost as little as $250 million.

Many people argue that the extra money needed to put people into space would be better spent at home. Furthermore, flights to Mars and beyond would require years, subjecting humans to the risks of solar radiation exposure and prolonged weightlessness, which over months leads to breakdowns of the immune system and bone structure.

Others, however, believe there are reasons besides scientific research for sending people into space. John Logsdon, director of the Space Policy Institute at George Washington University, says, "We do not give parades for robots. There are intangible benefits from human presence in space—national pride, role models for youth—that are real if not measurable."

The debate about sending people into space is an evaluation argument. People make evaluations all the time. Newspapers and magazines have picked up on this love of evaluation by running "best of" polls. They ask their readers what's the best Mexican, Italian, or Chinese restaurant; the best pizza; the best local band; the best coffeehouse; the best dance club; the best neighborhood park; the best swimming hole; the best bike ride (scenic and challenging); the best volleyball court; the best place to get married; and so on. If you ask one of your friends who voted in a "best" poll why she picked a particular restaurant as the best of its kind, she might respond by saying simply, "I like it." But if you ask her why she likes it, she might start offering good reasons such as these: The food is good, the service prompt, the prices fair, and the atmosphere comfortable. It's really not a mystery why these polls are often quite predictable and why the same restaurants tend to win year after year. Many people think that evaluations are matters of personal taste, but when we begin probing the reasons, we often discover that the criteria that different people use to make evaluations have a lot in common.

People opposed to sending humans into space use the criteria of cost and safety. Those who argue for sending people into space use the criteria of expanding human presence and human experience. The key to convincing other people that your judgment is sound is establishing the criteria you will use to make your evaluation. Sometimes it will be necessary to argue for the validity of those criteria that

> Evaluation arguments depend on the criteria you select.

you think your readers should consider. If your readers accept your criteria, it's likely they will agree with your conclusions.

Kinds of Evaluations

Arguments of evaluation are structured much like arguments of definition. Recall that the criteria in arguments of definition are set out in because clauses: *SOMETHING is a_____ because it has these criteria.* In arguments of evaluation the claim takes the form

> SOMETHING is a good (bad, the best, the worst) _____ if measured by these criteria

The key move in writing most evaluative arguments is first deciding what kind of criteria to use.

Imagine that the oldest commercial building in your city is about to be torn down. Your goal is to get the old store converted to a museum, which is a proposal argument. First you will need to make an evaluative argument that will form the basis of your proposal. You might argue that a downtown museum would be much better than more office space because it would draw more visitors. You might argue that the stonework in the building is of excellent quality and deserves preservation. Or you might argue that it is only fair that the oldest commercial building be preserved because the oldest house and other historic buildings have been saved.

Each of these arguments uses different criteria. An argument that a museum is better than an office building because it would bring more visitors to the downtown area is based on **practical criteria**. An argument that the old building is beautiful and that beautiful things should be preserved uses **aesthetic criteria**. An argument that the oldest store building deserves the same treatment as the oldest house is based on fairness, a concept that relies on **ethical criteria**. The debate over the value of sending people versus sending robots into space employs all these criteria but with different emphases. Both those who favor and those who oppose human space travel make practical arguments that much scientific knowledge and many benefits result from space travel. Those who favor sending humans use aesthetic arguments: Space travel is essential to the way we understand ourselves as humans and Americans. Those who oppose sending humans question the ethics of spending so much money for manned space vehicles when there are pressing needs at home and point out that robots can be used for a fraction of the cost. (See Figure 8.1.)

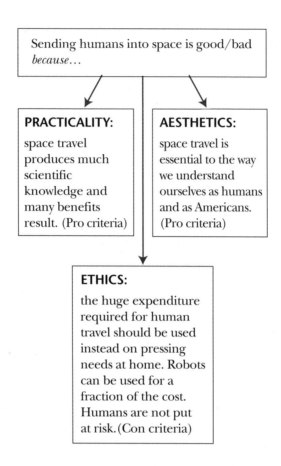

Figure 8.1

WHERE DO CRITERIA COME FROM?

The basic advice of this chapter probably makes sense to you: Making an evaluation argument is essentially a matter of finding appropriate criteria for evaluation and then measuring the topic or issue against those criteria. The criteria are, in effect, the basis for one or more because-clauses that support the overall judgment of the argument. Such-and-such is good *because of x* and *because of y;* or such-and-such is better than something else *because of x* and *because of y.* "Cleveland is a surprisingly good vacation spot *because* there's a lot to do, *because* there's a lot of beauty around Lake Erie, *because* the crowds and prices are reasonable, *and because* there are no friendlier people anywhere." "Despite his failure with the Vietnam War, President Johnson was actually a good president *because* the Civil

WHERE DO CRITERIA COME FROM? *(continued)*

Rights Act of 1964 and Voting Rights Act of 1965 made lasting improvements in American life, *because* Johnson presided with honor during calamitous times, *and because* his War on Poverty was actually a huge success."

But where do you find those criteria?

Traditionally evaluative criteria emerge from three sources: practicality, aesthetics, and ethics. Things are usually judged as good (or not so good) either because they work well (practicality), because they are beautiful (aesthetics), or because they are fair or morally just (ethics). All three of these sources of criteria may not appear in every evaluative argument, but one of them certainly will—and often all three will show up.

Practicality means that the thing being evaluated works efficiently or leads to good outcomes: Things are seen as good if they improve conditions, work well, are cost effective, and so forth. *Aesthetics* refers to beauty, but it also has to do with matters often associated with beauty, such as image and tradition. *Ethics* has to do with moral rightness, with legality or constitutionality, with fair play and human decency: Things are rarely evaluated positively if there are ethical improprieties to worry about.

Try out those sources of criteria on a few simple examples. Are you evaluating a consumer product, like a pair of skis, before you buy them? Of course you'll consider how well they work and fit and how much they cost; but you will also consider whether they are good looking and perhaps what image they project. And before you buy you will probably think about ethical issues as well. Were the skis manufactured in a sweatshop of some kind, for example? Does the store selling them have a good reputation? Or maybe you are evaluating various study-abroad programs to support your major in Spanish. Of course you will consider the quality of the educational experience (where will you learn the most?), cost, safety, and other practical matters; but you will also think about how beautiful or interesting the possible locations are as well as ethical issues such as the kind of government that is in place in the country or how the institution treats students.

Or maybe you are evaluating a public policy of some kind. A new gun control measure proposed for a certain community, for example, will have to be measured against its cost, enforceability, and effectiveness, of course. But you will also have to consider legal and constitutional issues—and even aesthetic considerations (such as what kind of community you wish to project your community to be, or what kind of traditions your community stands for). Or recall how you chose the college or university you attended: You evaluated it according to the quality of education it offered, according to cost, and according to other practical considerations (e.g., dorm quality, the availability of work opportunities), but you

(continued)

WHERE DO CRITERIA COME FROM? *(continued)*

also thought about other, less practical matters: Does it offer an aesthetically pleasing environment? Does it project a respected image? Does it have a tradition of encouraging certain values? Is it respected as an institution that is fair and honorable? Colleges and universities generally enjoy good reputations, so fairness and morality do not often show up in discussions of the relative merits of colleges; but if a college or university does something to compromise its reputation— because its sports teams are caught up in sports recruiting scandals, for example, or because it misuses research funds or is involved in a discrimination suit—its quality is perceived to be profoundly affected.

Or even take the example of a movie or book or musician. Typically those things are evaluated according to aesthetic merit, and evaluations of those things will therefore depend on aesthetic criteria like the ones celebrated in the Academy Awards or Grammy Awards shows: cinematography, acting, writing, direction, musical quality. And yet it is also true that movies, music, and other forms of entertainment are also evaluated on moral grounds. Look at the arguments that erupt daily over the work of Britney Spears or Eminem, for example. When a movie or song is truly controversial, as in the case of the recent movie by Mel Gibson, *The Passion of the Christ*, you can be sure that discussions about it will be based on aesthetics (e.g., was the torture of Christ in the movie too prolonged for it to be considered beautiful? was the acting inspirational or overly melodramatic?), on morality (e.g., is the movie anti-Semitic? does it promote values that run contrary to post–Vatican II Catholic values? is it sadistic?), and on pragmatics (e.g., will the movie inspire imitations? will it encourage church attendance, increase devotionalism, and renew Christian faith? is it really true to the Gospel accounts?).

Later in this chapter you will find a sample evaluative essay that considers an institutional policy: the quality of a university's health care plan. Examine it carefully to see whether it bases its evaluation on all three sources of criteria— practicality, aesthetics, and ethics—or whether it depends on one or two of them. Does it look at the health plan only as a question of practicality (e.g., affordability and effectiveness), or does it bring ethics and even aesthetics into the argument? Are certain criteria missing—and if they are, does that matter?

Building an Evaluation Argument

Most people have a lot of practice making consumer evaluations, and when they have enough time to do their homework, they usually make an informed decision. But sometimes, criteria for evaluations are not so obvious, and evaluations are much more difficult to make. Sometimes, one set of criteria favors one choice, while another set of criteria favors another. You might have encountered this problem when you chose a college. If you were able to leave home to go to school, you had a potential choice of over 1,400 accredited colleges and universities. Until twenty years ago, there wasn't much information about choosing a college other than what colleges said about themselves. You could find out the price of tuition and what courses were offered, but it was hard to compare one college with another.

In 1983 the magazine *U.S. News & World Report* began ranking U.S. colleges and universities from a consumer's perspective. Those rankings have remained highly controversial ever since. Many college officials have attacked the criteria that *U.S. News* uses to make its evaluations. In an August 1998 *U.S. News* article, Gerhard Casper, the president of Stanford University (which is consistently near the top of the rankings), says, "Much about these rankings—particularly their specious formulas and spurious precision—is utterly misleading." Casper argues that using graduation rates as a criterion of quality rewards easy schools. Other college presidents have called for a national boycott of the *U.S. News* rankings (without much success).

U.S. News replies in its defense that colleges and universities themselves do a lot of ranking, beginning with ranking students for admissions, using their SAT or ACT scores, high school GPA, ranking in high school class, quality of high school, and other factors, and then grading the students and ranking them against each other when they are enrolled in college. Furthermore, schools also evaluate faculty members and take great interest in the national ranking of their departments. They care very much about where they stand in relation to each other. Why, then, *U.S. News* argues, shouldn't people be able to evaluate colleges and universities, since colleges and universities are so much in the business of evaluating people?

Arguing for the right to evaluate colleges and universities is one thing; actually doing comprehensive and reliable evaluations is quite another. *U.S. News* uses a formula in which 25 percent of a school's ranking is based on a survey of reputation in which the president, provost, and dean of admissions at each college rate the quality of schools in the same category, and the remaining 75 percent is based on statistical criteria of quality. These statistical criteria fall into six major categories: retention of students, faculty resources, student selectivity, financial resources, alumni giving, and (for national universities and liberal arts colleges only) "graduation rate performance," the difference between the proportion of students who are expected to graduate and the proportion that actually do. These major categories are made up of factors that are weighted for their importance. For example, the faculty resources category is determined by the size of classes (the proportion of classes with fewer than twenty students and the proportion of classes with fifty or more students), the average faculty pay weighted by the cost of living in different regions of the country, the percentage of professors with the highest degree in their field, the overall student-faculty ratio, and the percentage of faculty who are full time.

Those who have challenged the *U.S. News* rankings argue that the magazine should use different criteria or weight the criteria differently. *U.S. News* answers those charges on its Web site (http://www.usnews.com/usnews/edu/college/corank.htm) by claiming that it has followed a trend toward emphasizing outcomes such as graduation rates. If you are curious about where your school ranks, take a look at the *U.S. News* Web site.

Sample Student Evaluation Argument

Houston native DeMarcus Taylor wrote "An Unhealthy Practice" in his first-year composition course at the University of Texas at Austin. DeMarcus is a government major who intends to go to law school. He is a member of the Beta Alpha Rho Pre-Law fraternity and loves to play volleyball.

```
                                                Taylor 1

     DeMarcus Taylor

     Professor Kim

     RHE 306

     9 March 2004

                    An Unhealthy Practice

          Let me tell you a story. During my second semester

     at the University of Texas, I began having headaches.

     Taking Tylenol helped, but the headaches returned. So I

     made an appointment with one of the doctors at

     University Health Services. This facility provides fully

     certified doctors and nurses for students as part of

     mandatory fees that are tacked on to each semester's
```

Taylor 2

tuition bill. (As it stands, the university charges students approximately sixty dollars each semester for what it dubs a "medical services fee.") The doctor told me that the headaches could be caused by many different things and recommended that I get an MRI to rule out any serious physical problems. I soon found out that that it stands for Magnetic Resonance Imaging and that I would have to go off campus to a radiology facility to have the procedure done. I had the MRI and the results brought a sigh of relief—no brain tumor. To my surprise, however, I then received a bill for $1,642 that my student medical plan did not cover. I called the accounting office and was told that I had to have purchased additional coverage to pay for the MRI. I had improperly assumed that my medical fees would cover any procedures directly ordered by the health center. In fact, these fees only cover minor treatment and office visits, though the specifics are quite vague and answers are hard to find.

Inconsistent with other university policies, detrimental to students' academic growth, and a threat to parents' and students' well-being, the current university policy for medical services falls short of being efficient, effective, or educational. Overall, UT has established an admirable tradition of providing—free of charge—various programs and services to aid students in expanding their minds within and beyond the classroom and coping with the challenges of college life. As the university fosters an image of paternal compassion and

Taylor 3

concern, programs such as Freshman Interest Groups (FIGs) and Achieving College Excellence (ACE) strive to provide new and at-risk students with tools helpful in reaching their academic and social goals. Similarly, academic services such as the Undergraduate Writing Center help students augment their in-class learning and bolster their writing skills, while the Counseling and Mental Health Center provides students with onsite psychiatrists and psychologists. A student will never receive a surprise bill for two hours of help on a writing assignment for Introduction to Biology or two sessions of counseling for depression. Sessions are either totally free or limits are clearly articulated through staff interaction or program literature. These types of offerings stand as a symbol of a university that cares about its enrollees as people, not just tuition payers.

In contrast, the current medical services plan keeps students in the dark. Aside from my personal experience with the unexpected MRI charge, I have heard other students discussing issues such as nurses, doctors, and administrators ordering laboratory tests and directly stating that they did not know if the student would owe any additional fees. Even if students do carefully read the university Web site and talk to representatives, he or she has no guarantee that either source will provide an accurate answer to questions. All in all, the school's health services protocol fails to encourage its students to excel in the university's main goal: learning.

Taylor 4

In addition to being at odds with the university's other policies and programs, the current medical services plan places students, parents, and the university at risk of suffering various levels of economic and educational hardships. Though my family was able to pull together funds to pay the MRI charge, incurring exorbitant and unexpected health costs could force and has forced students to drop out of school altogether. Many students (and often those who are targeted for special programs) come from lower socio-economic backgrounds and would be hard-pressed to cover surprise medical bills. Very possibly, many of these same students come from one of the millions of American families who are lacking employer- or personally funded family health insurance. For these two reasons, a non-communicative staff and unclear billing policies could result in students dropping out of the university because money saved for tuition and fees must be used to pay medical bills. One unexpected MRI bill could devastate a family. Is it fair for these students to have to risk their educations and futures because of an inefficient and ineffectively articulated policy? Moreover, this policy can result not only in students suffering as they are forced to give up their educational dreams, but can also cause the university to forfeit the tuition and other revenue it would be earning from continuing students. While this may seem like small change to such a big school, when coupled with the poor public image this policy produces, the stakes are high.

Taylor 5

Finally and on the most human and practical of levels, the current policy puts each individual student's health at risk. Bitten once by expensive fees or afraid of the unknowns attached to a vague system and an evasive staff, students may simply forego treatment. On their own for the first time, uninformed about medical costs, anxious about the university policy, and lacking personal insurance, some students may simply ignore health problems, resulting in poor attendance records, undiagnosed severe medical problems, or even the spread of contagions throughout the university community.

As young adults leave their homes to begin forging their own futures at UT, the university must be accountable for the physical—not just mental and educational—well being of the fifty-thousand plus students in its charge. The current health care policy of the University of Texas at Austin highlights its size and lack of intimacy and diminishes its ongoing attempts to welcome and cultivate the young minds and bodies of a culturally, ethnically, and economically diverse student body. By tweaking its procedures and training its staff, the university could convert its lackluster health services program into one which protects students and families, encourages the learning of life skills, and presents UT as an organization that seeks to go beyond the role of educator to one of overall mentor. As it currently stands, the program falls short on all counts.

Steps to Evaluation Argument

Step 1 Make a claim

Make an evaluative claim based on criteria.

Formula

- SOMETHING is good (bad, the best, the worst) ___ if measured by certain criteria (practicality, aesthetics, ethics).

Examples

- Write a book review or a movie review.
- Write a defense of a particular kind of music or art.
- Evaluate a controversial aspect of sports (e.g., the current system of determining who is champion in Division I college football by a system of bowls and polls) or evaluate a sports event (e.g., this year's WNBA playoffs) or a team.
- Evaluate the effectiveness of an educational program (such as your high school honors program or your college's core curriculum requirement) or some other aspect of your campus.
- Evaluate the effectiveness of a social policy or law such as legislating 21 as the legal drinking age, current gun control laws, or environmental regulation.

Step 2 Think about what's at stake

- Would nearly everyone agree with you? Then your claim probably isn't interesting or important. If you can think of people who would disagree, then something is at stake.
- Who argues the opposite of your claim?
- Why do they make a different evaluation?

Step 3 List the criteria

- Which criteria make something either good or bad?
- Which criteria are the most important?
- Which are fairly obvious and which will you have to argue for?

Step 4 Analyze your potential readers

- Who are your readers?
- How familiar will they be with what you are evaluating?
- What are they likely to know and not know?
- Which criteria are they most likely to accept with little explanation, and which will they disagree with?

Step 5 Write a draft

Introduction

- Introduce the person, group, institution, event, or object that you are going to evaluate. You might want to announce your stance at this point or wait until the concluding section.
- Give the background that your intended readers will need.

Body

- Describe each criterion and then analyze how well what you are evaluating meets that criterion.
- If you are making an evaluation according to the effects someone or something produces, describe each effect in detail.
- Anticipate where readers might question either your criteria or how they apply to your subject.
- Address opposing viewpoints by acknowledging how their evaluations might differ and by showing why your definition is better.

Conclusion

- If you have not yet announced your stance, then you can conclude that, on the basis of the criteria you set out or the effects you have analyzed, something is good (bad, best, worst).
- If you have made your stance clear from the beginning, then you can end with a compelling example or analogy.

Step 6 Revise, edit, proofread

- For detailed instructions, see Chapter 12.
- For a checklist to use to evaluate your draft, see pages 217–222.

CHAPTER 9

Narrative Arguments

In the months leading up to the second war against Iraq, which began on March 20, 2003, the United States and its allies enforced "no-fly" zones in northern and southern Iraq by increasing the number of surveillance flights. Occasionally, Iraqis shot at Coalition planes, which led to bombings of anti-aircraft sites. In October 2002, Coalition planes began dropping hundreds of thousands of propaganda leaflets on Iraqi military bases depicting what would happen if Iraqi soldiers shot at Coalition planes. (Notice that the "If" panel is on the right because Arabic is read from right to left.)

In 1980, 53,172 people were killed in traffic accidents in the United States, and over half the deaths involved alcohol. Americans had become accustomed to losing around 25,000 to 30,000 people every year to drunk drivers. But it was the tragic death in 1980 of Cari Lightner, a 13-year-old California girl who was killed by a hit-and-run drunk driver while walking along a city street, that made people start asking whether this carnage could be prevented. The driver had been out on bail only two days for another hit-and-run drunk driving crash, and he had three previous drunk driving arrests. He was allowed to plea-bargain for killing Cari and avoided going to prison. Cari's mother, Candy Lightner, was outraged that so little was being done to prevent needless deaths and injuries. She and a small group of other women founded Mothers Against Drunk Driving (MADD) with the goals of getting tougher laws against drunk driving, stiffer penalties for those who kill and injure while driving drunk, and greater public awareness of the seriousness of driving drunk.

Cari Lightner's story aroused to action other people who had been injured themselves or lost loved ones to drunk drivers. Chapters of MADD spread quickly across the country, and it has become one of the most effective citizen groups ever formed, succeeding in getting much new legislation against drunk driving on the books. These laws and changing attitudes about drunk driving have had a significant impact. The National Highway Traffic Safety Administration reported that in 2002, 17,419 people were killed in alcohol-related traffic accidents in the United States compared to 24,045 in 1986, a 30 percent reduction.

The success of MADD points to why arguing by narrating succeeds sometimes when other kinds of arguments have little effect. The story of Cari Lightner appealed to shared community values in ways that statistics did not. The story vividly illustrated that something was very wrong with the criminal justice system if a repeat drunk driver was allowed to run down and kill a child on a sidewalk only days after committing a similar crime.

> Like visual arguments, narrative arguments invite the audience to co-create the claims and links.

Martin Luther King, Jr., was another master of using narratives to make his points. In "Letter from Birmingham Jail," he relates in one sentence the disappointment of his 6-year-old daughter when he had to explain to her why, because of the color of her skin, she could not go to an amusement park in Atlanta advertised on television. This tiny story vividly illustrates the pettiness of segregation laws and their effect on children.

Kinds of Narrative Arguments

Using narratives for advocating change is nothing new. As far back as we have records, we find people telling stories and singing songs about their own lives that argue for change. Folk songs have always given voice to political protest and have celebrated marginalized people. When workers in the United States began to organize in the 1880s, they adapted melodies that soldiers had sung in the Civil War. In the 1930s, performers and songwriters such as Paul Robeson, Woody Guthrie, Huddie Ledbetter (Leadbelly), and Aunt Molly Jackson relied on traditions of hymns, folk songs, and African American blues to

Folk singer/songwriter Shawn Colvin is one of many contemporary folk and blues singers who continue the tradition of making narrative arguments in their songs.

protest social conditions. In the midst of the politically quiet 1950s, folk songs told stories that critiqued social conformity and the dangers of nuclear war. In the 1960s, the civil rights movement and the movement against the Vietnam War brought a strong resurgence of folk music. The history of folk music is a continuous recycling of old tunes, verses, and narratives to engage new political situations. What can be said for folk songs is also true for any popular narrative genre, be it the short story, novel, drama, movies, or even rap music.

Narrative arguments work in a way different from those that spell out their criteria and argue for explicit links. A narrative argument succeeds if the experience being described invokes the life experiences of the readers. Anyone who has ever been around children knows that most kids love amusement parks. Martin Luther King, Jr., did not have to explain to his readers why going to an amusement park advertised on television was so important for his daughter. Likewise, the story of Cari Lightner was effective because even if you have not known someone who was killed by a drunk driver, most people have known someone who died tragically and perhaps needlessly. Furthermore, you often read about and see on television many people who die in traffic accidents. Narrative arguments allow readers to fill in the conclusion. In the cases of King's arguments against segregation laws and MADD's campaign against drunk drivers, that's exactly what happened. Public outcry led to changes in laws and public opinion.

Narrative arguments can be representative anecdotes, as we have seen with the examples from MADD and Martin Luther King, Jr., or they can be longer accounts of particular events that express larger ideas. One such story is George Orwell's account of a hanging in Burma (the country that is now known as Myanmar) while he was a colonial administrator in the late 1920s. In "A Hanging," first published in 1931, Orwell narrates an execution of a nameless prisoner who was convicted of a nameless crime. Everyone quietly and dispassionately performs their jobs—the prison guards, the hangman, the superintendent, and even the prisoner, who offers no resistance when he is bound and led to the gallows. All is totally routine until a very small incident makes Orwell aware of what is happening:

> It was about forty yards to the gallows. I watched the bare brown back of the prisoner marching in front of me. He walked clumsily with his bound arms, but quite steadily, with that bobbing gait of the Indian who never straightens his knees. At each step his muscles slid neatly into place, the lock of hair on his scalp danced up and down, his feet printed themselves on the wet gravel. And once, in spite of the men who gripped him by each shoulder, he stepped lightly aside to avoid a puddle on the path.
>
> It is curious; but till that moment I had never realized what it means to destroy a healthy, conscious man. When I saw the prisoner step aside to avoid the puddle, I saw the mystery, the unspeakable wrongness, of cutting a life short when it is in full tide. This man was not dying, he was alive just as we are alive. All the organs of his body were working—bowels digesting food, skin renewing itself, nails growing, tissues forming—all toiling away in solemn foolery. His nails would still be growing when he stood on the drop, when he was falling through the air with a tenth-of-a-second to live. His eyes saw the yellow gravel and gray walls, and his brain still remembered, foresaw, reasoned—even about puddles. He and we were a party of men walking together, seeing, hearing, feeling, understanding the same world; and in two minutes, with a sudden snap, one of us would be gone—one mind less, one world less.

Orwell's narrative leads to a dramatic moment of recognition, which gives this story its lasting power.

Building a Narrative Argument

The biggest problem with narrative arguments is that anyone can tell a story. On the one hand, there are compelling stories that argue against capital punishment. For example, a mentally retarded man who was executed in Arkansas had refused a piece of pie at his last meal, telling the guards that he wanted to save the pie for later. On the other hand, there are also many stories about the victims of murder and other crimes. Many families have Web sites on which they call for killing those responsible for murdering their loved ones. They too have compelling stories to tell.

Violent deaths of all kinds make for especially vivid narrative arguments. In the late 1990s, there were several incidents in which schoolchildren used guns taken from the family home to kill other students. Stories of these tragedies provided strong arguments for gun control. Gun rights organizations, including the National Rifle Association (NRA), attempted to counter these stories by claiming that they are not truly representative. The NRA claims that between sixty million and sixty-five million Americans own guns and thirty million to thirty-five million own handguns. They argue that more than 99.8 percent of all guns and 99.6 percent of handguns will not be used to commit crimes in any given year. Thus, the NRA argues that narratives of tragic gun deaths are either not representative or the result of allowing too many criminals to avoid prison or execution.

There are two keys to making effective narrative arguments: establishing credibility and establishing representativeness. It's easy enough to make up stories that suit the point you want to make. Writing from personal experience can give you a great deal of impact, but that impact vanishes if your readers doubt that you are telling the truth. Second, the story you tell may be true enough, but the question remains how representative the incident is. We don't ban bananas because someone once slipped on a banana peel. Narratives are often useful for illustrating how people are affected by particular issues or events, but narrative arguments are more effective if you have more evidence than just one incident. The death of Cari Lightner was a tragedy, but the deaths of over 25,000 people a year caused by drunk drivers made Cari Lightner's death representative of a national tragedy, a slaughter that could be prevented. Cari Lightner's tragic story had power because people understood it to be representative of a much larger problem.

LESLIE MARMON SILKO

The Border Patrol State

Leslie Marmon Silko (1948–) was born in Albuquerque and graduated from the University of New Mexico. She now teaches at the University of Arizona. She has received much critical acclaim for her writings about Native Americans. Her first novel, Ceremony *(1977), describes the struggles of a veteran returning home after World War II to civilian life on a New Mexico reservation. Her incorporation of Indian storytelling techniques in* Ceremony *drew strong praise. One critic called her "the most accomplished Indian writer of her generation." She has since published two more novels,* Almanac of the Dead *(1991) and* Gardens in the Dunes *(1999); a collection of essays,* Yellow Woman and a Beauty of the Spirit: Essays on Native American Life Today *(1996); two volumes of poems and stories; and many shorter works. Silko's talents as a storyteller are evident in this essay, which first appeared in the magazine* Nation *in 1994.*

1   I used to travel the highways of New Mexico and Arizona with a wonderful sensation of absolute freedom as I cruised down the open road and across the vast desert plateaus. On the Laguna Pueblo reservation, where I was raised, the people were patriotic despite the way the U.S. government had treated Native Americans. As proud citizens, we grew up believing the freedom to travel was our inalienable right, a right that some Native Americans had been denied in the early twentieth century. Our cousin, old Bill Pratt, used to ride his horse 300 miles overland from Laguna, New Mexico, to Prescott, Arizona, every summer to work as a fire lookout.

2   In school in the 1950s, we were taught that our right to travel from state to state without special papers or threat of detainment was a right that citizens under communist and totalitarian governments did not possess. That wide open highway told us we were U.S. citizens; we were free. . . .

3   Not so long ago, my companion Gus and I were driving south from Albuquerque, returning to Tucson after a book promotion for the paperback edition of my novel *Almanac of the Dead*. I had settled back and gone to sleep while Gus drove, but I was awakened when I felt the car slowing to a stop. It was nearly midnight on New Mexico State Road 26, a dark, lonely stretch of two-lane highway between Hatch and Deming. When I sat up, I saw the headlights and emergency flashers of six vehicles— Border Patrol cars and a van were blocking both lanes of the highway. Gus stopped the car and rolled down the window to ask what was wrong. But the closest Border Patrolman and his companion did not reply; instead, the first agent ordered us to "step out of the car." Gus asked why,

but his question seemed to set them off. Two more Border Patrol agents immediately approached our car, and one of them snapped, "Are you looking for trouble?" as if he would relish it.

4   I will never forget that night beside the highway. There was an awful feeling of menace and violence straining to break loose. It was clear that the uniformed men would be only too happy to drag us out of the car if we did not speedily comply with their request (asking a question is tantamount to resistance, it seems). So we stepped out of the car and they motioned for us to stand on the shoulder of the road. The night was very dark, and no other traffic had come down the road since we had been stopped. All I could think about was a book I had read—*Nunca Mas*—the official report of a human rights commission that investigated and certified more than 12,000 "disappearances" during Argentina's "dirty war" in the late 1970s.

5   The weird anger of these Border Patrolmen made me think about descriptions in the report of Argentine police and military officers who became addicted to interrogation, torture and the murder that followed. When the military and police ran out of political suspects to torture and kill, they resorted to the random abduction of citizens off the streets. I thought how easy it would be for the Border Patrol to shoot us and leave our bodies and car beside the highway, like so many bodies found in these parts and ascribed to "drug runners."

6   Two other Border Patrolmen stood by the white van. The one who had asked if we were looking for trouble ordered his partner to "get the dog," and from the back of the van another patrolman brought a small female German shepherd on a leash. The dog apparently did not heel well enough to suit him, and the handler jerked the leash. They opened the doors of our car and pulled the dog's head into it, but I saw immediately from the expression in her eyes that the dog hated them, and that she would not serve them. When she showed no interest in the inside of the car, they brought her around back to the trunk, near where we were standing. They half-dragged her up into the trunk, but still she did not indicate any stowed-away human beings or illegal drugs.

7   The mood got uglier; the officers seemed outraged that the dog could not find any contraband, and they dragged her over to us and commanded her to sniff our legs and feet. To my relief, the strange violence the Border Patrol agents had focused on us now seemed shifted to the dog. I no longer felt so strongly that we would be murdered. We exchanged looks—the dog and I. She was afraid of what they might do, just as I was. The dog's handler jerked the leash sharply as she sniffed us, as if to make her perform better, but the dog refused to accuse us: She had an innate dignity that did not permit her to serve the murderous impulses of those men. I can't forget the expression in the dog's eyes; it was as if she were embarrassed to be associated with them. I had a small amount of medicinal marijuana in

my purse that night, but she refused to expose me. I am not partial to dogs, but I will always remember the small German shepherd that night.

8   Unfortunately, what happened to me is an everyday occurrence here now. Since the 1980s, on top of greatly expanding border checkpoints, the Immigration and Naturalization Service and the Border Patrol have implemented policies that interfere with the rights of U.S. citizens to travel freely within our borders. I.N.S. agents now patrol all interstate highways and roads that lead to or from the U.S.-Mexico border in Texas, New Mexico, Arizona and California. Now, when you drive east from Tucson on Interstate 10 toward El Paso, you encounter an I.N.S. check station outside Las Cruces, New Mexico. When you drive north from Las Cruces up Interstate 25, two miles north of the town of Truth or Consequences, the highway is blocked with orange emergency barriers, and all traffic is diverted into a two-lane Border Patrol checkpoint—ninety-five miles north of the U.S.-Mexico border.

9   I was detained once at Truth or Consequences, despite my and my companion's Arizona driver's licenses. Two men, both Chicanos, were detained at the same time, despite the fact that they too presented ID and spoke English without the thick Texas accents of the Border Patrol agents. While we were stopped, we watched as other vehicles—whose occupants were white—were waved through the checkpoint. White people traveling with brown people, however, can expect to be stopped on suspicion they work with the sanctuary movement, which shelters refugees. White people who appear to be clergy, those who wear ethnic clothing or jewelry and women with very long hair or very short hair (they could be nuns) are also frequently detained; white men with beards or men with long hair are likely to be detained, too, because Border Patrol agents have "profiles" of "those sorts" of white people who may help political refugees. (Most of the political refugees from Guatemala and El Salvador are Native American or mestizo because the indigenous people of the Americas have continued to resist efforts by invaders to displace them from their ancestral lands.) Alleged increases in illegal immigration by people of Asian ancestry mean that the Border Patrol now routinely detains anyone who appears to be Asian or part Asian, as well.

10   Once your car is diverted from the Interstate Highway into the checkpoint area, you are under the control of the Border Patrol, which in practical terms exercises a power that no highway patrol or city patrolman possesses: They are willing to detain anyone, for no apparent reason. Other law-enforcement officers need a shred of probable cause in order to detain someone. On the books, so does the Border Patrol; but on the road, it's another matter. They'll order you to stop your car and step out; then they'll ask you to open the trunk. If you ask why or request a search warrant, you'll be told that they'll have to have a dog sniff the car before they can request a search warrant, and the dog might not get there

for two or three hours. The search warrant might require an hour or two past that. They make it clear that if you force them to obtain a search warrant for the car, they will make you submit to a strip search as well.

11   Traveling in the open, though, the sense of violation can be even worse. Never mind high-profile cases like that of former Border Patrol agent Michael Elmer, acquitted of murder by claiming self-defense, despite admitting that as an officer he shot an "illegal" immigrant in the back and then hid the body, which remained undiscovered until another Border Patrolman reported the event. (Last month, Elmer was convicted of reckless endangerment in a separate incident, for shooting at least ten rounds from his M-16 too close to a group of immigrants as they were crossing illegally into Nogales in March 1992.) Or that in El Paso a high school football coach driving a vanload of players in full uniform was pulled over on the freeway and a Border Patrol agent put a cocked revolver to his head. (The football coach was Mexican-American, as were most of the players in his van; the incident eventually caused a federal judge to issue a restraining order against the Border Patrol.) We've a mountain of personal experiences like that which never make the newspapers. A history professor at U.C.L.A. told me she had been traveling by train from Los Angeles to Albuquerque twice a month doing research. On each of her trips, she had noticed that the Border Patrol agents were at the station in Albuquerque scrutinizing the passengers. Since she is six feet tall and of Irish and German ancestry, she was not particularly concerned. Then one day when she stepped off the train in Albuquerque, two Border Patrolmen accosted her, wanting to know what she was doing, and why she was traveling between Los Angeles and Albuquerque twice a month. She presented identification and an explanation deemed "suitable" by the agents, and was allowed to go about her business.

12   Just the other day, I mentioned to a friend that I was writing this article and he told me about his 73-year-old father, who is half Chinese and who had set out alone by car from Tucson to Albuquerque the week before. His father had become confused by road construction and missed a turnoff from Interstate 10 to Interstate 25; when he turned around and circled back, he missed the turnoff a second time. But when he looped back for yet another try, Border Patrol agents stopped him and forced him to open his trunk. After they satisfied themselves that he was not smuggling Chinese immigrants, they sent him on his way. He was so rattled by the event that he had to be driven home by his daughter.

13   This is the police state that has developed in the southwestern United States since the 1980s. No person, no citizen, is free to travel without the scrutiny of the Border Patrol. In the city of South Tucson, where 80 percent of the respondents were Chicano or Mexicano, a joint research project by the University of Wisconsin and the University of Arizona recently concluded that one out of every five people there had

been detained, mistreated verbally or nonverbally, or questioned by
I.N.S. agents in the past two years.

14   Manifest Destiny may lack its old grandeur of theft and blood—
"lock the door" is what it means now, with racism a trump card to be
played again and again, shamelessly, by both major political parties.
"Immigration," like "street crime" and "welfare fraud," is a political
euphemism that refers to people of color. Politicians and media people
talk about "illegal aliens" to dehumanize and demonize undocumented
immigrants, who are for the most part people of color. Even in the days
of Spanish and Mexican rule, no attempts were made to interfere with
the flow of people and goods from south to north and north to south. It
is the U.S. government that has continually attempted to sever contact
between the tribal people north of the border and those to the south.[1]

15   Now that the "Iron Curtain" is gone, it is ironic that the U.S. government and its Border Patrol are constructing a steel wall ten feet high
to span sections of the border with Mexico. While politicians and multi-
national corporations extol the virtues of NAFTA and "free trade"
(in goods, not flesh), the ominous curtain is already up in a six-mile section at the border crossing at Mexicali; two miles are being erected but
are not yet finished at Naco; and at Nogales, sixty miles south of Tucson,
the steel wall has been all rubber-stamped and awaits construction likely
to begin in March. Like the pathetic multimillion-dollar "antidrug" border surveillance balloons that were continually deflated by high winds
and made only a couple of meager interceptions before they blew away,
the fence along the border is a theatrical prop, a bit of pork for contrac-
tors. Border entrepreneurs have already used blowtorches to cut passageways through the fence to collect "tolls," and are doing a brisk business.
Back in Washington, the I.N.S. announces a $300 million computer con-
tract to modernize its record-keeping and Congress passes a crime bill
that shunts $255 million to the I.N.S. for 1995, $181 million earmarked
for border control, which is to include 700 new partners for the men who
stopped Gus and me in our travels, and the history professor, and my
friend's father, and as many as they could from South Tucson.

16   It is no use; borders haven't worked, and they won't work, not now,
as the indigenous people of the Americas reassert their kinship and solidarity with one another. A mass migration is already under way; its roots
are not simply economic. The Uto-Aztecan languages are spoken as far
north as Taos Pueblo near the Colorado border, all the way south to Mexico
City. Before the arrival of the Europeans, the indigenous communities
throughout this region not only conducted commerce, the people shared

[1]The Treaty of Guadalupe Hidalgo, signed in 1848, recognizes the right of Tohano O'Odom
(Papago) people to move freely across the U.S.-Mexico border without documents. A treaty
with Canada guarantees similar rights to those of the Iroquois nation in traversing the U.S.-
Canada border. [Author's note]

cosmologies, and oral narratives about the Maize Mothers, the Twin Brothers and their Grandmother, Spider Woman, as well as Quetzalcoatl the benevolent snake. The great human migration within the Americas cannot be stopped; human beings are natural forces of the Earth, just as rivers and winds are natural forces.

17   Deep down the issue is simple: The so-called "Indian Wars" from the days of Sitting Bull and Red Cloud have never really ended in the Americas. The Indian people of southern Mexico, of Guatemala and those left in El Salvador, too, are still fighting for their lives and for their land against the "cavalry" patrols sent out by the governments of those lands. The Americas are Indian country, and the "Indian problem" is not about to go away.

18   One evening at sundown, we were stopped in traffic at a railroad crossing in downtown Tucson while a freight train passed us, slowly gaining speed as it headed north to Phoenix. In the twilight I saw the most amazing sight: Dozens of human beings, mostly young men, were riding the train; everywhere, on flat cars, inside open boxcars, perched on top of boxcars, hanging off ladders on tank cars and between boxcars. I couldn't count fast enough, but I saw fifty or sixty people headed north. They were dark young men, Indian and mestizo; they were smiling and a few of them waved at us in our cars. I was reminded of the ancient story of Aztlán, told by the Aztecs but known in other Uto-Aztecan communities as well. Aztlán is the beautiful land to the north, the origin place of the Aztec people. I don't remember how or why the people left Aztlán to journey farther south, but the old story says that one day, they will return. ∎

Steps to a Narrative Argument

Step 1 Identify an experience that makes an implicit argument

Think about experiences that made you realize that something is wrong or that things need to be changed. The experience does not have to be one that leads to a moral lesson at the end, but it should be one that makes your readers think.

Examples

- Being arrested and hauled to jail for carrying a glass soft drink bottle in a glass-free zone made you realize how inefficiently your police force is being used.
- After going through a complicated system of getting referrals for a serious medical condition and then having the treatment your physician recommends denied by your HMO, you want to tell your story to show just how flawed the HMO system really is.
- When you moved from a well-financed suburban school to a much poorer rural school, you came to realize what huge differences exist among school systems in your state.
- If you have ever experienced being stereotyped in any way, narrate that experience and describe how it affected you.

Step 2 List all the details you can remember

- When did it happen?
- How old were you?
- Why were you there?
- Who else was there?
- Where did it happen? If the place is important, describe what it looked like.

Step 3 Examine the significance of the event

- How did you feel about the experience when it happened?
- How did it affect you then?
- How do you feel about the experience now?
- What long-term effects has it had on your life?

Step 4 Analyze your potential readers

- Who are your readers?
- How much will your readers know about the background of the experience you are describing?
- Are they familiar with the place where it happened?
- Would anything similar ever likely have happened to them?
- How likely are they to agree with your feelings about the experience?

Step 5 Write a draft

- You might need to give some background first, but if you have a compelling story, often it's best to launch right in.
- You might want to tell the story as it happened (chronological order), or you might want to begin with a striking incident and then go back to tell how it happened (flashback).
- You might want to reflect on your experience at the end, but you want your story to do most of the work. Avoid drawing a simple moral lesson. Your readers should share your feelings if you tell your story well.

Step 6 Revise, edit, proofread

- For detailed instructions, see Chapter 12.
- For a checklist to use to evaluate your draft, see pages 217–222.

CHAPTER 10

Rebuttal Arguments

The Media Foundation, a Canadian media activist organization, challenges advertising it sees as harmful by subverting it. The Media Foundation publishes an ad-free magazine, *Adbusters*, and it supports the Adbusters Web site, both of which take on specific advertising campaigns with clever spoofs.

When you hear the word *rebuttal*, you might think of a debate team or the part of a trial when the attorney for the defense answers the plaintiff's accusations. Although rebuttal has those definitions, a **rebuttal argument** can be thought of in much larger terms. Indeed, much of what people know about the world today is the result of centuries of arguments of rebuttal.

In high school and college, you no doubt have taken many courses that required the memorization of knowledge and evidence, which you demonstrated by repeating these facts on tests. You probably didn't think much about how the knowledge came about. Once in a while, though, something happens that makes people think consciously about a piece of knowledge that they have learned. For example, in elementary school, you learned that the earth rotates on its axis once a day. Maybe you didn't think about it much at the time, but once, years later, you were out on a clear night and noticed the Big Dipper in one part of the sky, and then you looked for it later and found it in another part of the sky. Perhaps you became interested enough that you watched the stars for a few hours. If you've ever spent a clear night out stargazing, you have observed that the North Star, called Polaris, stays in the same place. The stars near Polaris appear to move in a circle around Polaris, and the stars farther away move from east to west until they disappear below the horizon.

> Effective rebuttal arguments depend on critical thinking.

If you are lucky enough to live in a place where the night sky is often clear, you can see the same pattern repeated night after night. And if you stop to think about why you see the stars circling around Polaris, you remember what you were taught long ago—that you live on a rotating ball, so the stars appear to move across the sky, but in fact, stars are so distant from the earth that their actual movement is not visible to humans over a short term.

An alternative explanation for these facts not only is possible but is the one that people believed from ancient times until about five hundred years ago. People assumed that their position on the earth was fixed and that the entire sky rotated on an axis connecting Polaris and the earth. The flaw in this theory for people in ancient times is the movement of the planets. If you watch the path of Mars over several nights, you will observe that it also moves across the sky from east to west, but it makes an anomalous backward movement during its journey and then goes forward again. The other planets also seem to wander back and forth as they cross the night sky. The ancient Greeks developed an explanation of the strange wanderings of the planets by theorizing that the planets move in small circles imposed on

larger orbits. By graphing little circles on top of circles, the course of planets could be plotted and predicted. This theory culminated in the work of
Ptolemy, who lived in Alexandria in the second century AD. Ptolemy
proposed displaced centers for the small circles called *epicycles,* which gave a
better fit for predicting the path of planets.

Because Ptolemy's model of the universe was numerically accurate in
its predictions, educated people for centuries assumed its validity, even
though there was evidence to the contrary. For example, Aristarchus of
Samos, who lived in the fourth century BCE, used the size of the earth's
shadow cast on the moon during a lunar eclipse to compute the sizes of the
moon and sun and their distances from the earth. Even though his calculations were inaccurate, Aristarchus recognized that the sun is much bigger
than the earth, and he advanced the heliocentric hypothesis: that the earth
orbits the sun.

Many centuries passed, however, before educated people believed that
the sun, not the earth, was the center of the solar system. In the early six-
teenth century, the Polish astronomer Nicolas Copernicus recognized that
Ptolemy's model could be greatly simplified if the sun was at the center of
the solar system. He kept his theory a secret for much of his life and saw the
published account of his work only a few hours before his death in 1543.
Even though Copernicus made a major breakthrough, he was not able to
take full advantage of the heliocentric hypothesis because he followed the
tradition that orbits are perfect circles; thus, he still needed circles on top of
circles to explain the motion of the planets but far fewer than did Ptolemy.

The definitive rebuttal of Ptolemy came a century later with the work
of the German astronomer Johannes Kepler. Kepler performed many
tedious calculations, which were complicated by the fact that he had to first
assume an orbit for the earth before he could compute orbits for the planets. Finally he made a stunning discovery: All the orbits of the planets could
be described as an ellipse with the sun at the center. The dominance of the
Ptolemaic model of the universe was finally over.

Critical Thinking

The relationship of facts and theories lies at the heart of the scientific
method. Both Ptolemy's theory and Kepler's theory explain why the stars
appear to move around Polaris at night. Kepler made a convincing argument by rebuttal to the Ptolemaic model because he could give a much

simpler analysis. The history of astronomy is a history of arguments of rebuttal. Modern astronomy was made possible because Copernicus challenged the established relationship of theory and evidence in astronomy. This awareness of the relationship of factual and theoretical claims in science is one definition of *critical thinking* in the sciences. What is true for the history of astronomy is true for the sciences; critical thinking in the sciences relies on arguments of rebuttal.

Similar kinds of arguments of rebuttal are presented today in the debate over global warming. One of the main sources of data for arguments of rebuttal against global warming is the twenty-year record of temperature readings from NASA weather satellites orbiting the earth at the North and South Poles. These satellites use microwave sensors to measure temperature variation in the atmosphere from the surface to about six miles above the earth. Computer models predict a gradual warming in the earth's lower atmosphere along with the surface because of the buildup of carbon dioxide and other greenhouse gases, the gases produced from burning fossil fuels. But while temperatures measured on the earth's surface have gradually increased, the corresponding rises in the atmosphere as recorded by satellites didn't appear to happen. In August 1998, however, two scientists discovered a flaw in the satellites that was making them lose altitude and therefore misreport temperature data. When adjusted, the satellite data confirm what thermometers on the ground tell us: The earth is getting warmer.

In some cases, particular disciplines have specialized training to assess the relationship of theory and evidence. But more often, people must engage in *general critical thinking* to assess the validity of claims based on evidence. Often, one has to weigh competing claims of people who have excellent qualifications. One group of nutritional experts says that people should take calcium supplements to strengthen their bones. Another group warns that people are in danger of suffering from kidney stones if they take too much calcium. Critical thinking is involved in all the kinds of arguments that are discussed in this book, but it is especially important in arguments of rebuttal.

Two Ways of Rebutting

When you rebut the argument of someone else, you can do one of two things. You can *refute* the argument, or you can *counterargue*. In the first case, **refutation**, you emphasize the shortcomings of the argument that you wish to undermine without really making a positive case of your own. In the second case, **counterargument**, you emphasize not so much the shortcomings of the argument that you are rebutting but the positive strengths of the position you wish to support. Often there is considerable overlap between refutation and counterargument, and often both are present in a rebuttal.

Refutation

If you think back to the basic model of how arguments work, you can quickly see that there are two primary strategies for refutation arguments. First, *you can challenge the assumptions* on which a claim is based. Copernicus did not question Ptolemy's data concerning how the stars and planets appear in the sky to an observer on the earth. Instead, he questioned Ptolemy's central assumption that the earth is the center of the solar system.

Second, *you can question the evidence* supporting the claim. Sometimes, the evidence presented is simply wrong, as was the case for the satellites that lost altitude and reported faulty temperature data. Sometimes, the evidence is incomplete or unrepresentative, and sometimes, counterevidence can be found. Often when you refute an argument, you make the case that your opponent has been guilty of one or more **fallacies of arguments** (see pages 51–52). Your opponent has engaged in the either-or fallacy, or jumped to a hasty generalization, or created a straw man. So you indicate how the conclusions do not follow from the reasons offered, or you show that the evidence in support of the reasons is faulty or incomplete.

Take, for example, the case of arguments about drug policy in the United States. Today, almost everyone who writes about illegal drugs in the United States says that the current drug policy is flawed in some way. Even though U.S. jails and prisons are bursting with people who have been convicted and sentenced for drug offenses, millions of people still use illegal drugs. The social, political, and economic costs of illegal drugs are staggering, and the debate continues over what to do about these substances. On one side are those who want more police, more drug users in jail, and military forces sent to other countries to stop the drug traffic. On the other are those who compare current efforts to stop the flow of drugs to those of failed efforts under Prohibition (1919–1933) to halt the sale of alcohol. They want most illegal drugs to be legalized or decriminalized.

On September 7, 1989, Nobel prize–winning economist Milton Friedman published in the *Wall Street Journal* an open letter to William Bennett, then the drug czar (director of the Office of National Drug Policy) under President George H. W. Bush. Friedman wrote this as his refutation:

Dear Bill:

In Oliver Cromwell's eloquent words, "I beseech you, in the bowels of Christ, think it possible you may be mistaken" about the course you and President Bush urge us to adopt to fight drugs. The path you propose of more police, more jails, use of the military in foreign countries, harsh penalties for drug users, and a whole panoply of repressive measures can only make a bad situation worse. The drug war cannot be won by those tactics without undermining the human liberty and individual freedom that you and I cherish.

You are not mistaken in believing that drugs are a scourge that is devastating our society. You are not mistaken in believing that drugs are tearing asunder our social fabric, ruining the lives of many young people, and imposing heavy costs on some of the most disadvantaged among us. You are not mistaken in believing that the majority of the public share your concerns. In short, you are not mistaken in the end you seek to achieve.

Your mistake is failing to recognize that the very measures you favor are a major source of the evils you deplore. Of course the problem is demand, but it is not only demand, it is demand that must operate through repressed and illegal channels. Illegality creates obscene profits that finance the murderous tactics of the drug lords; illegality leads to the corruption of law enforcement officials; illegality monopolizes the efforts of honest law forces so they are starved for resources to fight the simpler crimes of robbery, theft and assault.

Drugs are a tragedy for addicts. But criminalizing their use converts that tragedy into a disaster for society, for users and non-users alike. Our experience with the prohibition of drugs is a replay of our experience with the prohibition of alcoholic beverages. . . .

Had drugs been decriminalized 17 years ago [when Friedman first made an appeal that drugs be decriminalized], "crack" would never have been invented (it was invented because the high cost of illegal drugs made it profitable to provide a cheaper version) and there would today be far fewer addicts. The lives of thousands, perhaps hundreds of thousands of innocent victims would have been saved, and not only in the U.S. The ghettos of our major cities would not be drug-and-crime-infested no-man's-lands. Fewer people would be in jails, and fewer jails would have been built.

Colombia, Bolivia, and Peru would not be suffering from narco-terror, and we would not be distorting our foreign policy because of narco-terror. Hell would not, in the words with which Billy Sunday welcomed Prohibition, "be forever for rent," but it would be a lot emptier.

In the first two paragraphs, Friedman carefully identifies the common ground he shares with Bennett. Both are political conservatives, as Friedman reminds Bennett when he mentions the "human liberty and individual freedom that you and I cherish." Friedman also agrees with Bennett about the severity of the drug problem, noting that it is "tearing asunder our social fabric, ruining the lives of many young people, and imposing heavy costs on some of the most disadvantaged among us."

Where Friedman differs from Bennett is in Bennett's central assumption: Friedman feels that Bennett's conclusion—"more police, more jails, use of the military in foreign countries, harsh penalties for drug users, and a whole panoply of repressive measures"—does not follow from the evidence about drugs. Bennett has cause and effect reversed, says Friedman: "Your mistake is failing to recognize that the very measures you favor are a major source of the evils you deplore." If drugs are now illegal and still being used, then how can the solution be to make them even more illegal by increasing penalties and extending law enforcement beyond U.S. borders? Friedman calls attention to the centrality of Bennett's assumptions when he quotes Oliver Cromwell's famous words: "I beseech you, in the bowels of Christ, think it possible you may be mistaken." If, in fact, Bennett's central assumption is flawed, then the reason to spend millions of dollars, to violate civil liberties, and to antagonize other nations is suddenly taken away.

William Bennett responded to Friedman quickly. On September 19, 1989, the *Wall Street Journal* published another refutation, an open letter of reply from Bennett to Friedman. Here is part of Bennett's response, which has a much more strident tone than Friedman's letter:

Dear Milton:

There was little, if anything, new in your open letter to me calling for the legalization of drugs. As your 1972 article made clear, the legalization argument is an old and familiar one, which has recently been revived by a small number of journalists and academics who insist that the only solution to the drug problem is no solution at all. What surprises me is that you would continue to advocate so unrealistic a proposal without pausing to consider seriously its consequences.

If the argument for drug legalization has one virtue it is its sheer simplicity. Eliminate laws against drugs, and street crime will disappear. Take the profit out of the black market through decriminalization and regulation, and poor neighborhoods will no longer be victimized by drug dealers. Cut back on drug enforcement, and use the money to wage a public health campaign against drugs, as we do with tobacco and alcohol.

The basic premise of all these propositions is that using our nation's laws to fight drugs is too costly. To be sure, our attempts to reduce drug use do carry with them enormous costs. But the question that must be asked—and which is totally ignored by the legalization advocates—is, what are the costs of *not* enforcing laws against drugs?

In my judgment, and in the judgment of virtually every serious scholar in this field, the potential costs of legalizing drugs would be so large as to make it a public policy disaster.

Of course, no one, including you, can say with certainty what would happen in the U.S. if drugs were suddenly to become a readily purchased product. We do know, however, that wherever drugs have become cheaper and more easily obtained, drug use—and addiction—has skyrocketed. In opium and cocaine producing countries, addiction is rampant among the peasants involved in drug production.

Professor James Q. Wilson tells us that during the years in which heroin could be legally prescribed by doctors in Britain, the number of addicts increased forty-fold. And after the repeal of Prohibition—an analogy favored but misunderstood by legalization advocates—consumption of alcohol soared by 350%.

Could we afford such dramatic increases in drug use? I doubt it. Already the toll of drug use on American society—measured in lost productivity, in rising health insurance costs, in hospitals flooded with drug overdose emergencies, in drug caused accidents, and in premature death—is surely more than we would like to bear.

You seem to believe that by spending just a little more money on treatment and rehabilitation, the costs of increased addiction can be avoided. That hope betrays a basic misunderstanding of the problems facing drug treatment. Most addicts don't suddenly decide to get help. They remain addicts either because treatment isn't available or because they don't seek it out. . . .

As for the connection between drugs and crime, your unswerving commitment to a legalization solution prevents you from appreciating the complexity of the drug market. Contrary to your claim, most addicts do not turn to crime to support their habit. Research shows that many of them were involved in criminal activity before they turned to drugs. Many former addicts who have received treatment continue to commit crimes during their recovery. And even if drugs were legal, what evidence do you have that the habitual drug user wouldn't continue to rob and steal to get money for clothes, food or shelter? Drug addicts always want more drugs than they can afford, and no legalization scheme has yet come up with a way of satisfying that appetite.

In refuting Friedman, Bennett contends that Friedman has not told the whole story. He has omitted important information, namely the likelihood that drug use would increase (and with tragic consequences) if drugs are legalized: "the potential costs of legalizing drugs would be so large as to make it a public policy disaster."

Bennett goes on to maintain that "a true friend of freedom understands that government has a responsibility to craft and uphold laws that help educate citizens about right and wrong. That, at any rate, was the Founders' view of our system of government." He ends by describing Friedman's proposal as "irresponsible and reckless public policy."

Friedman was not content to let Bennett have the last word, so he in turn wrote another reply—yet another refutation—that appeared on September 29, 1989, in the *Wall Street Journal*. At this point, Friedman drops the open-letter strategy and writes instead a more conventional response, referring to Bennett as *he* instead of *you*:

> William Bennett is entirely right (editorial page, Sept. 19) that "there was little, if anything, new in" my open letter to him—just as there is little, if anything, new in his proposed program to rid this nation of the scourge of drugs. That is why I am so disturbed by that program. It flies in the face of decades of experience. More police, more jails, more-stringent penalties, increased efforts at interception, increased publicity about the evils of drugs—all this has been accompanied by more, not fewer, drug addicts; more, not fewer, crimes and murders; more, not less, corruption; more, not fewer, innocent victims.
>
> Like Mr. Bennett, his predecessors were "committed to fighting the problem on several fronts through imaginative policies and hard work over a long period of time." What evidence convinces him that the same policies on a larger scale will end the drug scourge? He offers none in his response to me, only assertion and the conjecture that legalizing drugs would produce "a public policy disaster"—as if that is not exactly what we already have.

Friedman, that is, challenges Bennett's lack of evidence: "What evidence convinces him that the same policies on a larger scale will end the drug scourge? He offers none in his response to me." Friedman then adds that "legalizing drugs is not equivalent to surrender" but rather the precondition for an effective fight against drug use. He concedes that the number of addicts might increase, but he argues that it is certain that the total number of innocent victims would drop drastically, including innocent victims in foreign nations when we base our foreign policy on drug control.

Friedman's sharpest refutation of Bennett comes over Bennett's claim to represent the tradition of the Founders of the United States. Friedman completely rejects Bennett's assertion that the Founders wanted government to educate citizens about what is right and what is wrong. Friedman says "that is a totalitarian view utterly unacceptable to the Founders. I do not believe, and neither did they, that it is the responsibility of government to tell free citizens what is right and wrong."

Counterargument

Rebuttals, therefore, frequently involve refutation: a demonstration of where an argument has gone wrong. Refuters say, in effect, "I hear your argument, and here is where you are in error." What follows that thesis in a refutation is a challenge to the reasoning process (to show that a conclusion does not necessarily follow from the premises offered) or a challenge to the evidence that supports the premises (to show that the premise itself is not necessarily true). A person who engages in refutation does not necessarily say what is right—though certainly Bennett and Friedman leave no doubt about what they think is right—only that the other party is wrong.

Another way to rebut, however, is to counterargue. In a counterargument, you do not really show the shortcomings of your opponent's point of view; you may not refer to the details of the other argument at all. Rather, you offer an argument of the other point of view, in the hope that it will outweigh the argument that is being rebutted. A counterarguer, in effect, says "I hear your argument. But there is more to it than that. Now listen while I explain why another position is stronger." A counterargument offered to Friedman might go this way, in effect: "I hear your argument about the benefits of decriminalizing illegal drugs. You contend that the war on drugs threatens civil liberties and creates crime problems when drug abusers need money to support their bad habits. I accept your argument, as far as it goes. But what you have not called sufficient attention to is the negative consequences of legalizing drugs. Now listen as I explain how a policy of decriminalization will be a disaster, especially because it will encourage many, many more people to abuse harmful substances."

The counterarguer depends on the wisdom of audience members to hear all sides of an issue and to make up their minds about the merits of the case. In the following short poem, Wilfred Owen, a veteran of the horrors of World War I trench warfare, offers a counterargument to those who argue that war is noble, to those who believe along with the Latin poet Horace that "dulce et decorum est pro patria mori"—that it is sweet and fitting to die for one's country. This poem gains in popularity whenever there is an unpopular war, for it rebuts the belief that it is noble to die for one's country in modern warfare.

Dulce Et Decorum Est

Bent double, like old beggars under sacks,
Knock-kneed, coughing like hags, we cursed through sludge,
Till on the haunting flares we turned our backs

And towards our distant rest began to trudge.
Men marched asleep. Many had lost their boots
But limped on, blood-shod. All went lame; all blind;
Drunk with fatigue; deaf even to the hoots
Of disappointed shells that dropped behind.

Gas! Gas! Quick, boys!—An ecstacy of fumbling,
Fitting the clumsy helmets just in time;
But someone still was yelling out and stumbling
And floundering like a man in fire or lime.—
Dim, through the misty panes and thick green light
As under a green sea, I saw him drowning.
In all my dreams, before my helpless sight,
He plunges at me, guttering, choking, drowning.

If in some smothering dreams you too could pace
Behind the wagon that we flung him in,
And watch the white eyes writhing in his face,
His hanging face, like a devil's sick of sin;
If you could hear, at every jolt, the blood
Come gargling from the froth-corrupted lungs,
Obscene as cancer, bitter as the cud
Of vile, incurable sores on innocent tongues,—
My friend, you would not tell with such high zest
To children ardent for some desperate glory,
The old Lie: Dulce et decorum est
Pro patria mori.

Wilfred Owen does not summarize the argument in favor of being willing to die for one's country and then refute that argument, premise by premise. Rather, his poem presents an opposing argument, supported by a narrative of the speaker's experience in a poison gas attack, that he hopes will more than counterbalance what he calls "the old lie." Owen simply ignores the good reasons that people give for being willing to die for one's country and essentially argues instead that there are also good reasons not to do so. And he hopes that the evidence that he summons for his countering position will outweigh for his audience ("My friend") the evidence in support of the other side.

Of course, this example, like the Friedman-Bennett exchange, shows that it can be artificial to oppose refutation and counterargument, particularly because all arguments, in a broad sense, are counterarguments. Rebuttal arguments commonly frequently offer both refutation and counterargument. In short, people who write rebuttals work like attorneys do in a trial: They make their own cases with good reasons and hard evidence, but they also do what they can to undermine their opponent's argument. In the end the jury, the audience, decides.

LINDA CHAVEZ

The "Separation of Church and State" Myth

Linda Chavez (1947–), the author of An Unlikely Conservative: The Transformation of an Ex-Liberal *(2002) and* Out of the Barrio: Toward a New Politics of Hispanic Assimilation *(1991), has been outspoken in the service of contemporary conservatism for many years. Director of the U.S. Commission on Civil Rights from 1983 to 1985, she frequently appears on television talk shows and news programs, and she writes for a variety of publications about affirmative action, immigration, bilingual education, voting rights, and other issues. The following rebuttal essay appeared in the* Jewish World Review *in July 2002 after a federal appeals court ruled that the words "under God" in the Pledge of Allegiance ought to be stricken because they are forbidden by the First Amendment clause that requires a separation of church and state. (In 2004, the Supreme Court reversed that court of appeals judgment, as Chavez had hoped.)*

1   As soon as the Ninth Circuit Court of Appeals handed down its decision on the Pledge of Allegiance last week, the e-mails started pouring into my mailbox. Most railed against the idea that a couple of judges on "the Left Coast," as one person put it, could strike down the words "under God," which Congress added to the pledge in 1954. But a few, mostly from readers of my column, suggested that if I didn't like the decision, maybe I should try thinking about how I'd feel if Congress had inserted the words "under no God" instead—a sentiment echoed by the Ninth Circuit. In order to protect religious liberty, they implied, we have to make sure government divorces itself from any expression of religious belief.

2   "Why did the Founding Fathers, a group of basically conservative, property-owning religious men find it necessary at all to put the separation of Church and State into the Constitution, if not because of the persecution suffered in the lands they left from those who felt that only they knew the truth?" wrote one of my interlocutors.

3   Good question, because it exposes one of the most widely held myths in modern America.

4   Ask most Americans what the First Amendment says about religion, and you'll get the standard reply (if you're lucky enough to get any answer at all) that it guarantees the separation of church and state.

5   It says no such thing, of course. What it says is careful and precise: "Congress shall make no law respecting an establishment of religion, or prohibiting the free exercise thereof."

6   The First Amendment guarantees the freedom of religion, not from religion.

7   The Founders understood that religious belief was not incidental to the American experiment in liberty but was the foundation on which it was built. The whole idea that individuals were entitled to liberty rests on the Judeo-Christian conception of man. When the colonists rebelled against their king—an action that risked their very lives—they did so with the belief that they were answering to a higher law than the king's. They were emboldened by "the laws of nature and nature's God," in Thomas Jefferson's memorable phrase to declare their independence.

8   "We hold these truths to be self-evident that all men are created equal and that they are endowed by their Creator with certain unalienable rights," he wrote.

9   It is impossible to overstate how important the Judeo-Christian tradition was guiding the Founder's deliberations. Yet, in recent years, we've virtually ignored this aspect of our history.

10   As scholar Michael Novak points out in his excellent little book *On Two Wings: Humble Faith and Common Source at the American Founding*, "Professor Donald Lutz counted 3,154 citations in the writings of the founders; of these nearly 1,100 references (34 percent) are to the Bible, and about 300 each to Montesquieu and Blackstone, followed at considerable distance by Locke and Hume and Plutarch."

11   Perhaps the most eloquent argument on behalf of the role of religion in preserving our democracy was George Washington's, who cautioned in his Farewell Address on Sept. 19, 1794, that virtue and morality were necessary to popular government.

12   "And let us with caution indulge the supposition, that morality can be maintained without religion" he said. "Whatever may be conceded to the influence of refined education on minds of peculiar structure, reason and experience both forbid us to expect that national morality can prevail in exclusion of religious principle."

13   The Constitutional Convention of 1787 opened with a prayer, as does each session of Congress today. The motto "In God We Trust" is on our currency, and similar expressions adorn public buildings across the Nation. Even the U.S. Supreme Court, which has been the locus of so much recent confusion on the First Amendment, begins its proceedings with the phrase "God save the United States and this honorable court."

14   Perhaps our plea should be "God save us from the courts."

15   As Jefferson, perhaps the least devout of our Founders, once said to the Rev. Ethan Allen, as recorded in Allen's diary now in the Library of Congress, and quoted by Michael Novak: "No nation has ever yet existed or been governed without religion. Nor can be."

16   Let us hope the Supreme Court in reviewing the Ninth Circuit's opinion does not insist on testing whether Jefferson was right. ∎

Steps to a Rebuttal Argument

Step 1 Identify an argument to argue against as well as its main claim(s)

- What exactly are you arguing against?
- Are there secondary claims attached to the main claim?
- A fair summary of your opponent's position should be included in your finished rebuttal.

Example

- If you are taking on affirmative action admissions policies for colleges and universities, then what do those policies involve and whom do they affect?

Step 2 Examine the facts on which the claim is based

- Are the facts accurate?
- Are the facts a truly representative sample?
- Are the facts current?
- Is there another body of facts that you can present as counterevidence?
- If the author uses statistics, is evidence for the validity of those statistics presented?
- Can the statistics be interpreted differently?
- If the author quotes from sources, how reliable are those sources?
- Are the sources treated fairly, or are quotations taken out of context?
- If the author cites outside authority, how much trust can you place in that authority?

Step 3 Examine the assumptions on which the claim is based

- What is the primary assumption of the claim you are rejecting?
- What other assumptions support that claim?
- How are those assumptions flawed?
- If you are arguing against a specific piece of writing, then how does the author fall short?
- Does the author resort to name calling? use faulty reasoning? ignore key facts?
- What fallacies is the author guilty of committing?

Step 4 Analyze your potential readers

- To what extent do your potential readers support the claim that you are rejecting?
- If they strongly support that claim, then how might you appeal to them to change their minds?
- What common assumptions and beliefs do you share with them?

Step 5 Decide whether to write a refutation, a counterargument—or both

- Make your aim clear in your thesis statement.
- For example, a thesis statement like this one promises a refutation and a counterargument: "Friedman's argument is flawed in several ways. Not only that, he ignores the fact that laws in the United States are frequently developed in order to protect individuals against themselves."

Step 6 Write a draft

Identify the issue and the argument you are rejecting

- If the issue is not familiar to most of your readers, you might need to provide some background.
- Even if it is familiar, it might be helpful to give a quick summary of the competing positions.
- Remember that offering a fair and accurate summary is a good way to build credibility with your audience.

Take on the argument that you are rejecting

- You might want to question the evidence that is used to support the argument.
- You can challenge the facts, present counterevidence and countertestimony, cast doubt on the representativeness of the sample, cast doubt on the currency and relevance of the examples, challenge the credibility of any authorities cited, question the way in which statistical evidence is presented and interpreted, and argue that quotations are taken out of context.

Conclude on a firm note

- In your conclusion you should have a strong argument that underscores your objections.
- You might wish to close with a counterargument or counterproposal.

Step **7** Revise, edit, proofread

- For detailed instructions, see Chapter 12.
- For a checklist to use to evaluate your draft, see pages 217–222.

CHAPTER 11

Proposal Arguments

The major football programs in NCAA Division I generate millions of dollars in ticket and television revenue.

Not all NCAA Division I football programs are financially successful. Some lose millions every year.

The amateur tradition in college athletics continues at colleges in NCAA Division III, which do not offer athletic scholarships. The Williams College Ephs compete against the Tufts University Jumbos in a Division III game on a crisp fall Saturday in Williamston, Massachusetts.

Student athletes in big-time college football programs earn millions of dollars for their schools in ticket and television revenues, yet besides their scholarships, they receive barely enough money to live on. Should college athletes be paid? The Nebraska legislature thought so in April 2003 when it passed a bill allowing universities to pay student athletes. But the National Collegiate Athletic Association (NCAA) argues strongly to the contrary. The NCAA claims that paying players would destroy amateurism in college sports and make players third-rate professionals. Furthermore, only a handful of schools in NCAA Division I make a profit from athletics. At many schools athletics lose money, forcing administrators to cover these expenses from other revenues. Some people have proposed that schools should reduce expenses by offering fewer scholarships and by capping the salaries of coaches. These kinds of arguments are called proposal arguments, and they take the classic form:

We should (or should not) do SOMETHING.

At this moment, you might not think that there is anything you feel strongly enough about to write a proposal argument. But if you make a list of things that make you mad or at least a little annoyed, then you have a start toward writing a proposal argument. Some things on your list are not going to produce proposal arguments that many people would want to read. If your roommate is a slob, you might be able to write a proposal for that person to start cleaning up more, but who else would be interested? Similarly, it might be annoying to you that where you live it stays too hot for too long in the summer or too cold for too long in the winter, but unless you have a direct line to God, it is hard to imagine a serious proposal to change the climate. (Cutting down on air pollution, of course, is something that people *can* change.) Short of those extremes, however, are a lot of things that you might think, "Why hasn't someone done something about this?" If you believe that others have something to gain if a problem is solved or at least the situation made a little better, then you might be able to develop a good proposal argument.

For instance, suppose you are living off campus, and you buy a student parking sticker when you register for courses so that you can park in the student lot. However, you quickly find out that there are too many cars and trucks for the number of available spaces, and unless you get to campus by 8:00 AM, you aren't going to find a place to park in your assigned lot. The situation makes you angry because you believe that if you pay for a sticker, you should have a reasonable chance of finding a space to park. You see that there are unfilled lots reserved for faculty and staff next to the student parking lot, and you wonder why more spaces aren't allotted to students. You decide to write to the president of your college. You want her to direct parking and traffic services to give more spaces to students or else build a parking garage that will accommodate more vehicles.

But when you start talking to other students on campus, you begin to realize that the problem may be more complex than your first view of it. Your college has taken the position that the fewer students who drive to campus, the less traffic there will be on and around your campus. The administration wants more students to ride shuttle buses, form car pools, or bicycle to campus instead of driving alone. You also find out that faculty and staff members pay ten times as much as students for their parking permits, so they pay a very high premium for a guaranteed space—much too high for most students. If the president of your college is your primary audience, you first have to argue that a problem really exists. You have to convince the president that many students have no choice but to drive if they are to attend classes. You, for example, are willing to ride the shuttle buses, but they don't run often enough for you to make your classes, get back to your car that you left at home, and then drive to your job.

> Proposal arguments often include definition, causal, evaluation, narrative, and rebuttal arguments.

Next, you have to argue that your solution will solve the problem. An eight-story parking garage might be adequate to park all the cars of students who want to drive, but parking garages are very expensive to build. Even if a parking garage is the best solution, the question remains: Who is going to pay for it? Many problems in life could be solved if you had access to unlimited resources, but very few people have such resources at their command. It's not enough to have a solution that can resolve the problem. You have to be able to argue for the feasibility of your solution. If you want to argue that a parking garage is the solution to the parking problem on your campus, then you must also propose how the garage will be financed.

Components of Proposals

Proposal arguments are often complex and involve the kinds of arguments that are discussed in Chapters 5 through 9. Successful proposals have four major components:

1. *Identifying the problem.* Sometimes, problems are evident to your intended readers. If your city is constantly tearing up the streets and then leaving them for months without doing anything to

repair them, then you shouldn't have much trouble convincing the citizens of your city that streets should be repaired more quickly. But if you raise a problem that will be unfamiliar to most of your readers, you will first have to argue that the problem exists. Recall that in Chapter 1, Rachel Carson had to use several kinds of arguments in *Silent Spring* to make people aware of the dangers of pesticides, including narrative arguments, definition arguments, evaluation arguments, and arguments of comparison. Often, you will have to do similar work to establish exactly what problem you are attempting to solve. You will have to define the scope of the problem. Some of the bad roads in your city might be the responsibility of the state, not city government.

2. *Stating your proposed solution.* You need to have a clear, definite statement of exactly what you are proposing. You might want to place this statement near the beginning of your argument, or later, after you have considered and rejected other possible solutions.

3. *Convincing your readers with good reasons that your proposed solution is fair and will work.* When your readers agree that a problem exists and a solution should be found, your next task is to convince them that your solution is the best one to resolve the problem. If you're writing about the problem your city has in getting streets repaired promptly, then you need to analyze carefully the process that is involved in repairing streets. Sometimes there are mandatory delays so that competing bids can be solicited, and unexpected delays when tax revenue falls short of expectations. You should be able to put your finger on the problem in a detailed causal analysis. You should be able to make an evaluation argument that your solution is fair to all concerned. You should also be prepared to make arguments of rebuttal against other possible solutions.

4. *Demonstrating that your solution is feasible.* Your solution not only has to work; it must be feasible to implement. Malaysia effectively ended its drug problem by imposing mandatory death sentences for anyone caught selling even small amounts of drugs. Foreign nationals, teenagers, and grandmothers have all been hanged under this law. Malaysia came up with a solution for its purposes, but this solution probably would not work in most countries because the punishment seems too

extreme. If you want a parking garage built on your campus and you learn that no other funds can be used to construct it, then you have to be able to argue that the potential users of the garage will be willing to pay greatly increased fees for the convenience of parking on campus.

Building a Proposal Argument

Proposal arguments don't just fall out of the sky. For any problem of major significance—gun control, poverty, teenage pregnancy, abortion, capital punishment, drug legalization—you will find long histories of debate. An issue with a much shorter history can also quickly pile up mountains of arguments if it gains wide public attention. In 1972, for example, President Richard Nixon signed into law the Education Amendments Act, including Title IX, which prohibits sex discrimination at

Girls' sports leagues were a rarity in many communities just thirty years ago.

colleges that receive federal aid. Few people at the time guessed that Title IX would have the far-reaching consequences it did. When Title IX was first passed, 31,000 women participated in intercollegiate athletics. In the academic year 2002–2003, over 160,000 women athletes participated in varsity college sports. Even more striking is the increase in girls' participation in high school sports. The number of boy athletes has risen gradually from about 3.6 million in 1971 to approximately 4 million 2003–2004, while the number of girl athletes increased tenfold—from 294,000 in 1971 to 2.9 million in 2003–2004.

Proponents of Title IX are justifiably proud of the increased level of participation of women in varsity athletics. But for all the good that Title IX has done to increase athletic opportunities for women, critics blame Title IX for decreasing athletic opportunities for college men. According to the U.S. General Accounting Office (GAO), more than three hundred men's teams have been eliminated in college athletics since 1993. In 2000 the University of Miami dropped its men's swimming team, which had produced many Olympians, including Greg Louganis, who won gold medals in both platform and springboard diving in two consecutive Olympics. In 2001 the University of Nebraska also discontinued its men's swimming team, which had been in place since 1922, and the University of Kansas dropped men's swimming and tennis. Wrestling teams have been especially hard hit, dropping from 363 in 1981 to 192 in 1999. The effects were noticeable at the 2000 Olympics in Australia, where U.S. freestyle wrestlers failed to win any gold medals for the first time since 1968.

College and university administrators claim that they have no choice but to drop men's teams if more women's teams are added. Their belief comes not from the original Title IX legislation, which does not mention athletics, but from a 1979 clarification by the Office of Civil Rights (OCR), the agency that enforces Title IX. OCR set out three options for schools to comply with Title IX:

1. Bring the proportion of women in varsity athletics roughly equal to the percentage of women students.
2. Prove a "history and continuing practice" of creating new opportunities for women.
3. Prove that the school has done everything to "effectively accommodate" the athletic interests of women students.

University administrators have argued that the first option, known as *proportionality*, is the only one that can be argued successfully in a courtroom if the school is sued.

Proportionality is difficult to achieve at schools with football programs. Universities that play NCAA Division I-A football offer eighty-five football scholarships to men. Since there is no equivalent sport for women, football throws the gender statistics way out of balance. Defenders of football ask that it be exempted from Title IX because it is the cash cow that pays most of the bills for both men's and women's sports. Only a handful of women's basketball programs make money. All other women's sports are money losers and, like men's "minor" sports, depend on men's football and basketball revenues and student fees to pay their bills. College officials maintain that if they cut the spending for football, football will bring in less revenue, and thus all sports will be harmed.

Those who criticize Title IX argue that it assumes that women's interest in athletics is identical to men's. They point out that male students participate at much higher rates in intramural sports, which have no limitations on who can play. In contrast, women participate at much higher rates in music, dance, theater, and other extracurricular activities, yet Title IX is not being applied to those activities.

Defenders of Title IX argue that women's interest in athletics cannot be determined until they have had equal opportunities to participate. They claim Title IX is being used as a scapegoat for college administrators who do not want to make tough decisions. They point out that in 2001, women made up 53 percent of all college students but only 42 percent of all college athletes. At major colleges and universities, men still received 73 percent of the funds devoted to athletics. Without Title IX, in their view, schools would have no incentive to increase opportunities for women. The battle over Title IX is not likely to go away soon.

Sample Student Proposal Argument

Lifetime Cleveland Indians fan Brian Witkowski wrote this proposal argument in spring 2004 for a research paper assignment in the Rhetoric of Sports. Brian is a computer sciences major who enjoys playing video games and riding mountain bikes.

Brain Witkowski

Professor Mendelsohn

RHE 309K

2 May 2004

Need a Cure for Tribe Fever?

How About a Dip in the Lake?

Everyone is familiar with the Cleveland Indians'
Chief Wahoo logo and I do mean everyone, not just
Clevelanders. Across America one can see individuals
sporting the smiling mascot on traditional Indians caps
and jerseys, and recent trends in sports merchandise have
popularized new groovy multicolored Indians sportswear.
In fact, Indians merchandise recently was ranked just
behind the New York Yankees' merchandise in terms of
sales (Adams). Because of lucrative merchandising
contracts between major league baseball and Little
League, youth teams all over the country don Cleveland's
famous (or infamous) smiling Indian each season as fresh-
faced kids scamper onto the diamonds looking like mini
major leaguers ("MLBP"). Various incarnations of the
famous Chief Wahoo—described by sportswriter Rick
Telander as "the red-faced, big-nosed, grinning, drywall-
toothed moron who graces the peak of every Cleveland
Indians cap"—have been around since the 1940s (qtd. in
Eitzen). Now redder and even more cartoonish than the
original hooknosed, beige Indian with a devilish grin,
Wahoo often passes as a cheerful baseball buddy like the
San Diego Chicken or the St. Louis Cardinals' Fredbird.
(See Fig. 1.)

Fig. 1. Many youth baseball and softball
teams use the Chief Wahoo logo, including
teams with American Indian players.

Though defined by its distinctive logo, Cleveland
baseball far preceded its famous mascot, changing from
the Forest Citys to the Spiders to the Bluebirds/Blues to
the Broncos to the Naps and finally to the Indians. Dubbed
the Naps in 1903 in honor of their star player and
manager Napoleon Lajoie, the team finally arrived at their
current appellation in 1915. After Lajoie was traded, the
team's president challenged sportswriters to devise a
suitable "temporary" label for the floundering club.
Publicity material has it that the writers decided on the
Indians to celebrate Louis Sockalexis, a Penobscot Indian
who played for the team from 1897 to 1899. With a heck of
a batting average and the notability of being the first
Native American in professional baseball, Sockalexis
was immortalized by the new Cleveland label (Schneider
10-23). (Contrary to popular lore, some cite alternate—
and less reverent—motivations behind the team's naming
and point to a lack of Sockalexis publicity in period
newspaper articles discussing the team's naming process
[Staurowsky 95-97].) Almost ninety years later, the
"temporary" name continues to raise eyebrows, both in its
marketability and ideological questionability.

Today the logo is more than a little embarrassing. Since the high-profile actions of the American Indian Movement (AIM) in the 1970s, sports teams around the country—including the Indians—have been criticized and cajoled over their less than racially sensitive mascots. Native American groups question the sensitivity of such caricatured displays—not just because of grossly stereotyped mascots, but also because of what visual displays of team support say about Native American culture. Across the country, professional sporting teams, as well as high schools and colleges, perform faux rituals in the name of team spirit. As Tim Giago, publisher of The Lakota Times, a weekly South Dakotan Native American newspaper, has noted, "The sham rituals, such as the wearing of feathers, smoking of so-called peace pipes, beating of tomtoms, fake dances, horrendous attempts at singing Indian songs, the so-called war whoops, and the painted faces, address more than the issues of racism. They are direct attacks upon the spirituality of the Indian people" (qtd. in Wulf). Controversy over such performances still fuels the fire between activists and alumni at schools such as the University of Illinois at Champaign-Urbana where the "Fighting Illini" observe football halftimes with a performance by an (often white) student dressed as Chief Illiniwek. For fifteen years, the symbol has been dividing alumni, students, faculty, and administration; one alumnus has spent upward of ten thousand dollars to preserve the Chief (Selingo A20). Since 1969, when

Oklahoma disavowed its "Little Red" mascot, more than 600 school and minor league teams have followed a more ethnically sensitive trend and ditched their "tribal" mascots for ones less publicly explosive (Price). High-profile teams such as Berkeley, St. Johns University, and Miami (Ohio) University have buckled to public pressure, changing their team names from the Indians to the Cardinals (1972), the Redmen to the Red Storm (1993), and the Redskins to the Redhawks (1996), respectively. While many see such controversies as mere bowing to the PC pressures of the late twentieth and early twenty-first centuries, others see the mascot issue as a topic well worthy of debate.

Cleveland's own Chief Wahoo has far from avoided controversy. Protests regarding the controversial figure have plagued the city. Multiple conflicts between Wahoo devotees and dissenters have arisen around the baseball season. At the opening game of 1995, fifty Native Americans and supporters took stations around Jacobs Field to demonstrate against the use of the cartoonish smiling crimson mascot. While protestors saw the event as a triumph for first amendment rights and a strike against negative stereotyping, one befuddled fan stated, "I never thought of [Chief Wahoo] that way. It's all how you think of it" (Kropk). Arrests were made in 1998 when demonstrators from the United Church of Christ burned a three-foot Chief Wahoo doll in effigy ("Judge"). Wedded to their memorabilia, fans proudly stand behind their Indian as others lobby vociferously for its removal. Splitting government officials, fans, social and religious groups, this issue draws hostility from both sides of the argument. In 2000 Cleveland Mayor Michael White came out publicly against the team mascot, joining an already established group of religious leaders, laypersons, and civil rights activists who had demanded Wahoo's retirement. African American religious and civic leaders such as the Rev. Gregory A. Jacobs had been speaking out throughout the 1990s and highlighting the absurdity of minority groups who embrace the Wahoo symbol. "Each of us has had to fight its [sic] own battle, quite frankly," Jacobs stated. "We cannot continue to live in this kind of hypocrisy that says, Yes, we are in solidarity with my [sic] brothers and sisters, yet we continue to exploit them" (qtd. in Briggs). These words clash with those of individuals such as former Indians owner Dick Jacobs, who said amidst protest that the Wahoo logo would remain as long as he was principal owner of the club (Bauman 1) and a delegate of the East Ohio Conference of the United Methodist Church, who quipped, "I would cease being a United Methodist before I would cease wearing my Chief Wahoo clothing" (Briggs).

This controversy also swirls outside of the greater Cleveland area. Individual newspapers in Nebraska, Kansas, Minnesota, and Oregon have banned the printing of Native American sports symbols and team names such as the Braves, Indians, or Redmen (Wulf), while the Seattle Times went so far as to digitally remove the Wahoo symbol from images of the Cleveland baseball cap

("Newspaper"). As other teams make ethnically sensitive and image conscious choices to change their mascots, Cleveland stands firm on its resolve to retain the Chief. Despite internal division and public ridicule fueled by the team icon, the city refuses to budge. Clevelanders consequently appear as insensitive and backward as those who continue to support the Redmen, Redskins, or Illini.

As the city of Cleveland continues to enjoy its recent improved image and downtown revitalization, must the plague of the Wahoo controversy continue? As a native of Cleveland, I understand the power of "Tribe Fever" and the unabashed pride one feels when wearing Wahoo garb during a winning (or losing) season. Often it is not until we leave northeastern Ohio that we realize the negative image that Wahoo projects. What then can Cleveland do to simultaneously save face and bolster its burgeoning positive city image? I propose that the team finally change the "temporary" Indians label. In a city so proud of its diverse ethnic heritage—African American, Italian American, and Eastern European American to name a few—why stand as a bearer of retrograde ethnic politics? Cleveland should take this opportunity to link its positive midwestern image to the team of which it is so proud. Why not take the advice of the 1915 Cleveland management and change the team's "temporary" name? I propose a shift to the Cleveland Lakers.

The city's revival in the last twenty years has embraced the geographic and aesthetic grandeur of Lake

Witowski 7

Erie. Disavowing its "mistake on the lake" moniker of
the late 1970s, Cleveland has traded aquatic pollution
fires for a booming lakeside business district.
Attractions such as the Great Lakes Science Center, the
Rock and Roll Hall of Fame, and the new Cleveland Browns
Stadium take advantage of the beauty of the landscape
and take back the lake. Why not continue this trend
through one of the city's biggest and highest-profile
moneymakers: professional baseball? By changing the
team's name to the Lakers, the city would gain national
advertisement for one of its major selling points, while
simultaneously announcing a new ethnically inclusive
image that is appropriate to our wonderfully diverse
city. It would be a public relations triumph for the
city.

Of course this call will be met with many
objections. Why do we have to buckle to pressure? Do we
not live in a free country? What the fans and citizens
alike need to keep in mind is that ideological pressures
would not be the sole motivation for this move. Yes,
retiring Chief Wahoo would take Cleveland off of AIM's
hit list. Yes, such a move would promote a kinder and
gentler Cleveland. At the same time, however, such a
gesture would work toward uniting the community. So much
civic division exists over this issue that a renaming
could help start to heal these old wounds.

Additionally, this type of change could bring added
economic prosperity to the city. First, a change in name
will bring a new wave of team merchandise. Licensed

Witkowski 8

sports apparel enjoys more than a 10 billion dollar
annual retail business in the U.S., and teams have
repeatedly proven that new uniforms and logos can provide
new capital. After all, a new logo for the Seattle
Mariners bolstered severely slumping merchandise sales
(Lefton). Wahoo devotees need not panic; the booming
vintage uniform business will keep him alive, as is
demonstrated by the current ability to purchase replica
1940s jerseys with the old Indians logo. Also, good press
created by this change will hopefully help increase
Cleveland tourism. If the good will created by the
Cleveland Lakers can prove half as profitable as The Drew
Carey Show or the Rock and Roll Hall of Fame, then local
businesses will be humming a happy tune. Finally, if
history repeats itself, a change to a more culturally
inclusive logo could, in and of itself, prove to be a
cash cow. When Miami University changed from the Redskins
to the Redhawks, it saw alumni donations skyrocket to an
unprecedented 25 million dollars (Price). Perhaps a less
divisive mascot would prove lucrative to the ball club,
city, and players themselves. (Sluggers with inoffensive
logos make excellent spokesmen.)

Perhaps this proposal sounds far fetched: Los
Angeles may seem to have cornered the market on Lakers.
But where is their lake? (The Lakers were formerly the
Minneapolis Lakers, where the name makes sense in the
"Land of 10,000 Lakes.") Various professional and
collegiate sports teams—such as baseball's San Francisco
Giants and football's New York Giants—share the same team

name, so licensing should not be an issue. If Los Angeles
has qualms about sharing the name, perhaps Cleveland
could persuade them to become the Surfers or the Stars—
after all, Los Angeles players seem to spend as much time
on the big and small screen as on the court.

Now is the perfect time for Cleveland to make this
jump. Sportscasters continue to tout the revitalized
young Cleveland team as an up-and-coming contender.
Perhaps a new look will help usher in a new era of
Cleveland baseball. The team has already begun to
minimize the presence of Wahoo on new Wahoo-less caps and
jerseys, and the owners should introduce a new look and
ethnically sensitive image to its upstart team. Like
expansion teams such as the Florida Marlins and the
Arizona Diamondbacks, Cleveland's new look could bring
with it a vital sense of civic pride and a World Series
ring to boot. Through various dry spells, the Cleveland
Indians institution has symbolically turned to the
descendants of Sockalexis, asking for good will or a
latter-generation Penobscot slugger (Fleitz 3). Perhaps
the best way to win good will, fortunes, and their first
World Series title since 1948 would be to eschew a
grinning life-size Chief Wahoo for the new and improved
Cleveland Laker, an oversized furry monster sporting
water wings, cleats, and a catcher's mask. His seventh-
inning-stretch show could include an air guitar solo with
a baseball bat as he quietly reminds everyone that the
Rock Hall is just down the street. Go Lakers and go
Cleveland!

Witkowski 10

Works Cited

Adams, David. "Cleveland Indians Investors Watch Case on
 Native American Names." Akron Beacon Journal
 6 Apr. 1999. LexisNexis Academic. LexisNexis.
 Perry-Casteñeda Lib., U of Texas at Austin. 20 Apr.
 2004 <http://www.lexisnexis.com/>.

Bauman, Michael. "Indians Logo, Mascot Are the Real
 Mistakes." Milwaukee Journal Sentinel 23 Oct. 1997:
 Sports 1.

Briggs, David. "Churches Go to Bat Against Chief Wahoo."
 Cleveland Plain Dealer 25 Aug. 2000: 1A.

Eitzen, D. Stanley and Maxine Baca Zinn. "The Dark Side
 of Sports Symbols." USA Today Magazine Jan. 2001:
 48.

Fleitz, David L. Louis Sockalexis: The First Cleveland
 Indian. Jefferson: McFarland, 2002.

"Judge Dismisses Charges Against City in Wahoo Protest."
 Associated Press 6 Aug. 2001. LexisNexis Academic.
 LexisNexis. Perry-Casteñeda Lib., U of Texas at
 Austin. 19 Apr. 2004 <http://www.lexisnexis.com/>.

Kropk, M. R. "Chief Wahoo Protestors Largely Ignored by
 Fans." Austin American Statesman 6 May 1995: D4.

Lefton, Terry. "Looks Are Everything: For New
 Franchises, Licensing Battles Must Be Won Long
 Before the Team Even Takes the Field." Sport
 89 (May 1998): 32.

"MLBP Reaches Youth League Apparel Agreements with
 Majestic Athletic, Outdoor Cap." 25 June 2004.
 Major League Baseball. 28 June 2004.

Witkowski 11

<http://mlb.mlb.com/NASApp/mlb/mlb/news/mlb_press_
release.jsp?ymd=20040625&content_id=780105&vkey=pr_
mlb&fext=.jsp>.

"Newspaper Edits Cleveland Indian Logo from Cap Photo."
Associated Press 31 Mar. 1997. LexisNexis Academic.
LexisNexis. Perry-Casteñeda Lib., U of Texas at
Austin. 17 Apr. 2004 <http://www.lexisnexis.com/>.

Price, S. L. "The Indian Wars." Sports Illustrated
4 Mar. 2002: 66+. Expanded Academic ASAP. Thomson
Gale. Perry-Casteñeda Lib., U of Texas at Austin.
20 Apr. 2004 <http://www.gale.com/>.

Schneider, Russell. The Cleveland Indians Encyclopedia.
Philadelphia: Temple UP, 1996.

Selingo, Jeffrey. "An Honored Symbol to Some, a Racist
Mascot to Others." Chronicle of Higher Education
18 June 2004: A20-23.

Staurowsky, Ellen J. "Sockalexis and the Making of the
Myth at the Core of the Cleveland's 'Indian'
Image." Team Spirits: The Native American Mascots
Controversy. Eds. C. Richard King and Charles
Fruehling Springwood. Lincoln: U of Nebraska P,
2001. 82-106.

Wulf, Steve. "A Brave Move." Sports Illustrated
24 Feb. 1992: 7.

Steps to a Proposal Argument

Step **1** Make a claim

Make a proposal claim advocating a specific change or course of action.

Formula

- *We should (or should not) do* SOMETHING. In an essay of five or fewer pages, it's difficult to propose solutions to big problems such as continuing poverty. Proposals that address local problems are not only more manageable; sometimes, they get actual results.

Examples

- The process of registering for courses (getting appointments at the health center, getting email accounts) should be made more efficient.
- Your community should create bicycle lanes to make bicycling safer and to reduce traffic (build a pedestrian overpass over a dangerous street; make it easier to recycle newspapers, bottles, and cans).

Step **2** Identify the problem

- What exactly is the problem?
- Who is most affected by the problem?
- What causes the problem?
- Has anyone tried to do anything about it? If so, why haven't they succeeded?
- What is likely to happen in the future if the problem isn't solved?

Step **3** Propose your solution

State your solution as specifically as you can.

- What exactly do you want to achieve?
- How exactly will your solution work?
- Can it be accomplished quickly, or will it have to be phased in over a few years?
- Has anything like it been tried elsewhere?
- Who will be involved?
- Can you think of any reasons why your solution might not work?
- How will you address those arguments?
- Can you think of any ways of strengthening your proposed solution in light of those possible criticisms?

Step **4** Consider other solutions

- What other solutions have been or might be proposed for this problem, including doing nothing?
- What are the advantages and disadvantages of those solutions?
- Why is your solution better?

Step **5** Examine the feasibility of your solution

- How easy is your solution to implement?
- Will the people most affected by your solution be willing to go along with it? (For example, lots of things can be accomplished if enough people volunteer, but groups often have difficulty getting enough volunteers to work without pay.)
- If it costs money, how do you propose to pay for it?
- Who is most likely to reject your proposal because it is not practical enough?
- How can you convince your readers that your proposal can be achieved?

Step **6** Analyze your potential readers

- Whom are you writing for?
- How interested will your readers be in this problem?
- How much does this problem affect them?
- How would your solution benefit them directly and indirectly?

Step **7** Write a draft

Define the problem

- Set out the issue or problem. You might begin by telling about your experience or the experience of someone you know. You might need to argue for the seriousness of the problem, and you might have to give some background on how it came about.

Present your solution

- You might want to set out your solution first and explain how it will work, then consider other possible solutions and argue that yours is better; or you might want to set out other possible solutions first, argue that they don't solve the problem or are not feasible, and then present your solution.

- Make clear the goals of your solution. Many solutions cannot solve problems completely. If you are proposing a solution for juvenile crime in your neighborhood, for example, you cannot expect to eliminate all juvenile crime.
- Describe in detail the steps in implementing your solution and how they will solve the problem you have identified. You can impress your readers by the care with which you have thought through this problem.
- Explain the positive consequences that will follow from your proposal. What good things will happen and what bad things will be avoided if your advice is taken?

Argue that your proposal is feasible

- Your proposal for solving the problem is a truly good idea only if it can be put into practice. If people have to change the ways they are doing things now, explain why they would want to change. If your proposal costs money, you need to identify exactly where the money would come from.

Conclude with a call for action

- Your conclusion should be a call for action. You should put your readers in a position such that if they agree with you, they will take action. You might restate and emphasize what exactly they need to do.

Step 8 Revise, edit, proofread

- For detailed instructions, see Chapter 12.
- For a checklist to use to evaluate your draft, see pages 217–222.

Revision: Putting It All Together

Skilled writers know that one secret to writing well is rethinking and rewriting. Even the best writers often have to reconsider their aims and methods in the course of writing and to revise several times to get the result they want. If you want to become a better writer, therefore, take three words of advice: revise, revise, revise.

The biggest trap you can fall into is seeking a fast resolution and skipping revision. The quality of an argument varies in direct proportion to the amount of time devoted to it. You cannot revise a paper effectively if you finish it at the last minute. You have to allow your ideas to develop, and you have to allow what you write to sit for a while before you go back through it. So try your best to write your arguments over a period of several days. Be patient. Test your ideas against your reading and the informal advice of trusted friends and advisors. And once you are satisfied with what you have written, allow at least a day to let what you write cool off. With a little time you gain enough distance to "resee" it, which, after all, is what revision means. To be able to revise effectively, you have to plan your time.

> Revise, revise, revise.

Most of all, keep your eyes focused on the big picture, especially early in the process of making your argument. Don't sweat the small stuff at the beginning. If you see a word that's wrong or if you are unsure about a punctuation mark, you may be tempted to drop everything and fix the errors first. Don't do that: If you start searching for the errors early in the process, then it's hard to get back to the larger concerns that ultimately make your argument successful or unsuccessful.

Over time you have to develop effective strategies for revising if you're going to be successful. These strategies include the following:

1. Keep your goals in mind—but stay flexible about them.
2. Read as you write.
3. Take the perspective of your reader.

4. Focus on your argument.

5. Attend to your style and proofread carefully.

In addition, plan to get responses to what you write in time for you to revise your work based on those responses.

Keep Your Goals in Mind—But Stay Flexible

People who argue effectively know what they want to achieve. They understand their readers' needs, know what they want to accomplish, and keep their goals in mind as they write and revise. But they also know that writing about a subject likely will change how they think about it, often in productive ways. Thus they remain flexible enough to modify their goals as they write. You may begin writing an argument because you have strong feelings about an issue; in fact, a rush of strong feelings can often motivate you to compose a strong statement at one sitting. That's good. But at some point before you commit what you write to a final version, give yourself a chance to rethink your goals. It may be that you can make a better argument in the end if you leave yourself open to adjustments in what you are arguing and to whom you are arguing it.

Consider, for example, the case of a student at a northeastern university, Nate Bouton (not his real name), who arrived on his campus in the midst of a controversy in 2000 over the raising of the Confederate Battle Flag over the South Carolina state capitol building. You may recall the controversy: In 1999 the NAACP, in the conviction that the Confederate flag was a symbol of racism, called on citizens to boycott South Carolina tourist venues until the flag no longer was displayed over the state capitol building. After contentious debate and considerable thought, legislators decided to remove the flag. On July 1, 2000, it was taken down and displayed instead in a nearby memorial to Confederate soldiers. But public opinion within and outside South Carolina remained divided: Some citizens continued to ask that the flag be restored to the capitol, while others demanded that it be removed from the Confederate memorial as well.

As a native of South Carolina, Nate felt that students at his university were coming to uninformed, premature conclusions, which stemmed from faulty assumptions about the flag issue in particular and South Carolinians in general. When the players on the baseball team at Nate's university decided not to play previously scheduled games in South Carolina, he was ready to join the argument. He decided to write about the flag issue, in his words, "in order to straighten people out. People in the northeast just didn't know the facts and that ticked me off. I wanted to write an argument supporting what was being done in South Carolina."

Nate's interest and enthusiasm for his topic generated a series of notes and several draft paragraphs, and he was able to explain his goals forcefully in class. Here is what he wrote when his teacher asked for an account of what he planned to do in his essay: "I would like to evaluate the decision to remove the Confederate Battle Flag from the statehouse dome in Columbia, South Carolina. I do not believe it was handled properly and I do not think the valiant soldiers that fought in the war between the states and defended their way of life should be dishonored by a bunch of politicians who use people's feelings to their disadvantage. Now that politicians have won a battle, many more are springing up all over the South wanting to destroy a way of life and turn it into a politically correct zombie. I want to show that the flag is about pride, not prejudice."

But as Nate wrote a first draft, his goals gradually changed. In the course of discussing his ideas with his classmates and with his friends, he discovered that they had a number of what he considered to be misperceptions. They did not know much about the South and its traditions, and their conclusions on the flag issue, he was convinced, followed from their lack of knowledge. Nate also learned that several of his friends and classmates had different notions of what the Confederate flag stood for. African Americans in his dorm explained that when they stopped at a restaurant and saw the Confederate flag in the window, they understood from experience that it meant, "We don't want black people eating here."

Nate decided that one of his goals would be to educate people about the thinking of many South Carolinians and that the Confederate flag was not necessarily a symbol of racism. He would defend the decision of the South Carolina legislature, which had attempted to find some middle ground on the issue. Rather than calling for the return of the flag to the capitol, he would support the legislature's decision to raise the flag only at the monument to Confederate soldiers.

Read as You Write

Nate's conversations with his friends indicated to him that he had to become more knowledgeable before he could complete his argument. He continued reading in the library as he developed his points, using many of the search strategies we discuss in Chapter 15. Nate's decision reflects an important fact about effective arguments: They usually emerge from substantial knowledge. If you have not explored your topic fully, then you must read widely about the subject before going further. Not only will your reading alert you to arguments that you can cite in support of your own points, but it will also clarify for you the thinking of those who disagree with you so that you can take into account their points of view. Finally, reading will allow you to take seriously what we advise early in this book: that arguing is often more a contribution to a continuing conversation than a final resolution of all doubts, and that you can sometimes do far more good by persuading people to cooperate with you than by fervently opposing them.

Nate's reading gave him a number of insights into the flag issue. He learned about the original design of the flag, which was related to the crosses of St. Andrew and St. George. He also learned about the history of the flag's display at the capitol—including the fact that the flag was first raised there in 1962, in the midst of the civil rights movement. He also found that George Wallace began displaying the Battle Flag in Alabama shortly after his confrontations with Robert Kennedy over the issue of segregation. Nate read about the NAACP and the reasons for its opposition to the flag. He sampled Web sites that supported the flag's display over the capitol (including one that quoted the famous historian Shelby Foote), and he considered others that opposed that position. After several hours of note taking, Nate was ready to assemble a serious draft.

Take the Perspective of Your Reader

In most first drafts, it makes sense to get your ideas on paper without thinking about readers. Such a practice makes positive use of strong feelings and reveals the skeleton of an argument. (Nate's first draft expressed ideas that he had been formulating for some time.) The first draft, however, is only the beginning. You need to take time to think about how your argument will come across to your readers.

First, pretend you are someone who is either uninformed about your subject or informed but holding an opposing viewpoint. If possible think of an actual person and pretend to be that person. (Nate could easily imagine a person holding an opposing view because he knew people in his dorm who disagreed with him on this issue.) Then read your argument aloud all the way through. When you read aloud, you often hear clunky phrases and catch errors, but do no more in this stage than put checks in the margins that you can return to later. Once again, you don't want to get bogged down with the little stuff. Rather, what you are after in this stage is getting an overall sense of how well you accomplished what you set out to do. Think in particular about these things:

1. *Your claim.* When you finish reading, can you summarize in one sentence what you are arguing? If you cannot, then you need to focus your claim. Then ask yourself what's at stake in your claim. Who benefits by what you are arguing? Who doesn't? How will readers react to what you are arguing? If what you are arguing is obvious to everyone and if all or nearly all would agree with you, then you need to identify an aspect on which people would disagree and restate your claim.

2. *Your good reasons.* What are the good reasons for your claim? Would a reader have any trouble identifying them? Will those readers be likely to accept your reasons? What evidence is offered to support these good reasons and how is the evidence relevant to the claim (the "so what?" question in Chapter 2)? Note any places where you might add evidence and any places where you need to explain why the evidence is relevant.

3. *Your representation of yourself.* To the extent you can, forget for a moment that you wrote what you are reading. What impression do you have of you, the writer? Is the writer believable? Trustworthy? Has the writer done his or her homework on the issue? Does the writer take an appropriate tone? Note any places where you can strengthen your credibility as a writer.

4. *Your consideration of your readers.* Do you give enough background if your readers are unfamiliar with the issue? Do you acknowledge opposing views that they might have? Do you appeal to common values that you share with them? Note any places where you might do more to address the concerns of your readers.

Here is a sample paragraph from a first draft of Nate's essay on the Confederate flag:

The Confederate Battle Flag is not a racist sign; it is the most powerful and widely recognized symbol of Southern valor and independence. The flag honors the Confederate dead, who fought for their way of life and defended their homes from Northern aggression in the War Between the

States. People today owe it to the men and women who fought for their belief in liberty and states' rights, a sacrifice rarely seen today. People ought to honor the memories of the Confederate fallen just as they remember people involved in every other war. While people are making monuments to war dead in Washington, including monuments to those who died in Vietnam and Korea, there are those who are trying to dishonor Confederate dead by taking the Battle Flag from the Confederate monument in Columbia.

When Nate put himself in the shoes of his readers, he quickly saw the need for substantial changes in that paragraph. He still felt strongly about his belief in the symbolism of the flag, but he also realized that people who disagreed with him—the people he was trying to persuade—would not appreciate his use of the term "War Between the States" because they would suspect him of thinking that the war was not fought over the issue of slavery and accuse him of resisting any racist notions associated with the flag. "States' rights" is a phrase that is honorable, but not when one of the rights is the right to own slaves. Here is how he revised his paragraph:

The Confederate Battle Flag is not a racist sign; it is the most powerful and widely recognized symbol of Southern valor and independence. It is true, unfortunately, that many racists today display the Confederate flag. But that unfortunate truth should not permit us to discontinue to honor the flag, any more than the use of the cross by the Ku Klux Klan should permit us to discontinue honoring the cross in our churches. It is also true that the Civil War was conducted in large part because of the issue of slavery, that many people therefore associate the Confederate flag with white supremacy, and that many whites during the Civil Rights era flew the flag as a sign of resistance to the end of segregation. But the Civil War was also fought for other reasons in the South by many people who neither owned slaves nor who had any use for slavery. The flag honors the Confederate dead who fought for their way of life and who believed they were defending their homes from Northern aggression. People today owe it to those who fought for their belief in liberty (our nation's most basic belief) to permit their monuments to include the flag they fought under. The Confederate flag needs to be restored to its original symbolism, and that can only take place if it continues to be displayed in honorable places. To change the Confederate monument in Columbia by taking away the Confederate flag would be to dishonor those who died under it. People ought to honor the memories of the Confederate fallen just as they remember people involved in every other war. Shelby Foote, the well known Southern historian and author of a three-volume history of the Civil War, said it best: "Many among the finest people this country ever produced died [under the Confederate flag]. To take it as a symbol of evil is a misrepresentation" (www.southerninitiative.com, April 30, 2001).

Do you think Nate's revisions were successful in answering his reader's objections and in creating a more effective ethos? How will his quotation from the Southern historian go over with his Northern readers?

REVISION CHECKLIST
Focus on Your Argument

1. Find your main claim.

What kind of claim is it? Are you writing a proposal, an evaluation, a rebuttal, a narrative, or what? What things follow from that? (All arguments, as we have emphasized in Chapters 6 through 11, tend to develop in certain ways, depending on their kind.) Nate's argument that the Confederate flag ought to be permitted to remain on the Confederate monument (but not over the state capitol building) is a proposal argument. Identifying the type of claim helps you to think about how it might be developed further (see Chapter 11).

2. How will you support your claim?

What good reasons will you use? Will you use definitions, an evaluation, a causal argument, a list of consequences, a comparison or contrast, or a combination of these? Nate's paragraph, one segment of his overall proposal, offers a definition: "The Confederate Battle Flag is not a racist sign; it is the most powerful and widely recognized symbol of Southern valor and independence." If Nate can get his readers to accept that definition—that "good reason" for agreeing to his overall thesis—he will have gone a long way toward achieving his goals. It may take him several paragraphs to argue for the definition, but eventually it will be worth the effort. Nate might also use other good reasons to support his overall position on the flag issue: the good consequences that will follow if his advice is heeded (e.g., goodwill; an end to polarization in the community), the bad consequences that might be avoided (e.g., continued controversy and divisiveness in South Carolina), the useful comparisons or contrasts that can be cited as support (e.g., the comparison between the Klan's use of the cross and racists' use of the Confederate flag), and so forth. Altogether, those good reasons will make up a complete and satisfactory argument.

3. Analyze your organization.

Turn to one of the writing guides at the end of Chapters 6 though 11 that best fits your argument (or Chapter 4 if you are doing an rhetorical analysis or Chapter 5 if you are doing a visual analysis). The guides will help you determine what kind of overall organization you need. For example, if you have a definition argument, go to the Steps at the end of Chapter 6. You should be able to identify the criteria for your definition. How many criteria do you offer? Where are they located? Are they clearly connected to your claim? In what order should they be offered?

In addition, think about other effective ordering principles. Since readers often remember things that come first or last, do you want to put your strongest good reasons early and repeat them toward the end? Or do you want to build toward a climactic effect by ordering your reasons from least important to most important? Can you group similar ideas? Should you move from least controversial to most controversial? Or from most familiar to least familiar?

4. Examine your evidence.

If you noted places where you could use more evidence when you first read through your draft, now is the time to determine what kinds of additional evidence you need. Evidence can come in the shape of examples, personal experiences, comparisons, statistics, calculations, quotations, and other kinds of data that a reader will find relevant and compelling. Decide what you need and put it in.

5. Consider your title and introduction.

Many students don't think much about titles, but titles are important: A good title makes the reader want to discover what you have to say. Be as specific as you can in your title and, if possible, suggest your stance. In the introduction get off to a fast start and convince your reader to keep reading. You may need to establish right away that a problem exists. You may have to give some background. You may need to discuss an argument presented by someone else. But above all, you want to convince your reader to keep reading.

6. Consider your conclusion.

Restating your claim usually isn't the best way to finish. The worst endings say something like "in my paper I've said this." Think about whether there is a summarizing point you can make, an implication you can draw, or another example you can include that sums up your position. If you are writing a proposal, your ending might be a call for action or a challenge. If you have a telling quotation from an authority, sometimes that can make an effective clincher.

7. Analyze the visual aspects of your text.

Do the font and layout you selected look attractive? Do you use the same font throughout? If you use more than one font, have you done so consistently? Would headings and subheadings help to identify key sections of your argument? If you include statistical data, would charts be effective? Would illustrations help to establish key points? For example, a map could be very useful if you are arguing about the location of a proposed new highway.

REVISION CHECKLIST
Focus on Your Style and Proofread Carefully

In our advice about revision, we have ignored so far issues of style and correctness. We did that not because we think style and correctness are unimportant but because some people forget that revision can involve much more than those things. In your final pass through your text, you should definitely concentrate on the style of your argument and eliminate as many errors as you can. Here are some suggestions that may help.

1. Check the connections between sentences.

Notice how your sentences are connected. If you need to signal the relationship from one sentence to the next, use a transitional word or phrase. For example, compare the following:

> *Silent Spring* was widely translated and inspired legislation on the environment in nearly all industrialized nations. *Silent Spring* changed the way we think about the environment. $\longrightarrow$

> *Silent Spring* was widely translated and inspired legislation on the environment in nearly all industrialized nations. **Moreover**, the book changed the way we think about the environment.

2. Check your sentences for emphasis.

When most people talk, they emphasize points by speaking louder, using gestures, and repeating themselves. You should know that it is possible to emphasize ideas in writing too.

- **Things in main clauses tend to stand out more than things in subordinate clauses.** Compare these two sentences: "Kroger, who studied printing in Germany, later organized a counterfeiting ring"; and "Before he organized a counterfeiting ring, Kroger studied printing in Germany." These two sentences contain exactly the same information, but they emphasize different things. The second sentence suggests Kroger studied printing in order to organize a counterfeiting ring. Signal what you want to emphasize by putting it into main clauses, and put less important information in subordinate clauses or in modifying phrases. (If two things are equally important, signal that by using coordination: "Kroger studied printing in Germany; he later organized a counterfeiting ring.")

- **Things at the beginning and at the end of sentences tend to stand out more than things in the middle.** Compare these three sentences: "After he studied printing in Germany, Kroger organized a counterfeiting ring"; "Kroger, after he studied printing in Germany, organized a counterfeiting ring"; and "Kroger organized a counterfeiting ring after he studied printing in Germany." All three sentences contain the exact same words and use the same main clause and subordinate clause, but they emphasize different things, depending on which items are placed in the beginning, middle, and end.

- **Use punctuation for emphasis.** Dashes add emphasis; parentheses de-emphasize. Compare these two sentences: "Kroger (who studied printing in Germany) organized a counterfeiting ring"; and "Kroger—who studied printing in Germany—organized a counterfeiting ring."

3. Eliminate wordiness.

Drafts often contain unnecessary words. When you revise, often you can find long expressions that can easily be shortened ("at this point in time" ⟶ "now"). Sometimes you become repetitive, saying about the same thing you said a sentence or two before. See how many words you can take out without losing the meaning.

4. Use active verbs.

Anytime you can use a verb besides a form of *be* (*is, are, was, were*), take advantage of the opportunity to make your style more lively. Sentences that begin with "There is (are)" and "It is" often have better alternatives:

> "It is true that exercising a high degree of quality control in the manufacture of our products will be an incentive for increasing our market share."
> ⟶ "If we pay attention to quality when we make our products, more people will buy them."

Notice too that active verbs often cut down on wordiness.

5. Know what your spelling checker can and can't do.

Spelling checkers are the greatest invention since peanut butter. They turn up many typos and misspellings that are hard to catch. But spelling checkers do not catch wrong words (e.g., "to much" should be "too much"), incorrect word endings ("three dog" should be "three dogs"), and other, similar errors. You still have to proofread carefully to eliminate misspellings and word choice errors.

6. Use your handbook to check items of mechanics and usage.

Nothing hurts your credibility more than leaving mechanics and usage errors in what you write. A handbook will help you identify the most common errors and answer questions of usage. Readers probably shouldn't make such harsh judgments when they find errors, but in real life they do. We've seen job application letters tossed in the rejected pile because an applicant made a single, glaring error. The conventions of punctuation, mechanics, and usage aren't that difficult to master, and you'll become a lot more confident when you know the rules or at least know how to look up the rules. You should also trust your ear: If you noticed that a sentence was hard to read aloud or that it doesn't sound right, think about how you might rephrase it. If a sentence seems too long, then you might break it into two or more sentences. If you notice a string of short sentences that sound choppy, then you might combine them. If you notice any run-on sentences or sentence fragments, fix them.

Get Help on Your Draft

Don't trust your own ears (and eyes) exclusively. Most good writers let someone else—a trusted advisor or several of them—read what they write before they share it with their audience. You too need to develop a way of getting advice that you can use to shape your revisions. Be sure to leave enough time for someone else to review your work and for you to make revisions.

A good reviewer is one who is willing to give you her time and honest opinion, and who knows enough about the subject of your paper to make useful suggestions. A roommate or close friend can serve, but often such a friend will be reluctant to give negative evaluations. Perhaps you can develop a relationship with people with whom you can share drafts—you read theirs; they read yours. Whomever you choose, give that person time to read your work carefully and sympathetically. You need not take every piece of advice you get, but you do need to consider suggestions with an open mind.

Making Effective Arguments

Designing, Presenting, and Documenting

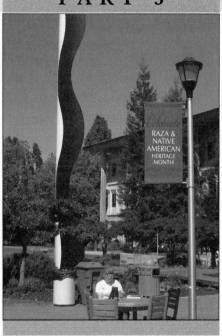

Advances in digital technology have made it possible for almost anyone to publish color images along with text, both on paper and on the World Wide Web. Programs such as PowerPoint make it easy to prepare visuals for oral presentations. Furthermore, many students now routinely publish animations, audio, and video clips along with images on Web sites. What is now possible using relatively common and inexpensive computers and software is staggering in comparison to what could be done just a decade ago.

But if new technologies for writing have given us a great deal of potential power, they have also presented us with a variety of challenges. Designing a piece of writing wasn't much of an issue with a typewriter. You could either single or double space, and increase or decrease the margins. But today with a word processing program you can change the typeface, insert illustrations, create charts and other graphics, and print in color. If you are publishing on the Web, you can introduce sound, animation, and video. Sometimes it seems like there are too many choices.

Likewise when you do research on the Web, you often find too much rather than too little. Much of what you find is of little value for a serious argument. And if the physical act of making changes to what you write is easier with a computer, the mental part is still hard work. Even experienced writers struggle with getting what they write into the shape they want it. In the chapters in Part 3, we offer you strategies for creating effective arguments using both new and old technologies.

CHAPTER 13

Effective Visual Design

Arguments do not communicate with words alone. Even written arguments that do not contain graphics or images have a look and feel that also communicates meaning. In daily life we infer a great deal from what we see. Designers are well aware that, like people, all writing has a body language that often communicates a strong message. Designers organize words, graphics, and images to achieve a desired effect for a particular audience and purpose. The principles of graphic design are not so very different from the rhetorical principles that were discussed in the previous chapters. It all has to do with understanding how particular effects can be achieved for particular readers in particular situations. Becoming more attentive to design will make your arguments more effective.

Perhaps the most important thing to know about design is that there are very few hard-and-fast rules. As for all arguments, everything depends on the rhetorical situation. All your decisions hinge on your purpose, your subject, the type of document you are writing, your intended audience(s), and how you want your reader(s) to perceive you. Sometimes, you succeed by breaking the rules.

Design Basics

Before discussing principles of graphic design, it is important to think about how language and visual design work. Language is extremely well adapted for describing things that fall into a linear order. Because humans perceive time as linear, language allows us from a very young age to tell stories. But when you describe a place, you have to decide what to tell about first. Suppose someone asks you how your house is laid out. You might begin by saying that inside the front door, there is an entryway that goes to the living room. The dining room is on the right, and the kitchen is adjacent. On the left is a hallway, which connects to two bedrooms on the right, one on the left, and a bathroom at the end. But if you draw a floor plan, you can show at once how the house is arranged. That's the basic difference between describing with spoken language and describing with visual images. Spoken language forces you to put things in a *sequence*; visual design forces you to arrange things in *space*. Written language—especially writing on a computer—permits you to do both: to use sequence and space simultaneously. Some of the same principles apply for both language and design when you write. Three of the most important groups of design principles are arrangement, consistency, and contrast.

Arrangement

Many people get through high school by mastering the five-paragraph theme. When they get the assignment, they first have to figure out exactly three points about the topic. Then they write an introduction announcing that they have three points, write a paragraph on each of the three points, and conclude with a paragraph that repeats the three points. It

> Place every item on a page in a visual relationship with the other items.

is amazing how useful that formula is. The basic structure of announcing the subject, developing it sequentially, and concluding with a summary works well enough in a great many circumstances—from business letters to short reports. Even many PhD dissertations are five-paragraph themes on a larger scale.

But if you translate the five-paragraph formula to space, it's not so simple. Think about putting it on a business card. How would you do it?

Introduction		Point 1
	My Topic	
Conclusion	Point 3	Point 2

Your eyes naturally go to the center, where the topic is boldfaced. But where do they go after that? It's not a given that a reader will start in the upper left-hand corner and go clockwise around the card.

Let's switch to an example of a business card.

```
┌─────────────────────────────────────────────────┐
│  (919) 684-2741              23 Maple Street      │
│                              Durham, NC 27703     │
│                                                   │
│                                                   │
│                  Todd Smith                       │
│                                                   │
│                                                   │
│  Westin Associates          Management           │
│                             Consulting            │
└─────────────────────────────────────────────────┘
```

Again, the name in the middle is where you go first, but where do your eyes go after that? The problem is that nothing on the card has any obvious visual relationship with anything else.

The way beginning designers often solve this problem is to put everything in the center. This strategy forces you to think about what is most important, and you usually put that at the top. On the next card, the information is grouped so that the relationship of the elements is clear. One of the most important design tools—white space—separates the main elements.

```
┌─────────────────────────────────────────────────┐
│                                                   │
│                  Todd Smith                       │
│                                                   │
│                Westin Associates                  │
│                                                   │
│              Management Consulting                │
│                                                   │
│                                                   │
│                 23 Maple Street                   │
│                 Durham, NC 27703                  │
│                 (919) 684-2741                    │
│                                                   │
└─────────────────────────────────────────────────┘
```

But centering everything isn't the only solution for showing the relationship of elements. Another way is by *alignment*. In the next example, the elements are aligned on the right margin and connected by an invisible line. This alignment is often called *flush right*.

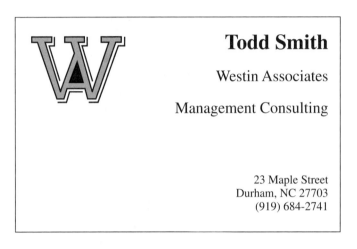

If you are in the habit of centering title pages and other elements, try using the flush left and flush right commands in your word processing program along with grouping similar elements. You'll be surprised what a difference it makes and how much more professional and persuasive your work will appear.

Consistency

You learned the principle of consistency in elementary school when your teacher told you to write on the lines, make the margins even, and indent your paragraphs. When you write using a computer, your word processing program takes care of these small concerns. However, too many people stop there when they use a computer to write. You can do a whole lot more.

> Make what is similar look similar.

Sometime during your college years, you likely will write a report or paper that uses headings. Readers increasingly expect you to divide what you write into chunks and label those chunks with headings.

It's easy enough to simply center every heading so that your report looks like this:

Title

Saepe et multum hoc mecum cogitavi, bonine an mali plus attulerit hominibus et civitatibus copia dicendi ac summum eloquentiae studium.

Heading 1

Ac me quidem diu cogitantem ratio ipsa in hanc potissimum sententiam ducit, ut existimem sapientiam sine eloquentia parum prodesse civitatibus, eloquentiam vero sine sapientia nimium obesse plerumque, prodesse numquam.

Heading 2

Ac si volumus huius rei, quae vocatur eloquentia, sive artis sive studii sive exercitationis cuiusdam sive facultatis ab natura profectae considerare principium, reperiemus id ex honestissimis causis natum atque optimis rationibus profectum.

If you write a report that looks like this one, you can make it much more visually appealing by devising a system of consistent headings that indicates the overall organization. You first have to determine the level of importance of each heading by making an outline to see what fits under what. Then you make the headings conform to the different levels so that what is equal in importance will have the same level of heading.

Title

Saepe et multum hoc mecum cogitavi, bonine an mali plus attulerit hominibus et civitatibus copia dicendi ac summum eloquentiae studium.

Major Heading

Ac me quidem diu cogitantem ratio ipsa in hanc potissimum sententiam ducit, ut existimem sapientiam sine eloquentia parum prodesse civitatibus, eloquentiam vero sine sapientia nimium obesse plerumque, prodesse numquam.

Level 2 Heading Ac si volumus huius rei, quae vocatur eloquentia, sive artis sive studii sive exercitationis cuiusdam sive facultatis ab natura profectae considerare principium, reperiemus id ex honestissimis causis natum atque optimis rationibus profectum.

Other useful tools that word processing programs offer are ways of making lists. Bulleted lists are used frequently to present good reasons for claims and proposals. For example:

The proposed new major in Technology, Literacy, and Culture will:

• Prepare our students for the changing demands of the professions and public citizenship
• Help students to move beyond technical skills and strategies to understand the historical, economic, political, and scientific impacts of new technologies
• Allow students to practice new literacies that mix text, graphics, sound, video, animation, hypermedia, and real-time communication
• Help to ensure that wise decisions are made about the collection, organization, storage, and distribution of and access to information via new technologies
• Provide students with a deeper, richer, and more profound understanding of the dynamic relationships among technology, culture, and the individual

---

A bulleted list is an effective way of presenting a series of items or giving an overview of what is to come. However, bulleted lists can be ineffective if the items in the list are not similar.

Contrast

We tend to follow the principle of consistency because that's what we've been taught and that's what writing technologies—from typewriters to computers—do for us. But the principle of contrast takes some conscious effort on our part to implement. Take a simple résumé as an example.

> Make what is different
> look different.

Roberto Salazar

Address: 3819 East Jefferson Avenue, Escondido, CA 92027

Send email to: salazar@capaccess.org

Job Title: Financial Consultant, Credit Reviewer, Financial Analyst

Relocation: Yes—particular interest in Central and South America.

Experience

2004–present. Credit Services Group, Carpenter & Tokaz LLP, 3000 Wilshire Boulevard, Los Angeles, California 90017

CONSULTING: Presented Directorate with report findings, conclusions, and recommendations for operation improvements. Coordinated a process improvement engagement for a large finance company, which resulted in the consolidation of credit operations.

SUPERVISION: Supervised, trained, and assessed the work of staff (1–4) involved in audit assists. Reviewed real estate investments, other real estate owned, and loan portfolios for documentation, structure, credit analysis, risk identification, and credit scoring.

Education

2004 San Diego State University, San Diego, California, Bachelor of Business Administration

Languages

Fluent in English and Spanish. Experience in tutoring students with Spanish lessons at San Diego State University, San Diego, California

Computers

Proficient with Microsoft Word and Excel, Lotus Notes, AmiPro, Lotus 1-2-3, WordPerfect, and Sendero SV simulation modeling software. Familiarity with several online information retrieval methods.

References available on request.

The résumé has consistency, but there is no contrast between what is more important and what is less important. The overall impression is that the person is dull, dull, dull.

Your résumé, along with your letter of application, might be the most important piece of persuasive writing you'll do in your life. It's worth taking some extra time to distinguish yourself. Your ability to write a convincing letter and produce a handsome résumé is a good reason for an employer to hire you. Remember why you are paying attention to graphic design. You want your readers to focus on certain elements, and you want to create the right image. Use of contrast can emphasize the key features of the résumé and contribute to a much more forceful and dynamic image.

Roberto Salazar

3819 East Jefferson Avenue
Escondido, CA 92027
salazar@capaccess.org

Position Titles Sought

Financial Consulting
Credit Reviewer
Financial Analyst
(Willing to relocate, especially to Central or South America)

Education

2004	**Bachelor of Business Administration.** San Diego State University.

Experience

2004–present	**Credit Services Group, Carpenter & Tokaz, LLP.** 3000 Wilshire Boulevard Los Angeles, California 90017
	Consulting: Presented Directorate with report findings, conclusions, and recommendations for operation improvements. Coordinated a process improvement engagement for a large finance company, which resulted in the consolidation of credit operations.
	Supervision: Supervised, trained, and assessed the work of four staff involved in audit assists. Reviewed real estate investments, other real estate owned, and loan portfolios for documentation, structure, credit analysis, risk identification, and credit scoring.

Languages

Fluent in English and Spanish. Experience as a Spanish Tutor at SDSU.

Computer Skills

Proficient with Microsoft Word & Excel, Lotus Notes, AmiPro, Lotus 1-2-3, WordPerfect, and Sendero SV simulation modeling software. Familiarity with several online information retrieval methods.

References

Available on request.

Notice that arrangement and consistency are also important to the revised résumé. Good design requires that all elements be brought into play to produce the desired results.

Understanding Typefaces and Fonts

Until computers and word processing software came along, most writers had little or no control over the type style they used. If they typed, they likely used Courier, a fact that many typists didn't even know. Furthermore, the typewriter gave no choice about type size. Writers worked with either 10-point type or 12-point type. (A point is a printer's measure. One inch equals 72 points.) You had no way to include italics. The convention was to underline the word so that the printer would later set the word in italics. Boldfacing could be accomplished only by typing the word over again, making it darker.

Even if the general public knew little about type styles and other aspects of printing before computers came along, printers had five hundred years' experience learning about which type styles were easiest to read and what effects different styles produced. Type styles are grouped into families of **typefaces**. When you open the pull-down font menu of your word processing program, you see a small part of that five-hundred-year tradition of developing typefaces. At first, many of the typefaces will look about the same to you, but after you get some practice with using various typefaces, you will begin to notice how they differ.

The two most important categories of typefaces are **serif** and **sans serif**. Serif (rhymes with "sheriff") type was developed first, imitating the strokes of an ink pen. Serifs are the little wedge-shaped ends on letter forms, which scribes produced with wedge-tipped pens. Serif type also has thick and thin transitions on the curved strokes. Five of the most common serif typefaces are the following:

Times

Palatino

Bookman

Garamond

New Century Schoolbook

If these typefaces look almost alike to you, it's not an accident. Serif typefaces were designed to be easy to read. They don't call attention to themselves. Therefore, they are well suited for long stretches of text and are used frequently.

Sans serif type (*sans* is French for "without") doesn't have the little wedge-shaped ends on letters, and the thickness of the letters is the same. Popular sans serif typefaces include the following:

Helvetica

Verdana

Arial

Sans serif typefaces work well for headings and short stretches of text. They give the text a crisp, modern look. And some sans serif typefaces are easy to read on a computer screen.

Finally, there are many script and decorative typefaces. These typefaces tend to draw attention to themselves. They are harder to read, but sometimes they can be used for good effects. Some script and decorative typefaces include the following:

Zapf Chancery

STENCIL

Mistral

Tekton

Changing typefaces will draw attention. It is usually better to be consistent in using typefaces within a text unless you want to signal something.

It's easy to change the size of type when you compose on a computer. A specific size of a typeface is called a **font**. The font size displays on the menu bar. For long stretches of text, you probably should use at least 10-point or 12-point type. For headings, you can use larger type.

type	8 point
type	10 point
type	12 point
type	14 point
type	18 point
type	24 point
type	36 point

type

48 point

type

72 point

Fonts also have different weights. *Weight* refers to the thickness of the strokes. Take a look at the fonts on your font menu. You probably have some fonts that offer options ranging from light to bold, such as Arial Condensed Light, Arial, Arial Rounded MT Bold, and Arial Black. Here's what each of these looks like as a heading:

1. Arial Condensed Light

Position Titles Sought

Financial Consultant

Credit Reviewer

Financial Analyst
(Willing to relocate, especially to Central or South America)

2. Arial

Position Titles Sought

Financial Consultant

Credit Reviewer

Financial Analyst
(Willing to relocate, especially to Central or South America)

3. Arial Rounded MT Bold

Position Titles Sought

Financial Consultant

Credit Reviewer

Financial Analyst
(Willing to relocate, especially to Latin America)

4. Arial Black

Position Titles Sought

Financial Consultant

Credit Reviewer

Financial Analyst
(Willing to relocate, especially to Latin America)

You can get strong contrasts by using heavier weights of black type for headings and using white space to accent what is different.

Finally, most word processing programs have some special effects that you can employ. The three most common are **boldface**, *italics*, and underlining. All three are used for emphasis, but underlining should be avoided because it makes text harder to read.

Creating Images and Other Graphics

Pictures, drawings, and other graphics can have powerful impacts on readers. They can support or emphasize your claims and make concrete the ideas you express in words. They can introduce additional details and even show other points of view.

The main thing you want to avoid is using images strictly for decoration. Readers quickly get tired of pictures and other graphics that don't contribute to the content. Think of pictures, charts, and graphics as alternative means of presenting information. Good use of images contributes to your overall argument.

Pictures

Digital cameras and scanners enable you to create digital images, which you can then easily insert into a word processing file or a Web site. Having the capability to create and publish images, however, doesn't tell you when to use images or for what purposes.

The first step is to determine what images you might need. The majority of images should be used to illustrate content. After you decide that you need a particular image, the next step is to find or create it. If you use someone else's images, including those you find on the Web, you need to obtain permission from the owner, and you need to credit the image just as you would a quotation (see Chapter 15).

When you have images in a digital format, you may need to edit or resize them. Many computers now come equipped with image editors, and you can also download shareware from the Web. If you own a digital camera, it likely includes some type of image editor. Before you begin working, make a copy from the original image. Once you alter and save the original, you cannot get its original image again.

One feature on all image editors is a **cropping** command, which allows you to select part of an image to keep while discarding the rest. You can crop out distracting or unneeded detail and thus create a stronger focus on what you want to emphasize. Cropping also reduces file size, allowing images to load faster on a Web site. To crop an image, select the rectangle or cropping tool, and when you have identified the area you want to keep, select the crop or trim command to discard the rest.

Other Graphics

Charts and graphs create visual summaries of data and are especially useful for illustrating comparisons, patterns, and trends. Popular software, including Microsoft Excel and PowerPoint, allows you to make charts and graphs by typing the data into a datasheet and then selecting the type of graph or chart. The program then creates the chart or graph. You must provide labels for the data, and you should include a caption that describes the content. See pages 92–96 for a discussion of charts and graphs.

Cropping enables you to select the part of the image that is important and to discard the rest.

Writing Arguments for the Web

The Web is a grassroots medium with millions of people putting up Web sites, so it's no surprise that the Web has turned out to be a vast forum for arguments. It seems that if anyone has an opinion about anything, there's a Web site representing that position. If you have strong feelings about any broad issue, you can find on the Web people who think like you do.

The problem with many argument sites on the Web is that they don't provide much depth. Their links, if any, take you to similar sites, with no context for making the link. It's up to you to figure out the relevance of the link. This strategy works for people who are already convinced of the position being advocated, but it's not a strategy that works well with people who haven't made up their mind. When you create a Web site that advocates a position, the ease of linking on the Web doesn't make your work any easier. Good arguments still require much thought and careful planning. You cannot expect your readers to do your work for you. You still have to supply good reasons.

Web authoring software makes it easy to compose Web pages, but the software doesn't tell you how reading on the Web is different from reading print materials. In most printed books, magazines, and newspapers, the text is continuous. Even though printed text isn't necessarily linear—witness the boxes and sidebars in this book—the basic movement in print is linear and the basic unit is the paragraph. By contrast, the basic movement on the Web is nonlinear and the basic unit is the screen. Perhaps the most important fact to remember when composing for the Web is that fewer than 10 percent of people who click on a Web site ever scroll down the page. Their eyes stop at the bottom of the screen. And those who do scroll down usually don't scroll down very far.

The First Page Is the Most Important

People who browse Web sites don't stay long if they aren't interested or if it takes too long to find out what's on the Web site. That's why the first page is critical. If you have something to tell your visitors, tell them right away. They probably aren't going to click or scroll through a bunch of pages to find out where you stand on an issue. You have to let your readers know on the first page what your site is about.

The first page is also the front door to your site, and when visitors enter your front door, they need to know where to go next. Supplying navigation tools on the first page is critical. These can take the form of menu bars, buttons, or clickable images. Whatever form you choose, the labels should indicate what the visitor will find on the next screen.

The Web page in Figure 13.1 was created by Grace Bernhardt for a class project on the conflict surrounding the Balcones Canyonlands Preserve (BCP), a nature reserve located within the city limits of Austin, Texas, and the habitat for six endangered species. The text on the first page describes the place and the various stakeholders in the Balcones Canyonlands Preserve. It also provides a menu to the main areas of the site.

Divide Your Text into Chunks

Long stretches of text on the Web tend not to get read. Effective Web designers try to divide text into chunks whenever possible. For example, when they present a list of facts, they often put space between items or use a bulleted list rather than a long paragraph. The page in Figure 13.2 is from a student Web site designed by Chungpei Hu on safety issues for Sixth Street, the entertainment district in Austin, Texas. It uses a bulleted list to enumerate frequent fire code violations in bars and clubs along Sixth Street.

You can put a great deal of background information about a topic on a Web site, connected by links to the main argument. You can thus offer a short summary on the main page, with links to other pages that give background and evidence. One advantage of this strategy is that you

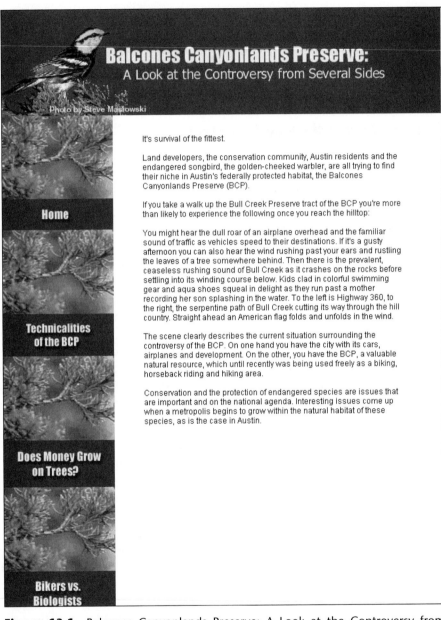

It's survival of the fittest.

Land developers, the conservation community, Austin residents and the endangered songbird, the golden-cheeked warbler, are all trying to find their niche in Austin's federally protected habitat, the Balcones Canyonlands Preserve (BCP).

If you take a walk up the Bull Creek Preserve tract of the BCP you're more than likely to experience the following once you reach the hilltop:

You might hear the dull roar of an airplane overhead and the familiar sound of traffic as vehicles speed to their destinations. If it's a gusty afternoon you can also hear the wind rushing past your ears and rustling the leaves of a tree somewhere behind. Then there is the prevalent, ceaseless rushing sound of Bull Creek as it crashes on the rocks before settling into its winding course below. Kids clad in colorful swimming gear and aqua shoes squeal in delight as they run past a mother recording her son splashing in the water. To the left is Highway 360, to the right, the serpentine path of Bull Creek cutting its way through the hill country. Straight ahead an American flag folds and unfolds in the wind.

The scene clearly describes the current situation surrounding the controversy of the BCP. On one hand you have the city with its cars, airplanes and development. On the other, you have the BCP, a valuable natural resource, which until recently was being used freely as a biking, horseback riding and hiking area.

Conservation and the protection of endangered species are issues that are important and on the national agenda. Interesting issues come up when a metropolis begins to grow within the natural habitat of these species, as is the case in Austin.

Figure 13.1 Balcones Canyonlands Preserve: A Look at the Controversy from Several Sides

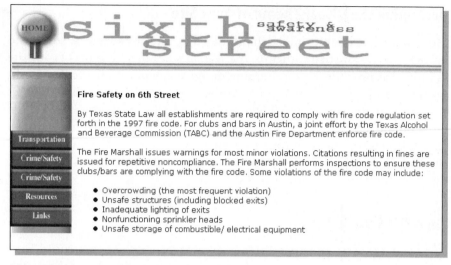

Figure 13.2 Sixth Street Safety & Awareness

design a single site both for those who know a great deal about the subject and want to skip the background information, and for those who know little and need to know the background. You can include additional evidence that would be hard to work into a paper otherwise. Furthermore, the act of clicking on particular words can make readers aware of the links in an argument.

Make the Text Readable

Above all, make your text readable. Remember that other people's monitors may be smaller than yours; thus what appears as small type on your monitor may require a magnifying glass for others. Also, dark backgrounds make for tough reading. If you use a dark background and want people to read what you write, be sure to increase the font size, make sure the contrast between text and background is adequate, and avoid using all caps and italics.

TEXT IN ALL CAPS IS HARD TO READ ON A BLACK BACKGROUND,
ESPECIALLY IF THE TEXT IS IN ITALICS.

Determine the Visual Theme of Your Site

Most Web sites contain more than one page, and because it is so easy to move from one site to another on the Web, it's important to make your site as unified as possible. Using common design elements, such as color, icons, typeface, and layout, contributes to the unity of the site. The Balcones Canyonlands Preserves site shown in Figure 13.1 repeats the image of its most famous resident—the endangered golden-cheeked warbler—on each page, along with images of foliage. Even without the text, the images on the site make it evident that the site deals with environmental issues.

Keep the Visuals Simple

The students who produced the Web sites in this chapter could have included many large pictures if they had chosen to. But they deliberately kept the visual design simple. A less complicated site is not only more friendly because it loads faster, but if it is well designed, it can be elegant. Simple elements are also easier to repeat. Too many icons, bullets, horizontal rules, and other embellishments give a page a cluttered appearance. A simple, consistent design is always effective for pages that contain text.

Finally, keep in mind that although good graphic design provides visual impact and can help the visitor navigate a Web site, it has little value if it is not supported by substance. People still expect to come away from a Web site with substantial information. Good visual design makes your Web site more appealing, but it does not do the work of argument for you.

Make Your Site Easy to Navigate

People don't read Web sites the same way they read a book. They scan quickly and move around a lot. They don't necessarily read from top to bottom. If you are trying to make an argument on the Web, you have to think differently about how the reader is going to encounter your argument. If you put the argument on more than one page, you have to plan the site so that readers can navigate easily.

First, you should determine the overall structure of your Web site, assuming you plan to include more than one page. Web sites that have a main page should have clear navigation tools. For example, the transportation section of Sixth Street Safety & Awareness (Figure 13.3) offers sections for both the general public and University of Texas students. The navigation icons make the possibilities obvious.

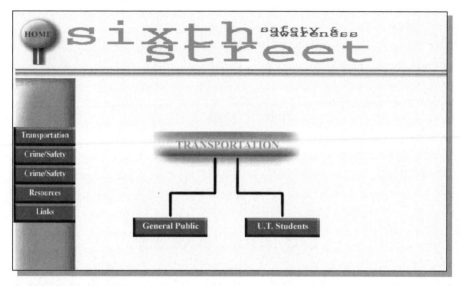

Figure 13.3 Sixth Street Safety & Awareness

EVALUATING A WEB SITE

You can use the following criteria to evaluate Web sites you have designed or those designed by others.

1. **Audience:** How does the site identify its intended audience? How does it indicate what else is on the site?

2. **Content:** How informative is the content? Where might more content be added? What do you want to know more about? Are there any mechanical, grammar, or style problems?

3. **Readability:** Is there sufficient contrast between the text and the background to make the text legible? Are the margins wide enough? Are there any paragraphs that go on too long and need to be divided? Are headings inserted in the right places, and if headings are used for more than one level, are these levels indicated consistently? Is text in boldface and all caps kept short?

4. **Visual Design:** Does the site have a consistent visual theme? Where is the focal point on each page? Do the images contribute to the visual appeal or do they detract from it?

5. **Navigation:** How easy or difficult is it to move from one page to another on the site? Are there any broken links?

CHAPTER 14

Effective Oral Presentations

Becoming effective in oral communication is just as important as in written communication. You may be asked to give oral presentations in your later life and perhaps in your college career. Oral presentations can be developed from written assignments and supported by visual elements such as slides, overheads, video clips, and other media.

Planning an Oral Presentation

Getting Started

Successful oral arguments, like written arguments, require careful planning. You first step is to find out what kind of oral presentation you are being asked to give. Look closely at your assignment for key words such as *analyze, evaluate,* and *propose,* which often indicate what is expected.

Another important consideration is length. How much time you have to give a speech determines the depth you can go into. Speakers who ignore this simple principle often announce near the end of their time that they will have to omit major points and rush to finish. Their presentations end abruptly and leave the audience confused about what the speaker had to say.

You also should consider early on where you will be giving the speech. If you want to use visual elements to support your presentation, you need to make sure the room has the equipment you need. If you know the room is large or has poor acoustics, you may need to bring audio equipment.

Selecting Your Topic

Choosing and researching a topic for an oral presentation is similar to choosing and researching a topic for a written assignment. If you have a broad choice of topics, make a list of subjects that interest you. Then go through your list and ask yourself these questions:

- Will you enjoy speaking on this topic?
- Will your audience be interested in this topic?
- Does the topic fit the situation for your presentation?
- Do you know enough to speak on this topic?
- If you do not know enough, are you willing to do research to learn more about the topic?

Remember that enthusiasm is contagious, so if you are excited about a topic, chances are your audience will become interested too.

Research for an oral presentation is similar to the research you must do for a written argument. You will find guidelines in Chapter 15 for planning your research. Remember that you will need to develop a bibliography for an oral presentation that requires research, just as you would for a written argument. You will need to document the sources of your information and provide those sources in your talk.

Thinking About Your Audience

Unlike writing, when you give a speech, you have your audience directly before you. They will give you concrete feedback during your presentation by smiling or frowning, by paying attention or losing interest, by asking questions or sitting passively.

When planning your presentation, you should think about your audience in relation to your topic.

- What is your audience likely to know or believe about your topic?
- What does your audience probably not know about your topic?
- What key terms will you have to define or explain?
- What assumptions do you hold in common with your audience?
- Where is your audience most likely to disagree with you?
- What questions are they likely to ask?

Supporting Your Presentation

The steps for writing various kinds of arguments, listed at the ends of Chapters 4–11, can be used to organize an oral presentation. When you have organized your main points, you need to decide how to support those points. Look at your research notes and think about how best to incorporate the information you found. Consider using one or more of these strategies:

- **Facts.** Speakers who know their facts build credibility.
- **Statistics.** Good use of statistics gives the impression that the speaker has done his or her homework. Statistics also can indicate that a particular example is representative. One tragic car accident doesn't mean a road is dangerous, but an especially high accident rate relative to other nearby roads does make the case.
- **Statements by authorities.** Quotations from credible experts are another common way of supporting key points.
- **Narratives.** Narratives are small stories that can illustrate key points. Narratives are a good way of keeping the attention of the audience. Keep them short so they don't distract from your major points.
- **Humor.** In most situations audiences appreciate humor. Humor is a good way to convince an audience that you have common beliefs and experiences, and that your argument may be one they can agree with.

Planning Your Introduction

No part of your speech is more critical than the introduction. You have to get the audience's attention, introduce your topic, convince the audience that it is important to them, present your thesis, and give your audience either an overview of your presentation or a sense of your direction. Accomplishing all this in a short time is a tall order, but if you lose your audience in the first two minutes, you won't recover their attention. You might begin with a compelling example or anecdote that both introduces your topic and indicates your stance.

Planning Your Conclusion

The next most important part of your speech is your conclusion. You want to end on a strong note. First, you need to signal that you are entering the conclusion. You can announce that you are concluding, but you also can give signals in other ways. Touching on your main points again will help your audience to remember them. But simply summarizing is a dull way to close. Think of an example or an idea that captures the gist of your speech, something that your audience can take away with them.

Delivering an Oral Presentation

The Importance of Practice

There is no substitute for rehearsing your speech several times in advance. You will become more confident and have more control over the content. The best way to overcome nervousness about speaking in front of others is to be well prepared. When you know what you are going to say, you can pay more attention to your audience, making eye contact and watching body language for signals about how well you are making your points. When you rehearse you can also become comfortable with any visual elements you will be using. Finally, rehearsing your speech is the only reliable way to find out how long it will take to deliver.

Practice your speech in front of others. If possible, go to the room where you will be speaking and ask a friend to sit in the back so you can learn how well you can be heard. You can also learn a great deal by videotaping your rehearsal and watching yourself as an audience member.

Speaking Effectively

Talking is so much a part of our daily lives that we rarely think about our voices as instruments of communication unless we have some training in acting or public speaking. You can become better at speaking by becoming more aware of your delivery. Pay attention to your breathing as you practice your speech. When you breathe at your normal rate, you will not rush your speech. Plan where you will pause during your speech. Pauses allow you to take a sip of water and give your audience a chance to sum up mentally what you have said. And don't be afraid to repeat key points. Repetition is one of the easiest strategies for achieving emphasis.

Most of the time nervousness is invisible. You can feel nervous and still impress your audience as being calm and confident. If you make mistakes while speaking, know that the audience understands and will be forgiving. Stage fright is normal; sometimes it can be helpful in raising the energy level of a presentation.

Nonverbal Communication

While you are speaking, you are also communicating with your presence. Stand up unless you are required to sit. Move around instead of standing behind the podium. Use gestures to emphasize main points, and only main points; if you gesture continually, you may appear nervous.

Maintaining eye contact is crucial. Begin your speech by looking at the people directly in front of you and then move your eyes around the room, looking to both sides. Attempting to look at each person during a speech may seem unnatural, but it is the best way to convince all the members of your audience that you are speaking directly to them.

T I P S

For Effective Speeches

Usually more effective	Usually less effective
Practice in advance	Don't practice
Talk	Read
Stand	Sit
Make eye contact	Look down
Move around	Stand still
Speak loudly	Mumble
Use visual elements	Lack visual elements
Focus on main points	Get lost in details
Give an overview of what you are going to say in the introduction	Start your talk without indicating where you are headed
Give a conclusion that summarizes your main points and ends with a key idea or example	Stop abruptly
Finish on time	Run overtime

Handling Questions

Your presentation doesn't end when you finish. Speakers are usually expected to answer questions afterward. How you handle questions is also critical to your success. Speakers who are evasive or fail to acknowledge questions sometimes lose all the credibility they have built in their speech. But speakers who listen carefully to questions and answer them honestly build their credibility further.

Keep in mind a few principles about handling questions:

- Repeat the question so that the entire audience can hear it and to confirm you understood it.
- Take a minute to reflect on the question. If you do not understand the question, ask the questioner to restate it.
- Some people will make a small speech instead of asking a question. Acknowledge their point of view but avoid getting into a debate.
- If you cannot answer a question, don't bluff and don't apologize. You can offer to research the question or you can ask the audience if they know the answer.
- If you are asked a question during your speech, answer it if it is a short, factual question or one of clarification. Postpone questions that require long answers until the end to avoid losing the momentum of your speech.

Multimedia Presentations

Visual Elements

Visual elements can both support and reinforce your major points. They give you another means of reaching your audience and keeping them stimulated. Visual elements range from simple transparencies and handouts to elaborate multimedia presentations. Some of the more easily created visual elements are

- Outlines
- Statistical charts
- Flow charts
- Photographs
- Maps

At the very minimum, you should consider putting an outline of your talk on an overhead transparency. Some speakers think that they will kill interest in their talk if they show the audience what they are going to say in advance. Just the opposite is the case. An outline allows an audience to keep track of where you are in your talk. Outlines also help you to make transitions to your next point. Most printers can make transparencies from blank transparency sheets fed through the paper feeder. Charts, maps, photographs, and other graphics in digital format can thus be printed onto transparencies. Many photocopiers can also make transparencies.

Keep the amount of text short. You don't want your audience straining to read long passages on the screen and neglecting what you have to say. Except for quotations, use single words and short phrases—not sentences—on transparencies and slides.

One major difficulty with visual elements is that they tempt you to look at the screen instead of at your audience. You have to face your audience while your audience is looking at the screen. Needless to say, you have to practice to feel comfortable.

T I P S

Readable Transparencies and Slides

If you put text on transparencies or slides, make sure that the audience can read the text from more than 10 feet away. You may depend on your transparencies and slides to convey important information, but if your audience cannot read the slides, not only will the information be lost but the audience will become frustrated.

Use these type sizes for transparencies and slides.

	Transparencies	Slides
Title:	36 pt	24 pt
Subtitles:	24 pt	18 pt
Other text:	18 pt	14 pt

Preview your transparencies and slides from a distance equal to the rear of the room where you will be speaking. If you cannot read them, increase the type size.

Presentation Software

You likely have seen many presentations that use Microsoft PowerPoint because it has become a favorite of faculty who lecture. If you have Microsoft Word on your computer, you likely have PowerPoint since they are often sold together. PowerPoint is straightforward to use, which is one of the reasons it has become so popular. You can quickly get an outline of your presentation onto slides, and if projection equipment is available in the room where you are speaking, the slides are easily displayed.

PowerPoint offers a choice of many backgrounds, which is a potential pitfall. Light text on a dark background is hard to read. It forces you to close every window and turn off all the lights in order for your audience to see the text. Darkened rooms create problems. You may have difficulty reading your notes in a dark room, and your audience may fall asleep. Instead, always use dark text on a white or light-colored background. Usually your audience can read your slides with a light background in a room with the shades up or lights on.

You can leave a slide on the screen for about one to two minutes, which allows your audience time to read and connect the slide to what you are saying. You will need to practice to know when to display a new slide. Without adequate practice, you can easily get too far ahead or behind in your slide show and then be forced to interrupt yourself to get your slides back in sync with your speech. You also need to know how to darken the screen if you want the audience to focus on you during parts of your presentation.

Another pitfall of PowerPoint is getting carried away with all the special effects possible such as fade-ins, fade-outs, and sound effects. Presentations heavy on the special effects often come off as heavy on style and light on substance. They also can be time-consuming to produce.

CHAPTER 15

Effective Research

Research: Knowing What Information You Need

The writing that you do in school sometimes seems isolated from the real world. After all, when you write for a class, your real audience is usually the teacher. For the same reason, the research associated with writing for school tends to get isolated from real-world problems. Instead of asking questions such as "How may compounds that mimic estrogen be causing reproductive abnormalities in certain animal species?" students ask questions such as "What do I need to know to write this paper?" This approach tends to separate research from writing. If you've ever said to yourself, "I'll get on the Web or go to the library to do the research tonight, and then tomorrow afternoon I'll start writing the paper," you might be making some assumptions about the nature of research and writing that will actually make your task harder instead of easier. For now, set aside what you already know about how to do research and think instead in terms of gathering information to solve problems and answer questions.

Effective research depends on two things: knowing what kind of information you are looking for and knowing where to get it. What you already know about writing arguments will help you to make some decisions about what kind of information you should be looking for. For instance, if you have decided to write a proposal for solving the problem of HMOs limiting subscribers' health care options, you already know that you will need to find statistics (to help your readers understand the urgency and scope of the problem) and several different analyses of the situation by writers from different camps (to help you make sure your own understanding of the situation is accurate, complete, and fair to all participants). But if you keep thinking about the demands of the proposal as a type of argument, you might also decide that you need to look at how this problem has been solved in the British or Canadian health system or how programs like Medicare and Medicaid are dealing with it.

Even if you don't yet know enough about your subject to know what type of argument you will want to write, there are still some basic questions you can use to plan your research. To make a thoughtful and mature contribution to any debate in the realm of public discourse, you will need to know the background of the issue. As you begin your research, then, you can use the following questions as a guide.

1. Who are the speakers on this issue and what are they saying?

Subdividing the group of everyone who has something to say on this issue and everything that is being said into narrower categories will help you to gain a better understanding of what the debate looks like. For example, you might make the following divisions:

- Who are the experts on this issue? What do the experts say?
- Who else is talking about it? What do they say?
- Are the people whose interests are most at stake participating in the debate? What are they saying?

In addition to the categories of experts, nonexpert speakers, and those whose interests are at stake, there are other general categories you can begin from, such as supporters and opponents of a position, liberals and conservatives, and so on.

Also remember that any given debate will have its own specific set of opponents. In a debate about constructing a storage facility for nuclear waste in Nevada, for instance, conservationists and proponents of growth in the state of Nevada are lining up against the federal government. On another significant issue—water usage—proponents of growth stand in opposition to conservationists, who object to the demands Las Vegas makes on the waters of the Colorado River. On yet other issues, conservationists depend on the federal government to use its power to protect land, water, and other resources that are vulnerable to the activities of businesses and individuals.

2. What is at stake?

Political debates often boil down to arguments about control of, or access to, resources or power. Therefore, resources and power are good places to start looking for what is at stake in any given debate. Depending on the nature of the debate, you might also look at what is at stake in terms of ethical and moral issues. For example, as a country and as a human community, what does this nation stand to lose if many young Americans can no longer afford to go to college? To help narrow down your search, you might rephrase this question in several different ways:

- How or why does this issue matter: to the world, to the citizens of this country, to the people whose interests are at stake, to me?

■ What stands to be gained or lost for any of these stakeholders?

■ Who is likely to be helped and hurt the most?

3. What kinds of arguments are being made about this issue?

Just as it is helpful to subdivide the whole field of speakers on your issue into narrower groups that line up according to sides, it is also helpful to subdivide the whole field of what is being said according to types or categories of arguments. It might help to set up a chart of speakers and their primary arguments to see how they line up.

■ What are the main claims being offered?

■ What reasons are offered in support of these claims?

■ What are the primary sources of evidence?

■ Is some significant aspect of this issue being ignored or displaced in favor of others?

■ If so, why?

4. Who are the audiences for this debate?

Sometimes, the audience for a debate is every responsible member of society, everyone living in a certain region, or everyone who cares about the fate of the human species on this planet. More often, however, arguments are made to specific types of audiences, and knowing something about those audiences can help you to understand the choices that the writers make. Even more important, knowing who is already part of the audience for a debate can help you to plan your own strategies.

■ Do you want to write to one of the existing audiences to try to change its mind or make it take action?

■ Or do you want to try to persuade a new, as-yet-uninvolved audience to get involved in the debate?

■ How much do they know about the issues involved?

■ Where do they likely stand on these issues?

■ Will they define the issues the same way you do?

5. What is your role?

At some point, as you continue to research the issue and plan your writing strategies, you will need to decide what your role should be in this debate. Ask yourself:

- What do I think about it?
- What do I think should be done about it?
- What kind of argument should I write, and to whom?

Use these questions to take inventory of how much you already know about the issue and what you need to find out more about. When you have worked through these questions, you are ready to make a claim that will guide your research efforts. See steps in writing arguments at the ends of Chapters 6 through 11 to get started.

WHAT MAKES A GOOD SUBJECT FOR RESEARCH

- **Find a subject that you are interested in.** Research can be enjoyable if you are finding out new things rather than just confirming what you already know. The most exciting part of doing research is making small discoveries.
- **Make sure that you can do a thorough job of research.** If you select a topic that is too broad, such as proposing how to end poverty, you will not be able to do an adequate job.
- **Develop a strategy for your research early on.** If you are researching a campus issue such as a parking problem, then you probably will rely most on interviews, observations, and possibly a survey. But if you find out that one of the earliest baseball stadiums, Lakefront Park in Chicago (built in 1883), had the equivalent of today's luxury boxes and you want to make an argument that the trend toward building stadiums with luxury boxes is not a new development, then you will have to do library research.
- **Give yourself enough time to do a thorough job.** You should expect to find a few dead ends, and you should expect to better focus your subject as you proceed. If you are going to do research in the field, by survey, or in the library, remember the first principle of doing research: *Things take longer than you think they will.*

Planning Your Research

Once you have a general idea about the kind of information you need to make your argument, the next step is to decide where to look for it. People who write on the job—lawyers preparing briefs, journalists covering news stories, policy analysts preparing reports, engineers describing a manufacturing process, members of Congress reporting to committees, and a host of others—have general research strategies available to them. The first is to gather the information themselves, which is called **primary** or **firsthand evidence**. We can distinguish two basic kinds of primary research.

Experiential research involves all the information you gather just through observing and taking note of events as they occur in the real world. You meet with clients, interview a candidate, go to a committee meeting, talk to coworkers, read a report from a colleague, observe a manufacturing process, witness an event, or examine a patient. In all these ways, you are adding to your store of knowledge about a problem or issue. In many cases, however, the knowledge that is gained through experience is not enough to answer all the questions or solve all the problems. In those cases, writers supplement experiential research with empirical research and research in the library.

Empirical research is a way of gathering specific and narrowly defined data by developing a test situation and then observing and recording events as they occur in the test situation. Analysis of tissue samples and cell cultures in a laboratory, for instance, can add important information to what a doctor can learn by examining a patient. Crash tests of cars help automakers and materials engineers understand why crumpling is an important part of a car's ability to protect its passengers in a crash. Surveys of adult children of divorced parents make it possible for psychologists to identify the long-term effects of divorce on family members. Many people believe that this kind of research is what adds new information to the store of human knowledge; so for many audiences, reporting the results of empirical research is an important part of making a strong argument. (Therefore, writers often use statistics and reports of research done by experts in the field to support their claims.)

For the most part, however, debates about public issues occur outside the fairly narrow intellectual spaces occupied by the true experts in any given field. Experts do, of course, participate in public debates, but so do all other interested citizens and policymakers. The majority of speakers on an issue rely on the work of others as sources of information—what is known as **secondary** or **secondhand evidence**. Many people think of library research as secondary research—the process of gathering information by reading what other people have written on a subject. In the past, library research was based almost exclusively on collections of printed materials housed in libraries; in addition to public and university libraries, organizations of all kinds had their own collections of reference materials specific to their work. Today, the Web has brought significant changes in the way people record, store, view, distribute, and gain access to documents. For most issues, searching the Web will be an important part of your research.

INTERVIEWS, OBSERVATIONS, AND SURVEYS

Interviews

- Decide first why one or more interviews could be important for your argument. Knowing the goals of your interview will help you to determine whom you need to interview and to structure the questions in the interview. You might, for example, learn more about the history of a campus issue than you were able to find out in the campus newspaper archives.

- Schedule each interview in advance, preferably by email or letter. Let the person know why you are conducting the interview. Then follow up with a phone call to find out whether the person is willing and what he or she might be able to tell you.

- Plan your questions. You should have a few questions in mind as well as written down. Listen carefully so that you can follow up on key points.

- Come prepared with at least a notebook and pencil. If you use a tape recorder, be sure to get the person's permission in advance and be sure that the equipment is working.

Observations

- Make detailed observations that you can link to your claim. For example, if you believe that the long lines in your student services building are caused by inefficient use of staff, you could observe how many staff members are on duty at peak and slack times.

- Choose a place where you can observe without intrusion. Public places work best because you can sit for a long time without people wondering what you are doing.

- Carry a notebook and write extensive notes whenever you can. Write down as much as you can. Be sure to record where you were, the date, exactly when you arrived and left, and important details such as the number of people present.

INTERVIEWS, OBSERVATIONS, AND SURVEYS *(continued)*

Surveys

- Like interview questions, questions on surveys should relate directly to the issue of your argument. Take some time to decide what exactly you want to know first.

- Write a few specific, unambiguous questions. The people you contact should be able to fill out your survey quickly, and they should not have to guess what a question means. It's always a good idea to test the wording of the questions on a few people to find out whether your questions are clear before you conduct the survey.

- You might include one or two open-ended questions, such as "What do you like about X?" or "What don't you like about X?" Answers to these questions can be difficult to interpret, but sometimes they provide insights.

- Decide whom you want to participate in your survey and how you will contact them. If you are going to use your survey results to claim that the people surveyed represent the views of undergraduates at your school, then you should match the gender, ethnic, and racial balance to the proportions at your school.

- If you are going to mail or email your survey, include a statement about what the survey is for and how the results will be used.

- Interpreting your results should be straightforward if your questions require definite responses. Multiple-choice formats make data easy to tabulate, but they often miss key information. If you included one or more open-ended questions, you need to figure out a way to analyze responses.

Finding Library Sources

Large libraries can be intimidating, even to experienced researchers when they begin working on a new subject. You can save time and frustration if you have some idea of how you want to proceed when you enter the library. Libraries have two major kinds of sources: books and periodicals. Periodicals include a range of items from daily newspapers to scholarly journals that are bound and put on the shelves like books.

Most books are shelved according to the Library of Congress Classification System, which uses a combination of letters and numbers to direct you to a book's location in the library. The Library of Congress call number begins with a letter or letters that represent the broad subject area into which the book is classified. The Library of Congress system has the advantage of shelving books on the same subject together, so you can sometimes find additional books by browsing in the stacks. You can use the *Library of Congress Subject Headings,* available in print in your library's reference area or on the Web (http://lcweb.loc.gov), to help you find out how your subject might be indexed.

If you want to do research on cloning, you might type "cloning" in the subject index of your online card catalog, which would yield something like the following results:

1 Cloning—23 item(s)

2 Cloning—Bibliography.—1 item(s)

3 Cloning—Congresses.—2 item(s)

4 Cloning—Fiction.—6 item(s)

5 Cloning—Government policy—United States.—2 item(s)

6 Cloning—History.—1 item(s)

7 Cloning, Molecular—36 item(s) Indexed as: MOLECULAR CLONING

8 Cloning—Moral and ethical aspects.—13 item(s)

9 Cloning—Moral and ethical aspects—Government policy—United States.—1 item(s)

10 Cloning—Moral and ethical aspects—United States.—2 item(s)

11 Cloning—Religious aspects—Christianity.—2 item(s)

12 Cloning—Research—History.—1 item(s)

13 Cloning—Research—Law and legislation—United States.—1 item(s)

14 Cloning—Research—United States—Finance.—1 item(s)

15 Cloning—Social aspects.—1 item(s)

16 Cloning—United States—Religious aspects.—1 item(s)

This initial search helps you to identify more precisely what you are looking for. If you are most interested in the ethical aspects of cloning, then the books listed under number 8 would be most useful to you.

Finding articles in periodicals is accomplished in much the same way. To find relevant newspaper and magazine articles, use a periodical index. Print indexes are located in the reference area of your library, but many are now available on your library's Web site. These general indexes are now commonly known as databases because they often have full-text versions of the articles they index. Databases are sometimes listed on your library's Web site under the name of the vendor—the company that sells the database to your library (e.g., EBSCO, FirstSearch). Some of the more useful general databases include

> **Academic Search Premier** (EBSCO). Provides full text for over 3,000 scholarly publications, including social sciences, humanities, education, computer sciences, engineering, language and linguistics, literature, medical sciences, and ethnic studies journals.

> **ArticleFirst** (FirstSearch). Indexes over 15,000 journals in business, the humanities, medicine, science, and social sciences.

> **Expanded Academic ASAP** (Thomson Gale). Indexes 2,300 periodicals from the arts, humanities, sciences, social sciences, and general news, some with full-text articles available.

> **Factiva** (Dow Jones). Gives full-text access to major newspapers, market research reports, and business journals, including *The Wall Street Journal*.

> **Ingenta.com** (Ingenta). Gives citations to over 20,000 multidisciplinary journals.

> **LexisNexis Academic** (LexisNexis). Provides full text of a wide range of newspapers, magazines, government and legal documents, and company profiles from around the world.

> **WorldCat** (FirstSearch). Contains over 52 million records of books and other materials in libraries throughout the world but very few articles in journals.

In addition to these general periodical indexes, there are many specialized indexes that list citations to journal articles in various fields.

Follow these steps to find articles:

1. Select an index that is appropriate to your subject.
2. Search the index using the relevant subject heading(s).
3. Print or copy the complete citation to the article(s).
4. Check the periodicals holdings to see whether your library has the journal.

SCHOLARLY, TRADE, AND POPULAR JOURNALS

Some indexes give citations for only one kind of journal. Others include more than one type. Although the difference between types of journals is not always obvious, you should be able to judge whether a journal is scholarly, trade, or popular by its characteristics.

Characteristics of Scholarly Journals

- Articles are long with few illustrations.
- Articles are written by scholars in the field, usually affiliated with a university or research center.
- Articles have footnotes or a works-cited list at the end.
- Articles usually report original research.
- Authors write in the language of their discipline, and readers are assumed to know a great deal about the field.
- Scholarly journals contain relatively few advertisements.

Examples: *American Journal of Mathematics, College English, JAMA: Journal of the American Medical Association, Plasma Physics*

Characteristics of Trade Journals

- Articles are frequently related to practical job concerns.
- Articles usually do not report original research.
- Articles usually do not have footnotes or have relatively few footnotes.

SCHOLARLY, TRADE, AND POPULAR JOURNALS *(continued)*

- Items of interest to people in particular professions and job listings are typical features.
- Advertisements are aimed at people in the specific field.

Examples: *Advertising Age, Industry Week, Macworld, Teacher Magazine*

Characteristics of Popular Journals

- Articles are short and often illustrated with color photographs.
- Articles seldom have footnotes or acknowledge where their information came from.
- Authors are usually staff writers for the magazine or freelance writers.
- Advertisements are aimed at the general public.
- Copies can be bought at newsstands.

Examples: *Cosmopolitan, Newsweek, Sports Illustrated, GQ, People*

Finding Web Sources

Searches for sources on databases on your library's Web site and searches on Google may look similar on your computer, but there is a world of difference. Sources on library databases have the advantage of being screened by librarians along with the convenience of Web delivery. Your library pays for access to most databases, which is why they aren't available to the public. The results of a Google search, by contrast, often give you a series of commercial sites selling books and products related to the words you typed in.

Nonetheless, some important databases, including ERIC, Ingenta.com, and MEDLINE, have many resources available free of charge both through library Web sites and through the Web. Furthermore, a huge selection of government documents is available on the Web. Often it takes skill and patience to find what is valuable on the Web. The key to success is knowing where you are most likely to find current and accurate information about the particular question you are researching.

Kinds of Search Engines

A search engine is a set of programs that sort through millions of items with incredible speed. There are four basic kinds of search engines.

1. **Keyword search engines** (e.g., AltaVista, Google, Hotbot, Lycos, Mooter, MSN Search, Teoma). Keyword search engines give different results because they assign different weights to the information they find. Mooter, for example, uses algorithms to sort the results.

2. **Web directories** (e.g., Britannica.com, LookSmart, ProFusion, Yahoo!). Web directories classify Web sites into categories and are the closest equivalent to the cataloging system used by libraries. On most directories professional editors decide how to index a particular Web site. Web directories also allow keyword searches.

3. **Metasearch agents** (e.g., Dogpile, Metacrawler, WebCrawler). Metasearch agents allow you to use several search engines simultaneously. While the concept is sound, metasearch agents are limited by the number of hits they can return and their inability to handle advanced searches.

4. **Natural-language search engines** (e.g., Ask Jeeves). Natural- or real-language search engines allow you to search by asking questions such as "Where can I find a recipe for scallops?" Natural-language search engines are still in their infancy; no doubt they will become much more powerful in the future.

T I P S
Search Engines

If you don't have much experience with search engines, try out a few different ones until you find one or two favorites; then learn how to use them well. Keyword search engines can be frustrating because they turn up so much, but you become better at using them with practice.

- To start your search, open your browser and select "Search." You may be offered a selection of Web navigators and search engines.

- To use a keyword search, enter a word, name, or phrase. Some search engines require quotation marks to indicate a phrase or full name. If you type Gwyneth Paltrow without quotation marks, you will get hits for all instances of Gwyneth and all instances of Paltrow.

Search Engines *(continued)*

- When you want the search to retrieve any form of a word, use an asterisk—for example, for both child and children, you can use "child*" to get both terms. The asterisk is sometimes referred to as a wild card.

- Most search engines will retrieve only exact matches to the terms you use in your search request. Try all the variations you can think of if you want to do a thorough search.

- Some search engines use a plus sign (+) to indicate that a term is required (as in "+ ADHD + children") and a minus sign (−) to indicate that sites containing that term should not be included. For example, " + ADHD –children" will exclude sites on ADHD that mention children. Other search engines use AND, OR, and NOT in capital letters. The pluses, minuses, ANDs, ORs, and NOTs, are called Boolean operators.

- Advanced searches allow you to limit the results by domain. You can specify "only" to restrict a search to a specific domain such as .edu for college and university sites. For example, most current statistics are on .gov sites. Adding "site:.gov" to a search for statistics on Google will limit the search to government sites.

Evaluating Sources

Not only is the volume of information on the Web overwhelming, but the quality varies a great deal too. Because anyone with access to the Internet can put up a Web site, there is no quality control on the Web. Thus, much outdated, false, and deliberately deceptive information can be found on the Web.

How to determine the reliability and relevance of sources is not a new problem. Just as Web sources do, print sources contain their share of biased, inaccurate, and misleading information. Other print sources may be accurate but not suited to the purpose of your project. A critical review can help you to sort through the sources you have gathered. Even though print and Web sources differ in many ways, some basic principles of evaluation can be applied to both.

Traditional Criteria for Evaluating Print Sources

Over the years librarians have developed criteria for evaluating print sources.

1. **Source.** Who printed the book or article? Scholarly books that are published by university presses and articles in scholarly journals are assessed by experts in the field before they are published. Because of this strict review process, they contain generally reliable information. But since the review process takes time, scholarly books and articles are not the most current sources. For people outside the field, they also have the disadvantage of being written for other experts. Serious trade books and journals are also generally reliable, though magazines devoted to politics often have an obvious bias. Popular magazines and books vary in quality. Often, they are purchased for their entertainment value, and they tend to emphasize what is sensational or entertaining at the expense of accuracy and comprehensiveness. Many magazines and books are published to represent the viewpoint of a particular group or company, so that bias should be taken into account. Newspapers also vary in quality. National newspapers, such as the *New York Times, Washington Post,* and *Los Angeles Times,* employ fact checkers and do a thorough editorial review and thus tend to be more reliable than newspapers that lack such resources.

2. **Author.** Who wrote the book or article? Is the author's name mentioned? Are the author's qualifications listed?

3. **Timeliness.** How current is the source? Obviously, if you are researching a fast-developing subject such as cloning, then currency is very important. But if you are interested in an issue that happened years ago, then currency might not be as important.

4. **Evidence.** How adequate is the evidence to support the author's claims? Where does the evidence come from—interviews, observations, surveys, experiments, expert testimony, or counterarguments? Does the author acknowledge any other ways in which the evidence might be interpreted?

5. **Biases.** Can you detect particular biases of the author? Is the author forthright about his or her biases? How do the author's biases affect the interpretation that is offered?

6. **Advertising.** Is the advertising prominent in the journal or newspaper? Is there any way that ads might affect what gets printed? For example, some magazines that ran many tobacco ads refused to run stories about the dangers of smoking.

Traditional print criteria can be helpful in evaluating some Internet sources. For example, most messages sent to a list or newsgroup do not mention the qualifications of the author or offer any support for the validity of evidence. For this reason any information you gather via such a newsgroup should be verified with a more reliable source.

Sources on the Web present other difficulties. Some of these are inherent in the structure of the Web, with its capability for linking to other pages. When you are at a site that contains many links, you will often find that some links go to pages on the same site but others take you off the site. You have to pay attention to the URLs to know where you are in relation to where you started. Furthermore, when you find a Web page using a search engine, often you go deep into a complex site without having any sense of the context of that page. You might have to spend thirty minutes or more just to get some idea of what is on the overall site.

Additional Criteria for Evaluating Web Sources

Traditional criteria for evaluating print sources remain useful for evaluating sources on the Web, but you should keep in mind how the Web can be different.

1. **Source.** If a Web site indicates what organization or individual is responsible for the information found on it, then you can apply the traditional criteria for evaluating print sources. For example, most major newspapers maintain Web sites where you can read some of the articles that appear in print. If a Web site doesn't indicate ownership, then you have to make judgments about who put it up and why. Documents are easy to copy and put up on the Web, but they are also very easily quoted out of context or altered. For example, you might find something represented as an "official" government document that is in fact a fabrication.

2. **Author.** Often, it is difficult to know who put up a particular Web site. Even when an author's name is present, in most cases the author's qualifications are not listed.

3. **Timeliness.** Many Web pages do not list when they were last updated; therefore, you do not know how current they are. Furthermore, there are thousands of ghost sites on the Web—sites that the owners have abandoned but have not bothered to remove. You can stumble onto these old sites and not realize that the organization might have a more current site elsewhere.

4. **Evidence.** The accuracy of any evidence found on the Web is often hard to verify. There are no editors or fact checkers guarding against mistakes or misinformation. The most reliable information on the Web stands up to the tests of print evaluation, with clear indication of an edited source, credentials of the author, references for works cited, and dates of publication.

5. **Biases.** Many Web sites are little more than virtual soapboxes. Someone who has an ax to grind can potentially tell millions of people why he or she is angry. Other sites are equally biased but conceal their attitude with a reasonable tone and seemingly factual evidence such as statistics.

6. **Advertising.** Many Web sites are "infomercials" of one sort or another. While they can provide useful information about specific products or services, the reason the information was placed on the Web is to get you to buy the product or service. Advertising on the Web costs a fraction of broadcast ads, so it's no wonder that advertisers have flocked to the Web.

Taking Notes

Before personal computers became widely available, most library research projects involved taking notes on notecards. This method was cumbersome, but it had some big advantages. You could spread out the notecards on a table or pin them to a bulletin board and get an overview of how the information that you gathered might be connected. Today, many people make notes in computer files. If you make notes in a computer file, then you don't have to retype when you write your paper. For example, if you copy a direct quote and decide to use it, you can cut and paste it. It is, of course, possible to print all your notes from your computer and then spread them out, or you can even paste your notes on cards, which will let you enjoy the best of both systems. Whatever way works best for you, there are a few things to keep in mind.

Make sure you get the full bibliographic information when you make notes. For books, you should get the author's name, title of the book, place of publication, publisher, and date of publication. This information is on the front and back of the title page. For journals, you need the author's name, title of the article, title of the journal, issue of the journal, date of the issue, and page numbers. For Web sites, you need the name of the page, the author if listed, the sponsoring organization if listed, the date the site was posted, the date you visited, and the complete URL.

Make photocopies or print copies of sources you plan to use in your paper. Having a copy of the source lessens the chances you'll make mistakes. If you do take notes, be sure to indicate which words are the author's and which words are yours. It's easy to forget later. Attach the bibliographic information to photocopies and printouts so that you won't get mixed up about which source the material came from.

Finally, know when to say you have enough information. Many topics can be researched for a lifetime. It's not just the quantity of sources that counts. You should have enough diversity that you are confident you know the major points of view on a particular issue. When you reach a possible stopping point, group your notes and see whether a tentative organization for your paper becomes evident. People who like to work with notecards sometimes write comment cards to attach to each card, indicating how that piece of information fits. People who work with computer files sometimes type in caps how they see their notes fitting together. The method doesn't matter as much as the result. You should have a sketch outline by the time you finish the information-gathering stage.

CHAPTER 16

MLA Documentation

Intellectual Property and Scholastic Honesty

In the 1970s cassette tapes met with the ire of the recording industry, while the video recorder soon thereafter drove the motion picture studios to distraction. Why? These new technologies were enabling individuals to create unauthorized copies of music and movies. In 1999 the entertainment industry found a new foe in Shawn Fanning, the 19-year-old programmer and founder of Napster. Fanning's service allowed Internet users to "swap" MP3 formatted music files, circumventing royalty fees for each new copy of a song or album. While users reveled in the freedom of the new cyber-trend, musicians such as Metallica and Dr. Dre and trade organizations such as the Record Industry Association of America and the National Music Publishers Association hurled accusations of piracy. Ultimately, the courts upheld the rights of the artists and those who licensed their music, ruling that copyrighted music is property and that file "sharing" is "stealing." The Napster altercation—as well as the ongoing controversy over illegal file sharing—indicates the complexity of the concept of intellectual property and its applications. Copyright laws were established in the 1700s to protect the financial interests of publishers and authors, but over the last century, the domain of intellectual property has spread to company trademarks, photographs, films, radio and television broadcasts, computer software, and—as the courts forced Fanning and users to acknowledge—music scores, lyrics, and recordings. With the rising ubiquity of the Internet, conflict over the unauthorized distribution of intellectual property continues to increase as art, scholarship, and countless other cerebral creations find their way onto the crowded information superhighway.

Intellectual property rights, however, are not the main reason that college writing requires strict standards of documentation. Writing at the college level follows a long tradition of scholarly writing that insists on accuracy in referencing other work so that a reader can consult a writer's sources. Often, scholarly arguments build on the work of others, and experiments almost always identify an area that other researchers have addressed. Sometimes, other pieces of writing are the primary data, as when a historian uses letters and public documents to construct what happened in the past. It is important for other historians to be able to review the same documents to confirm or reject a particular interpretation.

There is also a basic issue of fairness in recognizing the work of others. If you find an idea in someone else's work that you want to use, it seems only fair to give that person proper credit. In Chapter 7, we discuss Robert H. Frank and Phillip J. Cook's controversial argument that changes in attitudes help to account for the increasing divide between rich and poor people since 1973, a shift that they summarize as the winner-take-all society. The phrase "winner-take-all society" has become common enough that you might hear it in news features describing the contemporary United States, but certainly any extended treatment of the concept should acknowledge Frank and Cook for coming up with the idea. Many students now acknowledge the work of other students if they feel that their classmates have made an important contribution to their work. And why not? It's only fair.

In our culture in general and in the professions in particular, work that people claim is their own is expected to be their own. Imagine that you are the director of marketing at a company that paid a consulting firm to conduct a survey, only to find out that the work the firm presented to you had been copied from another survey. Wouldn't you be on the phone right away to your company's attorneys? Even though the unethical copying of the survey might have been the failure of only one employee, surely the reputation of the consulting firm would be damaged, if not ruined. Many noteworthy people in political and public life have been greatly embarrassed by instances of plagiarism; in some cases, people have lost their positions as a result. Short of committing a felony, plagiarism is one of the few things that can get you expelled from your college or university if the case is serious enough. So it's worth it to you to know what plagiarism is and isn't.

Avoiding Plagiarism

Stated most simply, you would be guilty of plagiarizing if you used the words or ideas of someone else without acknowledging the source. That definition seems easy enough, but when you think about it, how many new ideas are there? And how could you possibly acknowledge where all your ideas came from? In practical terms, you are not expected to acknowledge everything. You do not have to acknowledge what is considered general knowledge, such as facts that you could find in a variety of reference books. For example, if you wanted to assert that Lyndon Johnson's victory over

Barry Goldwater in the 1964 presidential election remains the largest popular vote percentage (61 percent) in presidential election history, you would not have to acknowledge the source. This information should be available in encyclopedias, almanacs, and other general sources.

But if you cite a more obscure fact that wouldn't be as readily verifiable, you should let your readers know where you found it. Likewise, you should acknowledge the sources of any arguable statements, claims, or judgments. The sources of statistics, research findings, examples, graphs, charts, and illustrations also should be acknowledged. People are especially skeptical about statistics and research findings if the source is not mentioned.

Where most people get into plagiarism trouble is when they take words directly from a source and use them without quotation marks, or else change a few words and pass them off as their own words. It is easiest to illustrate where the line is drawn with an example. Suppose you are writing an argument about attempts to censor the Internet, and you want to examine how successful other nations have been. You find the following paragraph about China:

> China is encouraging Net use for business, but not what it considers seditious or pornographic traffic and "spiritual pollution." So the state is building its communications infrastructure like a mammoth corporate system—robust within the country, but with three gateways to the world, in Beijing, Shanghai, and Shenzhen. International exchanges can then be monitored and foreign content "filtered" at each information chokepoint, courtesy of the Public Security Bureau.
>
> —Jim Erickson. "WWW.POLITICS.COM." *Asiaweek* 2 Oct. 1998: 42.

You want to mention the point about the gateways in your paper. You have two basic options: to paraphrase the source or to quote it directly.

If you quote directly, you must include all words you take from the original inside quotation marks:

```
According to one observer, "China is encouraging Net use for
business, but not what it considers seditious or pornographic
traffic and 'spiritual pollution'" (Erickson 42).
```

This example is typical of MLA style. The citation goes outside the quotation marks but before the period. The reference is to the author's last name, which refers you to the full citation in the works-cited list at the end. Following the author's name is the page number where the quotation can be located. Notice also that if you quote material that contains quotation marks, then the double quotation marks around the original quotation change to the single quotation mark. If you include the author's name, then you need to include only the page number in the parentheses:

> According to Jim Erickson, "China is encouraging Net use for
> business, but not what it considers seditious or pornographic
> traffic and 'spiritual pollution'" (42).

If an article appears on one page only, you do not need to include the page number:

> According to Jim Erickson, "China is encouraging Net use for
> business, but not what it considers seditious or pornographic
> traffic and 'spiritual pollution.'"

If the newspaper article did not include the author's name, you would include the first word or two of the title. The logic of this system is to enable you to find the reference in the works-cited list.

The alternative to quoting directly is to paraphrase. When you paraphrase, you change the words without changing the meaning. Here are two examples:

Plagiarized

> China wants its citizens to use the Internet for business, but
> not for circulating views it doesn't like, pornography, and
> "spiritual pollution." So China is building its communications
> infrastructure like a mammoth corporate system—well linked
> internally but with only three ports to the outside world. The
> Public Security Bureau will monitor the foreign traffic at each
> information choke-point (Erickson).

This version is unacceptable. Too many of the words in the original are used directly here, including much of one sentence: "is building its communications infrastructure like a mammoth corporate system." If an entire string of words is lifted from a source and inserted without using quotation marks, then the passage is plagiarized. The first sentence is also too close in structure and wording to the original. Changing a few words in a sentence is not a paraphrase. Compare the following example:

Acceptable paraphrase

```
The Chinese government wants its citizens to take advantage
of the Internet for commerce while not allowing foreign
political ideas and foreign values to challenge its
authority. Consequently, the Chinese Internet will have
only three ports to the outside world. Traffic through
these ports will be monitored and censored by the Public
Security Bureau (Erickson).
```

There are a few words from the original in this paraphrase, such as *foreign* and *monitored,* but these sentences are original in structure and wording while accurately conveying the meaning of the original.

Using Sources Effectively

The purpose of using sources is to *support* your argument, not to make your argument for you. Next to plagiarism, the worst mistake you can make with sources is stringing them together without building an argument of your own. Your sources help to show that you've done your homework and that you've thought in depth about the issue.

One choice you have to make when using sources is when to quote and when to paraphrase. Consider the following example about expressways:

```
Urban planners of the 1960s saw superhighways as the means to
prevent inner cities from continuing to decay. Inner-city
blight was recognized as early as the 1930s, and the problem
was understood for four decades as one of circulation (hence
expressways were called "arterials"). The planners argued
that those who had moved to the suburbs would return to the
city on expressways. By the end of the 1960s, the engineers
were tearing down thousands of units of urban housing and
small businesses to build expressways with a logic that was
similar to the logic of mass bombing in Vietnam—to destroy
the city was to save it (Patton 102). Shortly the effects
were all too evident. Old neighborhoods were ripped apart,
```

the flight to the suburbs continued, and the decline of inner
cities accelerated rather than abated.

Not everyone in the 1950s and 1960s saw expressways as
the answer to urban dilapidation. Lewis Mumford in 1958
challenged the circulation metaphor. He wrote: "Highway
planners have yet to realize that these arteries must not be
thrust into the delicate tissue of our cities; the blood they
circulate must rather enter through an elaborate network of
minor blood vessels and capillaries" (236). Mumford saw that
new expressways produced more congestion and aggravated the
problem they were designed to overcome, thus creating demand
for still more expressways. If road building through cities
were allowed to continue, he predicted the result would be "a
tomb of concrete roads and ramps covering the dead corpse of
a city" (238).

Notice that two sources are cited: Phil Patton, *Open Road: A Celebration of the American Highway*. New York: Simon, 1986; and Lewis Mumford, "The Highway and the City," *The Highway and the City*. New York: Harcourt, 1963. 234–46.

The writer decided that the point from Patton about tearing down thousands of units of urban housing and small businesses to build expressways in the 1960s should be paraphrased, but Mumford's remarks should be quoted directly. In both direct quotations from Mumford, the original wording is important. Mumford rejects the metaphor of arteries for expressways and foresees in vivid language the future of cities as paved-over tombs. As a general rule, you should use direct quotations only when the original language is important. Otherwise, you should paraphrase.

If a direct quotation runs more than four lines, then it should be indented one inch and double-spaced. But you still should *integrate* long quotations into the text of your paper. Long quotations should be attributed; that is, you should say where the quotation comes from in your text as well as in the reference. And it is a good idea to include at least a sentence or two after the quotation to describe its significance for your argument. The original wording in the long quotation in the following paragraph is important because it gives a sense of the language of the Port Huron Statement. The sentences following the quotation explain why many faculty members in the 1960s looked on the

Port Huron Statement as a positive sign (of course, college administrators were horrified). You might think of this strategy as putting an extended quotation in an envelope with your words before and after:

Critiques of the staleness and conformity of American education made the first expressions of student radicalism in the 1960s such as the "Port Huron Statement" from the Students for a Democratic Society (SDS) in 1962 appear as a breath of fresh air. The SDS wrote:

> Almost no students value activity as a citizen. Passive in public, they are hardly more idealistic in arranging their private lives; Gallup concludes they will settle for "low success, and won't risk high failure." There is not much willingness to take risks (not even in business), no setting of dangerous goals, no real conception of personal identity except one manufactured in the image of others, no real urge for personal fulfillment except to be almost as successful as the very successful people. Attention is being paid to social status (the quality of shirt collars, meeting people, getting wives or husbands, making solid contacts for later on); much, too, is paid to academic status (grades, honors, the med-school rat race). But neglected generally is real intellectual status, the personal cultivation of mind. (238)

Many professors shared the SDS disdain for the political quietism on college campuses. When large-scale ferment erupted among students during the years of the Vietnam War, some faculty welcomed it as a sign of finally emerging from the intellectual stagnation of the Eisenhower years. For some it was a sign that the promise of John F. Kennedy's administration could be fulfilled, that young people could create a new national identity.

Note three points about form in the long quotation. First, there are no quotation marks around the extended quotation. Readers know that the material is quoted because it is blocked off. Second, words quoted in the original retain the double quotation marks. Third, the page number appears *after* the period at the end of the quotation.

Whether long or short, make all quotations part of the fabric of your paper while being careful to indicate which words belong to the original. A reader should be able to move through the body of your paper without having to stop and ask: Why did the writer include this quotation? or Which words are the writer's and which are being quoted?

MLA Works-Cited List

Different disciplines use different styles for documentation. The two styles that are used most frequently are the APA style and the MLA style. APA stands for American Psychological Association, which publishes a style manual used widely in the social sciences (see Chapter 17). MLA stands for the Modern Language Association, and its style is the norm for humanities disciplines, including English and rhetoric and composition.

Both MLA and APA styles use a works-cited list placed at the end of a paper. Here is an example of an MLA works-cited list.

Center "Works Cited."

Double-space all entries. Indent all but the first line five spaces.

Alphabetize entries by last name of authors or by title if no author is listed.

> Smith 10
>
> Works Cited
>
> Bingham, Janet. "Kids Become Masters of
>   Electronic Universe: School Internet
>   Activity Abounds." Denver Post 3 Sept.
>   1996: A13.
> Dyrli, Odvard Egil, and Daniel E. Kinnaman.
>   "Telecommunications: Gaining Access to
>   the World." Technology and Learning 16.3
>   (1995): 79-84.

Smith 11

Ellsworth, Jill H. Education on the Internet:

A Hands-On Book of Ideas, Resources,

Projects, and Advice. Indianapolis:

Sams, 1994.

National Center for Education Statistics.

"Internet Access in Public Education." Feb.

1998. NCES. 4 Jan. 1999

<http://nces.ed.gov/pubs98/98021.html>.

Romano, Allison. "Oxygen: It Lives! Now Can It

Breathe? After Some Stumbles, the Women's

Network Is Working to Refine and Redefine

Its Image." Broadcasting and Cable

5 May 2003: 10.

"UK: A Battle for Young Hearts and Minds."

Computer Weekly 4 Apr. 1996: 20.

Underline the titles of books and periodicals.

The works-cited list eliminates the need for footnotes. If you have your sources listed on notecards, then all you have to do when you finish your paper is to find the cards for all the sources that you cite, alphabetize the cards by author, and type your works-cited list. For works with no author listed, alphabetize by the first content word in the title (ignore *a, an,* and *the*).

Some of the more common citation formats in MLA style are listed in the following section. If you have questions that these examples do not address, you should consult the *MLA Handbook for Writers of Research Papers* (6th edition, 2003) and the *MLA Style Manual and Guide to Scholarly Publishing* (2nd edition, 1998).

For a sample MLA-style research paper, see pages 196–206.

Citing Books

The basic format for listing books in the works-cited list is

1. Author's name (last name first)
2. Title (underlined)
3. Place of publication
4. Short name of publisher
5. Date of publication

   On the book's title page (not on the cover) you will find the exact title, the publisher, and the city (use the first city if several are listed). The date of publication is included in the copyright notice on the back of the title page.

Book by One Author

Lewis, Michael. Moneyball: The Art of Winning an Unfair Game.

   New York: Norton, 2003.

Book by Two or Three Authors

Sturken, Marita, and Lisa Cartwright. Practices of Looking: An

   Introduction to Visual Culture. New York: Oxford UP, 2001.

Book by Four or More Authors

Redkar, Arohi, et al. Pro MSMQ: Microsoft Message Queue

   Programming. Berkeley: Apress, 2004.

Two or More Books by the Same Author

Berger, John. About Looking. New York: Pantheon, 1980.

---. Ways of Seeing. New York: Viking, 1973.

Translation

Martin, Henri-Jean. The History and Power of Writing. Trans.

   Lydia G. Cochrane. Chicago: U of Chicago P, 1994.

Edited Book

Bizzell, Patricia, and Bruce Herzberg, eds. The Rhetorical

   Tradition: Readings from Classical Times to the Present.

   Boston: Bedford, 1990.

One Volume of a Multivolume Work

Arnold, Matthew. Complete Prose Works. Ed. R. H. Super.

Vol. 2. Ann Arbor: U of Michigan P, 1960.

Selection in an Anthology or Chapter in an Edited Collection

Merritt, Russell. "Nickelodeon Theaters, 1905-1914: Building

an Audience for the Movies." The American Film Industry.

Rev. ed. Ed. Tino Balio. Madison: U of Wisconsin P,

1985. 83-102.

Government Document

Malveaux, Julianne. "Changes in the Labor Market Status of

Black Women." A Report of the Study Group on Affirmative

Action to the Committee on Education and Labor. 100th

Cong., 1st sess. H. Rept. 100-L. Washington: GPO, 1987.

213-55.

Bible

Holy Bible. Revised Standard Version Containing the Old and

New Testaments. New York: Collins, 1973. [Note that

"Bible" is not underlined.]

Citing Articles in Periodicals

When citing periodicals, the necessary items to include are

1. Author's name (last name first)
2. Title of article inside quotation marks
3. Title of journal or magazine (underlined)
4. Volume number (for scholarly journals)
5. Date
6. Page numbers

Many scholarly journals are printed to be bound as one volume, usually by year, and the pagination is continuous for that year. If, say, a scholarly journal is printed in four issues and the first issue ends on page 278, then the second issue will begin with page 279. For journals that are continuously paginated, you do not need to include the issue number. Some scholarly journals, however, are paginated like magazines with each issue beginning on page 1. For journals paginated by issue, you should list the issue number along with the volume (e.g., for the first issue of volume 11, you would put "11.1" in the entry after the title of the journal).

Article in a Scholarly Journal—Continuous Pagination

Berlin, James A. "Rhetoric and Ideology in the Writing

Class." College English 50 (1988): 477-94.

Article in a Scholarly Journal—Continuous Pagination, Two or Three Authors

Roach, Bill, and Mary Roach. "Horatio Alger, Jr.: Precursor

of the Stratemeyer Syndicate." Journal of Popular

Culture 37 (2004): 450-62.

Article in a Scholarly Journal—Continuous Pagination, Four or More Authors

Domke, David, et al. "Insights Into U.S. Racial

Hierarchy: Racial Profiling, News Sources, and

September 11." Journal of Communication 53 (2003): 606-23.

Article in a Scholarly Journal—Pagination by Issue

Kolby, Jerry. "The Top-Heavy Economy: Managerial Greed and

Unproductive Labor." Critical Sociology 15.3 (1988): 53-69.

Review

Chomsky, Noam. Rev. of Verbal Behavior, by B. F. Skinner.

Language 35 (1959): 26-58.

Magazine Article

Engardio, Pete. "Microsoft's Long March." Business Week 24

June 1996: 52-54.

Newspaper Article

Bingham, Janet. "Kids Become Masters of Electronic Universe:

School Internet Activity Abounds." <u>Denver Post</u> 3 Sept.

1996: A13

Letter to the Editor

Luker, Ralph E. Letter. <u>Chronicle of Higher Education</u> 18 Dec.

1998: B9

Editorial

"An Open Process." Editorial. <u>Wall Street Journal</u> 30 Dec.

1998: A10

Citing Online Sources

Online sources pose special difficulties for systems of citing sources. Many online sources change frequently. Sometimes you discover to your frustration that what you had found on a Web site the previous day has been altered or in some cases no longer exists. Furthermore, basic information such as who put up a Web site and when it was last changed are often absent. Many print sources have also been put on the Web, which raises another set of difficulties. The basic format for citing a generic Web site is

1. Author's name (last name first)
2. Title of the document (in quotation marks)
3. Title of complete work or name of the journal (underlined)
4. Date of Web publication or last update
5. Sponsoring organization
6. Date you visited
7. URL (enclosed in angle brackets)

Book on the Web

Rheingold, Howard. <u>Tools for Thought: The People and Ideas of</u>

<u>the Next Computer Revolution</u>. New York: Simon, 1985. 14

Sept. 2004 <http://www.well.com/user/hlr/

texts/tftindex.html>.

Article in a Scholarly Journal on the Web

Browning, Tonya. "Embedded Visuals: Student Design in Web

Spaces." Kairos 2.1 (1997). 4 May 2004 <http://

www.as.ttu.edu/kairos/2.1/features/browning/index.html>.

Article in a Library Database

Pope, Nigel K. "The Impact of Stress in Self- and Peer

Assessment." Assessment and Evaluation in Higher

Education 30 (2005): 51-63. Academic Search Premier.

EBSCO. Zimmerman Lib., U of New Mexico. 14 Feb. 2005

<http://www.epnet.com/>.

Article in a Magazine on the Web

Layden, Tim. "Taking Action: Give Track and Field

Credit for Trying to Clean Up Its Doping

Problem." SI.com 3 July 2004. 28 July 2004

<http://sportsillustrated.cnn.com/2004/writers/

tim_layden/07/23/track.doping/index.html>.

Web Publication by an Organization

"ACLU Warns House Approval of Increased Indecency Fines Will

Have a Chilling Effect on Speech." 11 Mar. 2004.

American Civil Liberties Union. 28 July 2004 <http://

www.aclu.org/FreeSpeech/FreeSpeech.cfm?ID=15248&c=42>.

Personal Subscription Service (AOL)

Parascenzo, Marino A. "Zaharias, Babe Didrikson."

World Book Online Reference Center. 2004. America

Online. 29 July 2004. Keyword: Zaharias.

Newsgroup or Listserv Posting

Card, Lorin. "Re: Fahrenheit 9/11 Fahrenheit 451."

Online posting. 28 July 2004. H-NET List for

Scholarly Studies and Uses of Media. 28 July 2004

<http://h-net.msu.edu/>.

Entry in a Weblog (Blog)

Stereogum. "Dustin Hoffman Saves Bee Sting Victim." Weblog
posting. 28 July 2004. The Best Week Ever. 30 July 2004
<http://bestweekever.vh1.com/2004/07/
dustin_hoffman_.html>.

Personal Email

Fung, Richard. "Re: Invitation to University of Texas Speaking
Engagement." Email to the author. 13 Oct. 2003.

Course Web Site

Caristi, Dom. Programs and Audiences. Course home page
Sept. 2004-Apr. 2005. Dept. of Telecommunications,
Ball State U. 28 July 2004 <http://www.bsu.edu/classes/
caristi/tcom306/>.

Personal Web Site

Vitanza, Victor. Home page. 24 Apr. 2002. 7 Sept. 2004
<http://www.uta.edu/english/V/Victor_.html>.

CD-ROM

Boyer, Paul, et al. The Enduring Vision, Interactive Edition.
1993 ed. CD-ROM. Lexington: Heath, 1993.

Citing Visual Sources

Film

Harry Potter and the Prisoner of Azkaban. Dir.
Alfonso Cuarón. Perf. Daniel Radcliffe, Rupert
Grint, Emma Watson, David Thewlis, Michael
Gambon, Maggie Smith, Alan Rickman, Emma
Thompson, Robbie Coltrane, and Gary Oldman.
Warner Bros., 2004.

Television Program

"The Attitude." Perf. Calista Flockhart, Courtney
Thorne-Smith. Dir. Allan Arkush, Daniel Attias,
et al. Writ. David E. Kelley. Ally McBeal. Fox.
WFXT, Boston. 3 Nov. 1997.

Cartoon

Hamilton, Jane. "Little Rascals." Cartoon. Entertainment
Weekly. 14 Mar. 2003: 8.

Advertisement

"The Laughing Cow." Advertisement. People. 2 Aug. 2004: 20.

Painting, Sculpture, or Photograph

Hernandez, Anthony. Rome #17. Solomon R. Guggenheim Museum,
New York.

Citing Other Sources

Personal Interview

Williams, Errick Lynn. Telephone interview. 4 Jan. 1999.

Broadcast Interview

Reagan, Ron, Jr. Interview with Terry Gross. Fresh Air. Natl.
Public Radio. KUT-FM, Austin. 22 July 2004.

Unpublished Dissertation

Rouzie, Albert. "At Play in the Fields of Writing: Play and
Digital Literacy in a College-Level Computers and
Writing Course." Diss. U of Texas at Austin, 1997.

Recording

Glass, Phillip. "Low" Symphony. Point Music, 1973.

Speech

Khrushchev, Sergei. "Russia, Putin, and the War on
Terrorism." National Press Club, Washington. 6 Dec. 2001.

CHAPTER 17

APA Documentation

Disciplines in the social sciences (anthropology, government, linguistics, psychology, sociology) and in education most frequently use the APA (American Psychological Association) documentation style. This chapter offers a brief overview of the APA style. For a detailed treatment you should consult the *Publication Manual of the American Psychological Association*, fifth edition (2001).

The APA style has many similarities to the MLA style described in Chapter 16. Both styles use parenthetical references in the body of the text with complete bibliographical citations in the reference list at the end. The most important difference is the emphasis on the date of publication in the APA style. When you cite an author's name in the body of your paper with APA style, you always include the date of publication and the page number:

> By the end of the 1960s, the engineers were tearing down thousands of units of urban housing and small businesses to build expressways with a logic that was similar to the logic of mass bombing in Vietnam—to destroy the city was to save it (Patton, 1986, p. 102). Shortly the effects were all too evident. Old neighborhoods were ripped apart, the flight to the suburbs continued, and the decline of inner cities accelerated rather than abated.
>
> Not everyone in the 1950s and 1960s saw expressways as the answer to urban dilapidation. Mumford (1963) challenged the circulation metaphor: "Highway planners have yet to realize that these arteries must not be thrust into the delicate tissue of our cites; the blood they circulate must rather enter through an elaborate network of minor blood vessels and capillaries" (p. 236).

Notice that unlike MLA, a comma is placed after the author's name and the abbreviation for page is included (Patton, 1986, p. 102).

APA Reference List

The APA list of works cited is titled *References*:

New Technologies 5

References

Center "References"

Double-space all
entries. Indent all
but first line five
spaces.

Bingham, J. (1996, September 3). Kids become
    masters of electronic universe: School
    Internet activity abounds. *Denver Post*,
    p. A13.

Alphabetize entries
by last name of
authors or by title if
no author is listed.

Dyrli, O. E., & Kinnaman, D. E. (1995).
    Telecommunications: Gaining access to the
    world. *Technology and Learning*, *16*(3),
    79–84.

Notice that author's
initials are listed
rather than first
names.

Engardio, P. (1996, June 24). Microsoft's long
    march. *Business Week*, 52–54.

Notice that only the
first words and
proper nouns are
capitalized in titles
and subtitles of
articles and books.

The future just happened. (2001, July 29). *BBC*
    Online. Retrieved August 29, 2001, from
    http://news.bbc.co.uk/hi/english/
    static/in_depth/programmes/2001/
    future/tv_series_1.stm

Notice that article
titles are not placed
inside quotation
marks.

Lewis, M. (1989). *Liar's poker: Rising through*
    the wreckage on Wall Street. New York:
    Norton.

If an author has
more than one
entry, put the
earliest publication
first.

Lewis, M. (2000). *The next new thing: A Silicon*
    Valley story. New York: Norton.

Lewis, M. (2001). *Next: The future just*
    happened. New York: Norton.

```
                        New Technologies  6

National Center for Education Statistics.
        (1998, February). Internet access in
        public education. Retrieved May 21, 1998,
        from http://nces.ed.gov/ pubs98/98021.html
UK: A battle for young hearts and minds.
        (1996, April 4). Computer Weekly, 20.
```

> Italicize the titles of books and periodicals.

The reference list eliminates the need for footnotes. If you have your sources listed on notecards, all you have to do when you finish your paper is find the cards for all the sources that you cite, alphabetize the cards by author (or title), and type your reference list. For works with no author listed, alphabetize by the first significant word in the title (ignore *a, an,* and *the*).

Citing Books

The basic format for listing books in the reference list is

1. Author's name (last name first, initials)
2. Year of publication (in parentheses)
3. Title (in italics)
4. Place of publication
5. Name of publisher

Use the abbreviation for pages (pp.) for chapters in a book. Note that unlike MLA, APA includes the full range of pages (pp. 151–158).

Book by One Author

```
Wolf, S. (2002). A problem like Maria: Gender and sexuality
        in the American musical. Ann Arbor, MI: University of
        Michigan Press.
```

Book by Two or More Authors

Scribner, S., & Cole, M. (1981). *The psychology of literacy.*
    Cambridge, MA: Harvard University Press.

Two or More Books by the Same Author

Stagier, J. (2000). *Perverse spectators: The practices of film*
    reception. New York: New York University Press.

Stagier, J. (2001). *Blockbuster TV: Must-see-sitcoms in the*
    network era. New York: New York University Press.

Edited Book

Inness, S. (Ed.). (2004). *Action chicks: New images of*
    tough women in popular culture. New York: Palgrave
    Macmillan.

Translated Book

Homer. (2004). *The odyssey: Homer.* (E. McCrorie, Trans.).
    Baltimore, MD: Johns Hopkins University Press.

One Volume of a Multivolume Work

de Selincourt, E., & Darbishire, H. (Eds.). (1958). *The*
    poetical works of William Wordsworth (Vol. 5). Oxford,
    England: Oxford University Press.

Selection in an Anthology or Chapter in an Edited Collection

Merritt, R. (1985). Nickelodeon theaters, 1905–1914: Building
    an audience for the movies. In T. Balio (Ed.), *The*
    American film industry (Rev. ed., pp. 83–102). Madison:
    University of Wisconsin Press.

Unpublished Dissertation

Rouzie, A. (1997). *At play in the fields of writing: Play and*
    digital literacy in a college-level computers and writing
    course. Unpublished doctoral dissertation, University of
    Texas at Austin.

Citing Articles in Periodicals

When citing periodicals, the necessary items to include are

1. Author's name (last name first, initials)
2. Date of publication (in parentheses). For scholarly journals, give the year. For newspapers and weekly magazines, give the year followed by the month and day (2001, December 13)
3. Title of the article
4. Title of the journal or magazine (in italics)
5. Volume number (in italics)
6. Page numbers

For articles in newspapers, use the abbreviation for page or pages (p. or pp.).

Many scholarly journals are printed to be bound as one volume, usually by year, and the pagination is continuous for that year. If, say, a scholarly journal is printed in four issues and the first issue ends on page 278, then the second issue will begin with page 279. For journals that are continuously paginated, you do not need to include the issue number. Some scholarly journals, however, are paginated like magazines with each issue beginning on page 1. For journals paginated by issue, you should list the issue number along with the volume (e.g., for the first issue of volume 11, you would put *11*(1) in the entry after the title of the journal).

Article in a Scholarly Journal—Continuous Pagination

Berlin, J. A. (1988). Rhetoric and ideology in the writing
        class. *College English, 50*, 477-494.

Article in a Scholarly Journal—Pagination by Issue

Kolby, J. (1988). The top-heavy economy: Managerial greed
        and unproductive labor. *Critical Sociology, 15*(3), 53-69.

Article by Two Authors

Roach, B., & Roach, M. (2004). Horatio Alger, Jr.: Precursor
        of the Stratemeyer syndicate. *Journal of Popular Culture,
        37*(3), 450-462.

Article by Three or More Authors (if more than six, the seventh and subsequent authors can be abbreviated to *et al.*)

Domke, D., Garland, P., Billeaudeaux, A., & Hutcheson, J.

(2003). Insights into U.S. racial hierarchy: Racial

profiling, news sources, and September 11. *Journal of*

Communication, 53, 606-623.

Review

Chomsky, N. (1959). [Review of the book *Verbal behavior*].

Language, 35, 26-58.

Magazine Article

Engardio, P. (1996, June 24). Microsoft's long march.

Business Week, 52-54.

Magazine Article—No Author Listed

UK: A battle for young hearts and minds. (1996, April 4).

Computer Weekly, 20.

Newspaper Article

Bingham, J. (1996, September 3). Kids become masters of

electronic universe: School Internet activity abounds.

Denver Post, p. A13.

Citing Online Sources

The *Publication Manual of the American Psychological Association* specifies that those citing Web sources should direct readers to the exact source page if possible, not to menu or home pages. URLs have to be typed with complete accuracy to identify a Web site. If you type an uppercase letter for a lowercase letter, a browser will not find the site. To avoid typos in URLs, load the page in your browser, highlight the URL, and copy it (Control C on Windows or Command C on a Mac), and then paste it into the reference. You may have to change the font to match your text, but you will have the accurate URL.

The basic format for citing online sources is as follows:

1. Author's last name, initials
2. Date of document or last revision in parentheses
3. Title of document. Capitalize only the first word and any proper nouns.
4. Title of periodical (if applicable). Use italics and capitalize only the first word and any proper nouns.
5. Date of retrieval
6. URL or access path from a database. Notice that there is no period after a URL.

Article in a Scholarly Journal on the Web

Agre, P. (1998). The Internet and public discourse.
First Monday, 3(3). Retrieved July 10, 2001, from
http://www.firstmonday.dk/issues/issue3_3/agre/

Article Retrieved from a Database

Schott, G., & Selwyn, N. (2001). Examining the "male,
antisocial" stereotype of high computer users. *Journal of
Educational Computing Research, 23*, 291–303. Retrieved
November 2, 2004, from PsychINFO database.

Abstract Retrieved from a Database

Putsis, W. P., & Bayus, B. L. (2001). An empirical analysis
of firms' product line decisions. *Journal of Marketing
Research, 37*(8), 110–118. Abstract retrieved December 31,
2004, from PsychINFO database.

Article in a Newspaper on the Web

Mendels, P. (1999, May 26). Nontraditional teachers
more likely to use the Net. *New York Times on
the Web.* Retrieved September 19, 2001, from
http://www.nytimes.com/library/tech/99/05/cyber/
education/26education.html

Article from an Online News Service

Rao, M. (1999, February 10). WorldTel in $100 M community
　　initiative for Indian state. *Asia InternetNews*. Retrieved
　　April 15, 2001, from http://asia.internet.com/
　　1999/2/1003-india.html

Article in a Magazine on the Web

Happy new Euro. (1998, December 30). *Time Daily*. Retrieved
　　May 10, 2000, from http://www.time.com/
　　time/nation/article/0,8599,17455,00.html

Online Encyclopedia

Semiconductor. (1999). In *Encyclopaedia Britannica Online*.
　　Retrieved November 30, 2000, from http://search.eb.com/
　　bol/topic?eu=68433&sctn=1#s_top

Document on a Web Site

Kaplan, N. (1997, December 17). E-literacies:
　　Politexts, hypertexts and other cultural
　　formations in the late age of print. Retrieved
　　July 2, 2001, from http://raven.ubalt.edu/
　　staff/kaplan/lit/

Document on the Web Site of an Organization

National Audubon Society. (2001). Cowbirds and
　　conservation. Retrieved August 15, 2001,
　　from http://www.audubon.org/bird/research/

Electronic Version of a U.S. Government Report

U.S. Public Health Service. Office of the Surgeon
　　General. (2001, January 11). *Clean indoor air regulations
　　fact sheet*. Retrieved February 12, 2001,
　　from http://www.cdc.gov/tobacco/sgr/sgr_2000/factsheets/
　　factsheet_clean.htm

Graphic, Audio, or Video Files

East Timor awaits referendum. (1999, August 31). *NPR Online*.
Retrieved August 31, 1999, from http://www.npr.org/
ramfiles/atc/19990830.atc.10.ram

Electronic Mailing List Posting

Selzer, J. (1998, July 4). Ed Corbett. Message posted to
WPA-L@lists.asu.edu

Entry in a Weblog

Stereogum. (2004, July 28). Dustin Hoffman saves bee sting
victim. Message posted to http://bestweekever.vh1.com/
2004/07/dustin_hoffman_.html

Newsgroup Posting

Brody, P. (1999, May 9). Chamax. Message posted to news:
sci.archaeology.mesoamerican

Personal Email

APA omits personal email from the list of references. Personal communication can be cited in parenthetical references in the text. Provide a date if possible.

S. Wilson (personal communication, April 6, 2004)

Citing Other Sources

Government Report

U.S. Environmental Protection Agency. (1992). *Respiratory
health effects of passive smoking: Lung cancer and other
disorders*. (EPA Publication No. 600/6-90/006 F).
Washington, DC: Author.

Film

Spielberg, S. (Director). (1998). *Saving Private Ryan* [Motion
picture]. United States: Paramount Pictures.

Television Broadcast

Burns, K. (Writer). (1992, January 29). *Empire of the air: The men who made radio* [Television broadcast]. Walpole, NH: Florentine Films.

Television Series

Connelly, J. (Producer). (1957). *Leave it to Beaver* [Television series]. New York: CBS Television.

Music Recording

Glass, P. (1973). *"Low" symphony* [CD]. New York: Point Music.

Glossary

A

abstract Summary of an article or book

aesthetic criteria Evaluative criteria based on perceptions of beauty and good taste

AltaVista Internet portal with powerful search engine at http://www.altavista.digital.com

analogy An extended comparison of one situation or item to another

APA American Psychological Association

APA documentation Documentation style commonly used in social science and education disciplines

argument In speech and writing, a claim supported by at least one reason

assumption An unstated belief or knowledge that connects a claim with evidence

audience Real or assumed individuals or groups to whom a verbal or written communication is directed

B

bandwagon appeal A fallacy of argument based on the assumption that something is true or correct because "everyone" believes it to be so

bar chart Visual depiction of data created by the use of horizontal or vertical bars that comparatively represent rates or frequencies

because clause A statement that begins with the word *because* and provides a supporting reason for a claim

begging the question A fallacy of argument that uses the claim as evidence for its own validity

bias Personal beliefs which may skew one's perspective or presentation of information

bibliography List of books and articles on a specific subject

brainstorming A method of finding ideas by writing a list of questions or statements about a subject

C

causal argument An argument that seeks to identify the reasons behind a certain event or phenomenon

claim A declaration or assertion made about any given topic

claim of comparison A claim that argues something is like or not like something else

common factor method A method used by scientists identifying a recurring factor present in a given cause–effect relationship

consequence The cause–effect result of a given action

context Of a text, both the combination of author, subject, and audience and the broader social, cultural, and economic influences

contextual analysis A type of rhetorical analysis that focuses on the author, the audience, the time, and the circumstances of an argument

counterargument An argument offering an opposing point of view with the goal of demonstrating that it is the stronger of the two arguments

criteria Standards used to establish a definition or an evaluation

critical reading A process of reading which surpasses an initial understanding or impression of basic content and proceeds with the goal of answering specific questions or examining particular elements

cropping In photography, the process of deleting unwanted parts of an image

cultural assumptions Widely held beliefs in a particular culture that are considered common sense

D

database Large collection of digital information organized for efficient search and retrieval

debate A contest or game where two or more individuals attempt to use arguments to persuade others to support their opinion

definition, argument by An argument made by specifying that something does or does not possess certain criteria

diction The choice and use of words in writing and speech

E

either–or A fallacy of argument that presents only two choices in a complex situation

emotional appeal An argumentation strategy that attempts to persuade by stirring the emotions of the audience

empirical research Research that collects data from observation or experiment

ethos An appeal to the audience based on the character and trustworthiness of the speaker or writer

evaluation argument An argument that judges something based on ethical, aesthetic, and/or practical criteria

evaluation of sources The assessment of the relevance and reliability of sources used in supporting claims

evidence Data, examples, or statistics used to support a claim

experimental research Research based on obtaining data under controlled conditions, usually by isolating one variable while holding other variables constant

F

fallacy of argument Failure to provide adequate evidence to support a claim. See *bandwagon appeal, begging the question, false analogy, hasty generalization, name calling, non sequitur, oversimplification, polarization, post hoc fallacy, rationalization, slippery slope, straw man*

false analogy A fallacy of argument that compares two unlike things as if they were similar

feasibility The potential that a proposed solution can be implemented

figurative language The symbolic transference of meaning from one word or phrase to another, such as with the use of metaphor, synecdoche, and metonymy

firsthand evidence Evidence such as interviews, observations, and surveys collected by the writer

font The specific size and weight of a typeface

freewriting A method of finding ideas by writing as fast as possible about a subject for a set length of time

G

generalization A conclusion drawn from knowledge based on past occurrences of the phenomenon in question

GIF (Graphic Interchange Format) Preferred Web format for images with sharp lines, text, and small images

good reason A reason that the audience accepts as valid

Google Powerful search engine at www.google.com

H

hasty generalization A fallacy of argument resulting from making broad claims based on a few occurrences

HTML (HyperText Markup Language) Display language used for creating Web pages

hypertext Document that allows you to connect to other pages or documents by clicking on links. The Web can be thought of as one huge hypertext

I

idea map A brainstorming tool which visually depicts connections between different aspects of an issue

image editor Software program that allows you to create and manipulate images

intellectual property Any property produced by the intellect, including copyrights for literary, musical, photographic, and cinematic works, patents for inventions, trademarks, and industrial processes

J

JPEG (acronym for Joint Photographic Experts Group) Preferred Web format for photographs

journal A general category that includes popular, trade, and scholarly periodical publications

K

keyword search A Web-based search that uses a robot and indexer to produce results based on a chosen word or words

L

line graph Visual presentation of data represented by a continuous line or lines plotted on specific intervals

logos An appeal to the audience based on reasoning and evidence

M

metaphor A figure of speech using a word or phrase that commonly designates one thing to represent another, thus making a comparison

metonomy A type of figurative language that uses one object to represent another that embodies its defining quality

MLA Modern Language Association

MLA documentation Documentation style commonly used in humanities and fine arts disciplines

N

name calling A fallacy of argument resulting from the use of undefined and therefore meaningless names

narrative arguments A form of argument based on telling stories that suggest the writer's position rather than explicitly making claims

non sequitur A fallacy of argument resulting from connecting together two or more unrelated ideas

O

oversimplification A fallacy in argument caused by neglect of accounting for the complexity of a subject

P

pathos An appeal based on the audience's emotions or deeply-held values

periodical A journal, magazine, or newspaper published at standard intervals, usually daily, weekly, monthly, or quarterly

periodical index Paper or electronic resource that catalogs the contents of journals, magazines, and newspapers

pie chart A circular chart resembling a pie that illustrates percentages of the whole through the use of delineated wedge shapes

plagiarism The improper use of the unauthorized and unattributed words or ideas of another author

polarization A fallacy of argument based on exaggerating the characteristics of opposing groups to highlight division and extremism

popular journal A magazine aimed at the general public; usually includes illustrations, short articles, and advertisements

position argument A general kind of argument in which a claim is made for an idea or way of thinking about a subject

post hoc fallacy A fallacy of argument based on the assumption that events that follow each other have a causal relationship

practical criteria Evaluative criteria based on usefulness or likely results

primary research Information collected directly by the writer through observations, interviews, surveys, and experiments

process of elimination method A means of finding a cause by systematically ruling out all other possible causes

proposal argument An argument that either advocates or opposes a specific course of action

R

rationalization A fallacy of argument based on using weak explanations to avoid dealing with the actual causes

reason In an argument, the justification for a claim

rebuttal argument An argument that challenges or rejects the claims of another argument

reference librarian Library staff member who is familiar with information resources and who can show you how to use them. You can find a reference librarian at the reference desk in your library.

refutation A rebuttal argument that points out the flaws in an opposing argument

rhetorical analysis Careful study of a written argument or other types of persuasion aimed at understanding how the components work or fail to work

rhetorical situation Factors present at the time of writing or speaking, including the writer or speaker, the audience, the purpose of communicating, and the context

S

sans serif type A style of type recognized by blunt ends and a consistency in thickness

scholarly journals Contain articles written by experts in a particular field; also called "peer-reviewed" or "academic" journals

search engine A program that searches information in electronic formats. Web search engines like Google and AltaVista search the entire Web.

secondary research Information obtained from existing knowledge, such as research in the library

secondhand evidence Evidence from the work of others found in the library, on the Web, and elsewhere

serif type A style of type developed to resemble the strokes of an ink pen and recognized by wedge-shaped ends on letter forms

single difference method Finding a cause for differing phenomena in very similar situations by identifying the one element that varies

slippery slope A fallacy of argument based on the assumption that if a first step is taken, additional steps will inevitably follow

straw man A fallacy of argument based on the use of the diversionary tactic of setting up the opposing position in such a manner that it can be easily rejected

sufficiency Refers to the adequacy of evidence supporting a claim

synecdoche A type of figurative language in which a part is used to represent the whole

T

textual analysis A type of rhetorical analysis that focuses exclusively on the text itself

thesis One or more sentences that state the main idea of an argument

trade journals A magazine in which articles and advertisements target individuals of a specific occupation

typeface Styles of type such as serif, sans serif, and decorative

U

URL (Universal Resource Locator) Addresses on the Web

V

visual argument A type of persuasion with images, graphics, or objects

voice In writing, the distinctive style of a writer that gives a sense of the writer as a person

W

Web directory Subject guide to Web pages grouped by topic and sub-topic

Web editors Programs that allow you to compose Web pages

working thesis A preliminary statement of the main claim of an argument, subject to revision

Y

Yahoo Popular Web directory at http://www.yahoo.com

Text Credits

William Bennett, from open letter that appeared in the *Wall Street Journal* September 7, 19 and 29 to Milton Friedman by William Bennett. Used by permission of Dr. William J. Bennett.

Grace A. Bernhardt, from Balcones Canyonlands Preserve website, reprinted with permission of Grace A. Bernhardt.

Rachel Carson, "The Obligation to Endure" from *Silent Spring* by Rachel Carson. Copyright © 1962 by Rachel L. Carson, renewed 1990 by Roger Christie. Reprinted by permission of Houghton Mifflin Company. All Rights Reserved.

Linda Chavez, "The Separation of Church and State" Myth by Linda Chavez. Appeared in *Jewish World Review* July 3, 2002, reprinted by permission of Creators Syndicate.

Robert H. Frank and Phillip T. Cook, from a summary of their book, *The Winner-Take-All-Society*, by Robert H. Frank and Phillip T. Cook, which appeared in *Across the Board* 33:5 (May 1996). Copyright © 1996. Reprinted with permission of Professor Robert H. Frank.

Milton Friedman, excerpts from open letter to William Bennett from Milton Friedman which appeared in the *Wall Street Journal* September 19, 1989 Copyright © 1989 Dow Jones & Company, Inc. Reprinted by permission of Milton Friedman.

Chung-pei Hu, from Sixth Street Safety and Awareness Website, reprinted with permission of Chung-pei Hu.

Martin Luther King, Jr., from "Letter from Birmingham Jail." Reprinted by arrangement with the Estate of Martin Luther King, Jr., c/o Writers House as agent for the proprietor New York, NY. Copyright © 1963 by Martin Luther King Jr., copyright renewed 1991 by Coretta Scott King.

Jennifer May, "Why are Teenage Girls Dying to Be Thin?" by Jennifer May, copyright © 2004, reprinted by permission of the author.

Scott McCloud, "Setting the Record Straight" [pp. 2–9] from *Understanding Comics* by Scott McCloud. Copyright © 1993, 1994 by Scott McCloud. Reprinted by permission of HarperCollins Publishers Inc.

Wilfred Owen, "Dulce et Decorum Est" by Wilfred Owen, from *The Collected Poems of Wilfred Owen*, copyright © 1963 by Chatto & Windus, Ltd. Reprinted by permission of New Directions Publishing Corp.

Leslie Marmon Silko, "The Border Patrol State," copyright © 1994 by Leslie Marmon Silko, reprinted with the permission of the Wylie Agency, Inc.

Erica M. Strauser, "The NRA Blacklist: A Project Gone Mad?" by Erica M. Strauser, copyright © 2004, reprinted by permission of the author.

Excerpt from "Supreme Court Says 'No' to Army Engineers" from *Realty Times*, January 10, 2001, http://realtytimes.com/rtcpages/20010110_land.htm, copyright © 2001, reprinted by permission of Realty Times.

"The Impact of Global Warming," rendering of map and two text boxes (Global Warming fingerprint about Chesapeake Bay and the global warming harbinger about Southeast Arizona) from http://www.climatehotmap.org/namerica.html by Union of Concerned Scientists, reprinted by permission.

Screen shot from Yahoo! reproduced with permission of Yahoo! Inc., copyright © 2004 by Yahoo! Inc. YAHOO! and the YAHOO! logo are trademarks of Yahoo! Inc.

Photo credits are found on the copyright page.

Index